GORDON RAMSAY'S HOME COOKING

GORDON RAMSAY'S HOME COOKING

Everything You Need to Know to Make Fabulous Food

GRAND CENTRAL
Life & Style

NEW YORK · BOSTON

Grand Central Life & Style
Hachette Book Group
237 Park Avenue
New York, NY 10017

www.GrandCentralLifeandStyle.com

Printed in the United States of America
Q-MA

Originally published in Great Britain in 2012 by
Hodder & Stoughton, a Hachette UK Company.

First US Edition: April 2013
10 9 8 7 6 5 4 3 2 1

Grand Central Life & Style is an imprint of Grand
Central Publishing.
The Grand Central Life & Style name and logo are
trademarks of Hachette Book Group, Inc.

The Hachette Speakers Bureau provides a wide range
of authors for speaking events. To find out more,
go to www.HachetteSpeakersBureau.com or call
(866) 376-6591.

The publisher is not responsible for websites (or their
content) that are not owned by the publisher.

Library of Congress Control Number: 2012953718

ISBN: 978-1-455-52525-6

CONTENTS

CONTENTS

GETTING STARTED

A DECADE OR SO AGO, THERE WAS A FASHION FOR MICHELIN-STARRED CHEFS TO PRODUCE THESE INCREDIBLY COMPLICATED COOKBOOKS.

You know the sort of thing I mean—where following one recipe meant you had to turn to five other recipes to prepare the various stages before you could even begin to tackle the featured dish. It was crazy, and completely failed to recognize that home cooking and restaurant cooking are two very different things.

So the first thing I want to do is to reassure you that this book isn't going to be anything like that. I'm not setting out to turn you into Michelin-starred chefs here. I'm not expecting you to spend hours bent over plates, tweaking and primping in pursuit of perfection. I just want to teach you how to cook and enjoy good food at home. I'm going to strip away all the hard graft and complexity and show how, from humble beginnings, anyone can produce mouthwatering recipes. Put simply, I'm going to show you how to cook yourself into a better cook.

Not that I'm turning my back on my experience. Over the past 25 years I've been lucky enough to work with some of the best chefs in the world, from Albert and Michel Roux in London to Guy Savoy and Joel Robuchon in Paris. I've held Michelin stars in many of the major cities of the world, including three at Restaurant Gordon Ramsay in London for more than 10 years now. Like all chefs, I've learned an incredible amount along the way: techniques, tricks—cheats, even—that I incorporate instinctively into my cooking every day. Half the time I don't even know I'm using them, but they are always there, giving me confidence in the kitchen.

And believe me, the best thing you can have in a kitchen is confidence. I really think that's what separates good cooks from the mediocre ones. Sure, you need to be able to taste and to master a few basics, but being able to act boldly and decisively, to have the confidence to ramp up the seasoning, for example, or to turn the gas up high and use the heat to your advantage—that's the real secret. That's what takes your cooking to another level.

Some people say they can't cook—that given half a chance, they'll burn water. I just don't buy that.

I think they're just not very interested in trying. Fair enough. I'm not interested in needlepoint and I'll tell you that I can't sew. But in truth, there's no one with a genuine interest in learning who can't improve and, with enough practice, become a decent cook. They might not get to the stage where they can hold down a job in a professional kitchen, but they can learn to produce good home cooking and to get pleasure from it. And if you are already a good cook? Well, that's the great thing about cooking—there's always something new to learn, another way of doing things, a different way of combining flavors that takes a recipe in a new direction.

So where do we start? With the absolute basics, of course. Before you even get to turn on the gas, the first job in any new kitchen is always, always, always to get to know your environment, to get familiar with the layout and be comfortable with the location of everything in your kitchen. Are the pans within easy reach? Are your sieves close at hand? I'm not talking about major DIY here. I'm not suggesting you need to rip out your kitchen sink and shift it across the room. It's just a question of getting yourself familiar with where everything is. You don't want to be just about to finish off your risotto and have to spend 10 minutes looking for the cheese grater. That's the kind of thing that throws you off your stride and from then on you'll be playing catch-up.

Time spent getting yourself ready is never wasted. Get out the ingredients and the equipment you need. This *mise-en-place,* as we call it, is crucial. It sets you off on a calm course and takes the stress out of cooking. Without it, any professional kitchen would be dead in the water, and it's equally important for the home cook too. Get it right and you have won 90 percent of the battle.

KITCHEN EQUIPMENT

Speaking of equipment, what do you need? Less than you might think. I'm always suspicious of people who have every gadget under the sun because I suspect they collect them as a kind of displacement therapy, to make up for the lack of cooking they actually do. Like a footballer who's afraid to make a tackle for fear of getting grass stains on his uniform, they line up their blenders and juicers and pasta machines to look the part, and then let them collect dust. Better to be a poorly equipped doer than an over-equipped poseur.

Essential kitchen equipment starts and pretty much finishes with a good set of knives and pans. Armed with these, there are not a lot of jobs you can't tackle. A knife will do the job of both food processor and garlic press, a pan can be both meat mallet and flan tin. Buy the best quality you can, and by that I don't necessarily mean the most expensive— as in everything, you'll sometimes pay dearly for fashionable brands—but I do mean something built to last. Spend the money now and these kitchen workhorses will last you a lifetime, saving you a fortune in the long run.

HOW TO CHOP AN ONION

1. Cut the onion in half lengthwise, going through the pointed end and the root. Peel off the papery skin to get to the shiny layers, but leave the root intact or the juices will start to bleed and make you cry.

2. Make a series of parallel vertical cuts down the length of the onion, stopping just short of the root.

3. Holding the onion steady, make two horizontal cuts through the onion, again stopping just short of the root.

4. Now grip the onion like a tennis ball to hold it together, pushing down with your forefinger, middle finger, and ring finger on top and thumb and pinkie at the sides. Have your middle finger slightly ahead of its two neighbors and use the knuckle to guide the knife down to make repeated slices, inching your fingers back toward the root as you go.

5. You should be left with a pile of neatly diced onion, and a root, which you can trim more if you like or reserve for the stockpot.

KNIVES

Knives are the first thing every aspiring chef buys. I still remember the day I came home as a pimply teenager clutching my first set tightly under my arm. From day one, they stay with you, taken from kitchen to kitchen and guarded with your life. At cooking school I was taught that the test of a good knife was in the balance. The blade should be forged all the way through to the butt of the handle and you should be able to balance it on an extended forefinger where the blade and handle meet.

Most knives are made of stainless steel. French steel is softer, so easier to sharpen, but more vulnerable to wear. German steel is harder, so takes more skill to sharpen, but it will maintain its sharp edge for longer. Japanese knives, too, are made of very hard steel and tend to be lighter and more stylish-looking. I favor Wüsthof, a German brand, but the important thing is to find a make that feels comfortable in your hand. That way it will become your best friend.

A basic set of knives should include a 2- to 3-inch paring knife for peeling fruit and cutting small vegetables, an 8-inch chef's knife for chopping, a 5-inch boning knife with a slightly flexible blade for cutting around meat and bone, and a 10-inch serrated or bread knife. You'll also need a honing steel to keep them sharp. A blunt knife is far more dangerous than a sharp one as it can easily skid off what you are cutting and do serious damage to fingers. Get into the habit of brushing your knife against a steel every time you use it. Hold the steel confidently as you would a tennis racket in your left hand (or right, if you are left-handed) and place the heel of the blade (where the sharpened edge meets the handle) on top of the steel near its base. Now draw the knife up the steel in a sweeping motion so that you stroke the entire length of the blade against the steel, keeping the angle between the blade and the steel at a steady 20 degrees. Now hone the other side of the knife by placing the blade edge underneath the steel and repeating the motion. Do this five or six times, always alternating the side of the blade, until you have a sharp edge.

With practice, you'll be able to build up a rhythm and do this instinctively in fast and fluid movements, but speed isn't the issue—it's about keeping the blade in contact with the steel at a consistent angle and stroking it all the way to the tip.

If the knife has lost its edge, no amount of honing will bring it back. In that case you'll need to regrind the blade, either with a household knife sharpener or, better still, by asking your kitchen shop to do it for you.

When using a knife, always make sure you are cutting onto a solid surface such as a cutting board. Glass and marble boards may look the part, but they have no real place in the kitchen as they will blunt the knife. Heavy wooden boards, which are what I use at home, are more knife-friendly but still look good. They can be cleaned with hot water and a little detergent, but never leave them to soak. They should be treated periodically with oil (wood, vegetable,

it doesn't really matter, but probably not your best extra virgin). Plastic boards are highly practical as they can be put in the dishwasher. We use polyethylene boards in my restaurants—color-coded for meat, fish, and vegetables. That's probably overkill for the home kitchen, but do be aware of hygiene and certainly don't chop anything that isn't going to be thoroughly cooked on a board you previously used for raw meat. Don't forget, you can always flip a board over if you need a clean surface.

Make sure the board is steady (placing it on a damp dishcloth will prevent it from slipping) and press whatever you are cutting down firmly to hold it steady. Always cut forward, letting the weight of the knife do the work. If your knife is sharp enough, you shouldn't hear a loud chopping noise as the blade hits the board. You should be using more of a rocking motion, with the point of the knife staying largely in contact with the cutting board.

PANS

Again, buy the best you can afford. Good-quality construction is key; not only will the pans last longer, but the heavier they are, the more evenly they'll conduct heat, preventing hot spots from scorching your food. Look for a weighty pan with a copper or aluminium base, and a stainless steel inner lining for ease of cleaning. Most chefs prefer copper because it not only heats up quickly but also cools fast, meaning you have more control. It does need more looking after, though. Long, heatproof handles should be securely riveted, so check the fixings.

Three sizes—2-quart, 3- to 4-quart, and 6- to 8-quart, all with snugly fitting lids—should see you right for most jobs. One other pan worth considering is a saucier, which has sloping sides, making it ideal for reducing stocks because the liquid evaporates more easily. It's also good for making risotto or anything else that needs constant stirring. A large, cast-iron lidded casserole that can transfer from the stovetop to the oven is also invaluable, especially for slow braises and winter stews.

You'll also need a couple of frying pans: an 8-inch pan for omelettes and a 12-inch one for general frying. These should be ovenproof up to 400°F so that you can start cooking something on the stovetop and then finish it in the oven—a rack of lamb, say, or a tarte tatin.

If your pan doesn't already have a nonstick coating, you can season it by sprinkling it with salt and heating it to a high temperature on the stovetop. Then you throw away the salt and rub the pan with a thin layer of peanut or vegetable oil. This will give it a protective layer and prevent things from sticking. Once you've finished using it, simply wipe it out while it's still hot with oiled paper towels. Don't wash it in detergent or you will need to season it again.

I also use a grill pan for searing steaks. Pressing the meat down onto the ridged surface not only creates a professional-looking finish (especially if you give your steak a quarter turn halfway through cooking to give a cross-hatched pattern), but also gives some of the char-grilled flavor you'll get from a professional grill.

Well, that's the essentials out of the way. But there are some other good kitchen standbys you may find useful.

BLOWTORCH

We chefs love a blowtorch. It's great not just for caramelizing sugar—on top of a crème brûlée, for example—but for unmolding frozen desserts.

DIGITAL SCALE

The great thing about a digital scale is not just that you can weigh things down to the last ounce, but that you can weigh everything into the same bowl, setting the scale to zero between each addition, which saves both time and washing up.

FOOD PROCESSOR

For making pasta dough, pastry, and crumble toppings. Choose a processor that has a low starting speed as some are too powerful and will blow your flour and confectioners' sugar around the room when you switch them on.

ICE CREAM MAKER

You can make ice cream without a machine, but it will never be as smooth. There are two types: ones with built-in coolers, which are much bulkier and more expensive, and those where you have to freeze the bowl ahead of using it. What you buy depends on how much you think you'll use it.

IMMERSION OR STICK BLENDER

For puréeing soups and sauces, making smoothies, or quickly blending a batter.

MANDOLINE

No matter how good you get with a knife, you'll always be able to slice vegetables more finely and more quickly on a mandoline (a metal, wood, or plastic board with a sharp metal blade built in). Choose one with a good guard to protect your fingers.

MICROPLANE ZESTER

Not just for zesting oranges and lemons, but also for puréeing garlic or fresh ginger.

MORTAR AND PESTLE

Invaluable for crushing and grinding herbs and spices. It gives a coarser, more earthy texture than using an electric blender, which is ideal for Asian cooking. It's also great for pounding garlic to a paste. Choose a mortar with a large bowl and a heavy-weight pestle.

POTATO RICER

A bit like a giant garlic press, a ricer is essential if you want to make silky-smooth mashed potatoes. Boiled potatoes are pushed through to make thin strands, which can then be beaten with butter, milk, or cream. You can get a similar result with a mouli (a hand-operated stainless steel grinder that pushes cooked vegetables through perforated discs).

PROBE THERMOMETER

A handy device that takes the guesswork out of cooking meat. There are two types: instant-read thermometers for a one-shot reading, or alarm thermometers that will tell you when the temperature reaches a preset level. This is very useful if you are roasting meat, for example, and want to be sure it is cooked at the center.

SIEVE

Essential for straining stocks and sauces or for draining vegetables. Choose one with a long handle and a balancing hook so that you can rest it over a deep bowl or pan. Conical-shaped sieves, known as chinois, are particularly useful when you want to purée something, as you can push down with the back of a ladle and exert considerable force.

VEGETABLE PEELER

The swivel types make peeling so much less of a chore, although to be honest, I'll often leave vegetable skins on if I'm cooking at home. It's where so many of the vitamins and nutrients, and a lot of the flavor, are to be found, so why waste them?

WHISKS

Electric mixers are useful for meringues and sponges, but a balloon whisk gives you much more control and makes it less likely you'll overwhip cream.

So having started by saying you don't need much equipment, I realize I've gone on to mention rather a lot. I suppose the best advice is to buy things as and when you need them, rather than in one big preemptive shop. That way at least you know everything will be used at least once. But please, no egg separators or garlic peelers. That's what hands and fingers are for.

CLASSICS WITH A TWIST

ONCE UPON A TIME, WE TOOK COMFORT IN OUR ROUTINES.

People found it reassuring to follow the kind of weekly diet you could tell the day of the week by. As long as there was steak on Wednesdays, fish on Fridays, and a roast on Sundays, all was well with the world. And woe betide anyone who tried to change the way these things were cooked. You really could get by with just a handful of old faithful recipes.

In a way, there was a lot to be said for that. It was proper home cooking, and the meals you did cook you became absolutely expert at. There's no substitute for repetition when you want to master a dish, and the old ways certainly allowed for plenty of that. But the world's moved on. It's a faster place now, and we're spoiled for choice in everything we do, from going to the movies to buying a car. Going out to eat, you'll find that even the smallest town will offer plenty of choices, from the usual Italian, Chinese, or Mexican to Indian, Thai, or even Vietnamese. We've grown accustomed to new flavors and food that excites us. And yet back at home how many of us are guilty of getting stuck in a rut, of always doing the same old dishes the same old way? Let's be honest, how many of us see cooking as a chore?

That's what I want to change in this chapter. I want to show you that cooking can be fun and exciting. I want to encourage you to look afresh at some familiar ingredients, and to throw in a few new ones too. Because the more you cook, the more confident you become, and the more confident you become, the more you'll enjoy spending time in the kitchen.

Part of the problem is that you open the fridge door, see the usual ingredients, and instantly start cooking the recipes you are familiar with. You see a can of tomatoes and some onions, and you make pasta and tomato sauce. You see half a dozen eggs and you make a cheese omelette. There's nothing wrong with that. But I want to show you how just a few changes in your shopping habits and introducing a couple of new ingredients can take your cooking in a new direction.

This is always the best way to develop—to build on dishes you are already familiar with. If you are used to roasting a chicken, then it's a small step to start stuffing it with chorizo and lima beans, but it takes it to another level in terms of flavor. Add some dried chiles, capers, and anchovies to that tomato sauce and you've got the most beautiful, rich, spicy puttanesca sauce. If you are used to making a risotto, why not try pan-frying it in squares (see page 30) to give it a new twist? I'm not saying don't cook the basics ever again, but just try changing things up.

The best place to start is with your shopping. Ordering your supermarket items off the Internet is a real time-saver, no question, but it does tend to make us creatures of habit. It's very easy to order the same things week in, week out, and that's the death knell for creativity. I'd always suggest you walk around a market or some local shops and see what catches your eye. Ask the stallholder or shopkeeper what's good at the moment. Ask him how he would cook it. You'll be surprised at how much information you can pick up.

TASTING

The other thing I can't urge you enough to do is to get into the habit of really tasting your food as you cook. It's the first thing I teach any new chef in my kitchens and is the only way to understand how to combine new flavors. Cooking is far more intuitive than you might think, and you should learn to trust your palate—it will tell you if something is missing.

Often it comes down to building up layers of the five basic tastes—sweet, sour, salty, bitter, and umami. The first four tastes are self-explanatory. Sweetness, of course, comes mainly from sugar, but also from maple syrup, honey, fruit, etc., each bringing a subtle difference to the final dish. It's useful not only for countering acidity, but also for tempering too much heat. So if you think you've overdone it on the chiles, add a bit more sugar. I always add a pinch to a simple tomato sauce, too, as it just helps to bring out the tomatoes' natural sharpness.

Sourness normally comes in the form of lemon or lime juice, tamarind, or vinegar; and saltiness in a lot of Asian condiments, such as soy sauce, fish sauce, and oyster sauce.

Salt you should think of as the backbone taste on which to hang the others. It really helps other flavors to shine: a little salt in caramel, for example, exaggerates its sweetness.

Bitterness is found in beer, olives, citrus rind, coffee, cocoa, and some vegetables, such as chicory. It's the taste to use with the most caution as it can set people's teeth on edge and is difficult to disguise.

Umami was identified as a separate taste only in the last century. It means "meaty" or "savory" in Japanese, and describes that lip-smacking, more-ishness you find particularly in soy sauce, dashi, and other fermented or aged foods. It's also in foods such as Parmesan cheese and tomatoes.

Asian cooking, in particular, often calls for a balance of the basic tastes, especially the first three: sweet, sour, and salty. Once you understand this, you can start to experiment with more confidence. Taste your food. What is it lacking? Saltiness? Add a splash of soy sauce or fish sauce. A bit more acidity? Maybe lime juice or rice vinegar. Sweetness? Mirin or palm sugar. With practice, your cooking will become instinctive and all the richer for it.

PASTA WITH TOMATOES, ANCHOVIES, AND CHILES

SERVES 4

Pasta and tomato sauce has become a midweek standby in every home. In this classic Italian dish, we are taking that basic sauce to another level by adding a few pantry staples—chiles, anchovies, olives, and capers. Ready in the time it takes for the pasta to cook, and utterly delicious.

1 pound dried spaghetti or linguine
Olive oil
2–3 garlic cloves, peeled and finely chopped
1 dried red chile, crumbled or chopped
  into small pieces
One 2-ounce tin anchovies in oil, drained and
  finely chopped

8 ounces pitted black olives, roughly chopped
3 Tbsp capers, drained and rinsed
8 ounces cherry tomatoes, halved
Sea salt and freshly ground black pepper
Basil leaves, to garnish

1. Cook the pasta in boiling salted water until al dente, according to the package instructions.

2. Meanwhile, heat a wide high-sided frying pan or sauté pan over medium heat and add a glug of olive oil. Sauté the garlic, chile, and anchovies for 1–2 minutes until the garlic is aromatic and the anchovy is beginning to melt into the oil.

3. Add the olives, capers, and tomatoes to the pan and stir over medium heat for 4–5 minutes until the tomatoes have collapsed and everything is well combined.

4. Drain the pasta and toss in the pan with the sauce. Taste and adjust the seasoning as necessary (you probably won't need any salt because of the saltiness of the anchovies, olives, and capers).

5. Serve drizzled with a little olive oil and garnished with basil leaves.

HOW TO COOK PASTA
Always use well-salted water to cook pasta because it is impossible to season later. The Italians always use 2 teaspoons salt for every quart of water. Adding olive oil to the cooking water is helpful, but if you really want to make sure that your pasta doesn't stick as it cooks, use plenty of water and twist the pan from side to side a few times to get the pasta swirling around just after you've put it in.

BACON, PEA, AND GOAT CHEESE FRITTATA

SERVES 4–6

Don't limit yourself to cheese or ham when filling an omelette. This open Italian version is a meal in itself, and because it is finished under the broiler, doesn't involve any awkward folding or flipping. Check that one of your goat cheeses is firm enough to grate finely—if not, firm it up in the freezer first.

Olive oil
8 strips of smoked bacon, chopped into
  bite-sized pieces
1 red pepper, seeded and sliced
3 scallions, trimmed and sliced diagonally
1 cup frozen peas

Handful of basil, leaves roughly chopped
2 goat cheese crottins (about 4 ounces in total)
8 eggs, beaten
3–4 Tbsp grated Parmesan cheese
Freshly ground black pepper

1. Preheat the oven to 350°F.

2. Heat a glug of oil in a 10-inch nonstick ovenproof frying pan and cook the bacon for 2–3 minutes. Add the red pepper and continue to cook for another few minutes until the bacon is golden brown and crisp. Add the scallions and sweat for 4–5 minutes until everything is tender. Stir in the peas and heat through. Sprinkle in the basil, roughly mixing it through the vegetables. Cut one of the goat cheeses into chunks and scatter on top.

3. Preheat the broiler to the highest setting.

4. Put the beaten eggs in a bowl, add the Parmesan, and season generously with pepper. Pour into the pan over the vegetables and gently shake over medium heat. As the omelette begins to set at the bottom, grate the remaining goat cheese on top and season with pepper.

5. Place the pan under the broiler for 4–5 minutes until cooked through and golden on top.

6. Slide the frittata out of the pan and cut into wedges to serve.

TOMATO RISOTTO

**SERVES 4 AS A STARTER
OR 2 AS A MAIN COURSE**

The secret to making a good risotto is to add your
hot stock very gradually, stirring to make sure it has
all been absorbed before adding the next ladleful.
This way you can control the consistency better and
make sure the rice still has a slight bite to it—al
dente, as the Italians call it—when you take it off
the heat. This classic risotto just needs a garnish of
arugula or baby spinach.

2–3 Tbsp olive oil
1 cup risotto rice
2 cups chicken or vegetable stock
3½ Tbsp unsalted butter
8 ounces cherry tomatoes, halved
⅓ cup mascarpone cheese
1 ounce Parmesan cheese, grated
Sea salt and freshly ground black pepper

1. Heat the oil in a large frying pan, add the rice, and
stir well to coat the grains in the oil. Bring the stock
to a boil and add 1 ladleful of it at a time to the rice,
stirring well after each addition, until the liquid has
been absorbed and the rice is cooked but still al dente.
(This will take about 15–18 minutes.)

2. Meanwhile, heat the butter in a small saucepan,
add the tomatoes, and gently cook for about 10
minutes until soft. Pass through a mouli or coarse
sieve; alternatively, mash with a potato masher.

3. When the rice is cooked, fold in the mascarpone,
Parmesan, and the tomato mixture, adjust the
seasoning, and serve.

HOW TO SERVE RISOTTO AS A CAKE
To remove the need for last-minute stirring, you can
serve risotto as a cake. Make the risotto in advance,
taking it slightly beyond the al dente stage (about
20 minutes), then add the mascarpone, Parmesan,
and tomato. Spread the mixture out in
a square pan lined with wax paper, cover, and chill
for 2–4 hours. When ready to serve, heat 3½ Tbsp
butter in a large frying pan. Cut the risotto cake
into 4 squares and quickly pan-fry for about
3 minutes on each side until golden, taking care
when you flip them over. Serve immediately.

STUFFED ROAST CHICKEN

SERVES 4–6

This is a very simple twist guaranteed to impress. The chorizo, bean, and tomato stuffing helps the bird to cook evenly and perfumes the meat as it cooks. Serve it alongside the chicken with some steamed greens or a mixed green salad.

1 large free-range chicken, about 4½ pounds
Sea salt and freshly ground black pepper
1 lemon
Olive oil
1 heaping tsp paprika (sweet or smoked)
1½ cups white wine

FOR THE CHORIZO STUFFING
Olive oil
5–7 ounces chorizo, casings removed and cubed
1 onion, peeled and finely chopped
2 garlic cloves, peeled and thinly sliced
Bunch of thyme sprigs
Two 15-ounce cans cannellini beans, drained and
    rinsed in oil
One 7-ounce jar sun-dried tomatoes

1. Preheat the oven to 350°F.

2. First make the stuffing. Heat a little olive oil in a large frying pan, add the chorizo, and cook for about 3 minutes, until turning golden. Add the onion and cook for a minute or two until softened, then add the garlic. Cook for an additional couple of minutes before adding the leaves from 3 thyme sprigs. Stir in the cannellini beans, seasoning well. Cook for a minute or two to warm through. Add the tomatoes and a couple of tablespoons of the oil they are stored in. Stir to combine, then remove from the heat and cool.

3. Now prepare the chicken. Season the cavity with salt and pepper, then fill with the chorizo stuffing and place a whole lemon at the cavity opening, tucking any excess skin over it. Drizzle the chicken with olive oil, sprinkle over the paprika, and season with salt and pepper. Rub into the chicken skin.

4. Pour the wine and about ¾ cup of water into a roasting pan and season with salt and pepper. Add the chicken and the remaining sprigs of thyme from the chorizo, then cover with foil and roast for 1 hour in the preheated oven.

5. After 1 hour, remove the foil from the chicken, baste with the roasting juices, and turn the oven up to 400°F. Roast for another 25–30 minutes until the skin is golden brown and the juices from the thigh run clear. Remove from the oven and rest for 15 minutes before serving.

6. Remove the lemon from the chicken cavity, and squeeze the juice into the pan juices. Whisk together to create a light gravy—if you prefer a thicker gravy, reduce over a high heat.

HOW TO KEEP CHICKEN MOIST WHILE ROASTING
Roasting chicken under a tent of foil with stock and water is a lovely way to keep it moist during the first part of cooking. Once it has steamed for an hour, you simply remove the foil for the final 30 minutes to brown the breasts. The resulting chicken will be much plumper and fuller than if you had roasted it all the way.

MISO SALMON

SERVES 4

Miso is a salty paste made from fermented rice or soybeans and is traditional in Japanese cooking. It gives a rich and sumptuous flavor to this spicy broth. Kaffir lime leaves give an aromatic lime flavor; you can find them in Asian groceries. Poaching is a lovely, delicate way of cooking salmon. Keep the skin on to keep it from breaking up as the stock gently simmers.

3 Tbsp light miso paste
3 cups fish stock
Sea salt
2 kaffir lime leaves
1–2 red chiles, seeded and finely chopped,
    to taste
1-inch piece of fresh ginger, peeled and
    thinly sliced
1-pound side of salmon, skin on, scaled and
    pin-boned (see page 54, step 6)

1 bunch bok choy
5 ounces baby broccoli
2 small bunches of enoki mushrooms, separated
1 tsp toasted sesame oil
Cilantro leaves, to garnish (optional)

1. Place the miso paste in a pan and whisk in the stock. Taste and add a little salt if necessary. Bring to a simmer (don't boil too rapidly, or it may separate), then add the lime leaves, chiles, and ginger.

2. Cut the salmon in half widthwise, then add to the stock, skin side down, and gently simmer for 8–10 minutes, basting the salmon in the liquid until cooked through.

3. Separate the bok choy leaves from the stems. Chop the stems into bite-sized pieces and shred the leaves. Slice the broccoli into bite-sized pieces.

4. Carefully transfer the salmon to a plate with a fish spatula and pour a small ladleful of broth over it. Bring the stock remaining in the pan back to a boil.

5. Put the broccoli into the broth to cook, and after 30 seconds add the bok choy stems. Cook for an additional 1–2 minutes, then add the shredded bok choy leaves. Cook for about 1 minute until wilted. Meanwhile, flake the cooked salmon into large chunks, discarding the skin.

6. Just before serving, add half the mushrooms to the broth. Rub your serving bowls with a little toasted sesame oil, then divide the remaining mushrooms among them. Add some flaked salmon and vegetables to each bowl, then spoon over some broth. Serve immediately, garnished with cilantro if you like.

HOW TO COOK FIBROUS GREENS

With vegetables such as bok choy and Swiss chard, which have quite fibrous stalks, it is often best to remove the leaves and add them a few minutes later, or else they will be overcooked by the time the stalks are tender.

SLOW-COOKED
FIERY LAMB
SERVES 4

I love cooking with lamb shanks because the
longer you leave them, the better they taste.
Three hours may seem a long time, but trust me,
once you see the way the meat falls off the bone,
you'll understand. Marinate the lamb in the spice
mix overnight if you can as it will really improve
the flavor. Serve with couscous or mashed potatoes.

4 lamb shanks
Olive oil
2 carrots, peeled and sliced
1 onion, peeled and thickly sliced
2 bay leaves
One 750-ml bottle red wine
2 cups chicken stock
Small handful of mint leaves, to garnish

FOR THE MARINADE
1–2 green chiles, seeded and sliced, to taste
1–2 red chiles, seeded and sliced, to taste
2 tsp smoked paprika
2 tsp dried oregano
1 tsp cumin seeds
2 cinnamon sticks, snapped in half
3 garlic cloves, peeled, roughly chopped,
    and crushed
Olive oil
Sea salt and freshly ground black pepper

1. First prepare the marinade. Mix together the chiles
(use only one of each if you don't like hot dishes),
smoked paprika, oregano, cumin seeds, cinnamon
sticks, garlic, 1 tablespoon of olive oil, and salt and
pepper to taste. Rub the mixture into the lamb so that
it is well flavored. You can cook the lamb right away,
but if you have time, cover and leave to marinate for at
least 1 hour, or even overnight.

2. Preheat the oven to 325°F.

3. Heat a large casserole dish on the stovetop and add
a couple of tablespoons of olive oil. Brown the
lamb in it for about 6 minutes until colored on
all sides, then add the chiles and cinnamon from
the marinade.

4. Add the carrots, onion, and bay leaves to the
casserole and brown for a minute or two. Lift the lamb
so that it is resting on top of the onions and carrots.
Add the red wine to deglaze the pan, scraping up the
bits from the bottom, then bring to a boil and cook
for 7–8 minutes to reduce the liquid by half. Add the
chicken stock, bring to a boil, then transfer,
uncovered, to the preheated oven. Cook for 3 hours
until the meat is really tender and the sauce is reduced.
(If the tops of the shanks look like they might be
drying out, just baste and occasionally turn them.)

5. Remove the cooked meat from the oven and serve
garnished with torn mint leaves and the cooking
juices spooned on top.

BEEF WELLINGTONS

SERVES 4

You can dress up a beef Wellington with foie gras, porcini mushrooms, or even truffles, but in my opinion, that beautiful beef tenderloin should always be the star. The trick here is in wrapping the mushrooms and beef with Parma ham. That seals in the juices and keeps the pastry from getting soggy.

Two 14-ounce beef tenderloins
Olive oil
1 pound mixture of wild mushrooms, cleaned
1 thyme sprig, leaves only
Sea salt and freshly ground black pepper
One 12-ounce package frozen puff pastry, thawed
8 slices of Parma ham
2 egg yolks, beaten with 1 Tbsp water
  and a pinch of salt

FOR THE RED WINE SAUCE
2 Tbsp olive oil
7 ounces beef trimmings (ask the butcher to
  reserve these when trimming the tenderloin)
4 large shallots, peeled and sliced
12 black peppercorns
1 bay leaf
1 thyme sprig
Splash of red wine vinegar
One 750-ml bottle red wine
3 cups beef stock
Sea salt and freshly ground black pepper

1. Wrap each piece of beef tightly in a triple layer of plastic wrap to set its shape, then chill overnight.

2. Remove the plastic wrap, then quickly sear the beef in a hot pan with a little olive oil for 30–60 seconds until browned all over and rare in the middle. Remove from the pan and leave to cool.

3. Finely chop the mushrooms and sauté in a hot pan with a little olive oil, the thyme leaves, and some salt and pepper. When the mushrooms begin to release their juices, continue to cook over high heat for about 10 minutes until all the excess moisture has evaporated and you are left with a mushroom paste (known as a duxelle). Remove the duxelle from the pan and leave to cool.

4. Cut the pastry in half (if it doesn't already come in two pieces), place on a lightly floured surface, and roll each piece into a rectangle large enough to envelop one of the beef tenderloins. Chill in the refrigerator.

5. Lay a large sheet of plastic wrap on a work surface and place 4 slices of Parma ham in the middle, overlapping them slightly, to create a square. Spread half the duxelle evenly over the ham.

6. Season the beef tenderloins, then place them on top of the mushroom-covered ham. Using the plastic wrap, roll the Parma ham over the beef, then roll and tie the plastic wrap to get a nice, evenly thick log. Repeat this step with the other beef tenderloin, then chill for at least 30 minutes.

7. Brush the pastry with the egg wash. Remove the plastic wrap from the beef, then wrap the pastry around each ham-wrapped tenderloin. Trim the pastry and brush all over with the egg wash. Cover with plastic wrap and chill for at least 30 minutes.

8. Meanwhile, make the red wine sauce. Heat the oil in a large pan, then cook the beef trimmings for a few minutes until browned on all sides. Stir in the shallots with the peppercorns, bay leaf, and thyme and continue to cook for about 5 minutes, stirring frequently, until the shallots turn golden brown.

9. Pour in the vinegar and let it bubble for a few minutes until almost dry. Now add the wine and boil until almost completely reduced. Add the stock and bring to a boil again. Lower the heat and simmer gently for 1 hour, removing any foam from the surface of the sauce, until you have the desired consistency. Strain the liquid through a fine sieve lined with cheesecloth. Check for seasoning and set aside.

10. When you are ready to cook the beef Wellingtons, score the pastry lightly and brush with the egg wash again, then bake at 400°F for 15–20 minutes until the pastry is golden brown and cooked. Rest for 10 minutes before carving.

11. Meanwhile, reheat the sauce. Serve the beef Wellingtons sliced, with the sauce as an accompaniment.

HOW TO COOK BEEF TO PERFECTION
The only surefire way to ensure that your beef is perfectly pink is to check the internal temperature with a probe thermometer. It should read 85°F.

CHICKEN AND AUTUMN VEGETABLE PIES

SERVES 2–3

I've always loved serving individual pies. It instantly elevates a casual family dish into something a bit smarter, but without really increasing the work. The twist here is that the lids are cooked separately from the pie filling. If serving more than two or three people, simply double the quantities for the filling, but the amount of pastry required depends on the size of your dish(es). Use the meat from the chicken thigh and leg as it is less likely to dry out than the breast.

2 ounces pancetta, chopped
1 Tbsp olive oil
1 leek, trimmed and sliced
7 ounces celeriac, peeled and cut into small cubes
7 ounces butternut squash, peeled and cut into small cubes
Handful of thyme sprigs, leaves only
Sea salt and freshly ground black pepper
¼ cup dry sherry

1 cup chicken stock
½ cup crème fraîche
One 6-ounce sheet frozen puff pastry, thawed
All-purpose flour, for rolling
1 egg yolk, beaten with 1 tsp water
8 ounces cooked chicken, cut into chunks

1. Fry the pancetta in a hot, dry pan for 3–4 minutes until lightly golden. Tip onto a plate lined with paper towels. Wipe out the pan.

2. Heat the oil in the pan and sauté the vegetables with the thyme and some salt and pepper for about 7 minutes until softened. Pour in the sherry and bubble for 5 minutes until well reduced. Return the pancetta to the pan and pour in the stock.

3. Return the liquid to a boil and cook for 10–15 minutes until reduced by half. Stir in the crème fraîche and cook for about 5 minutes until the sauce has reduced by about a third. Check for seasoning, then remove from the heat and set aside.

4. Preheat the oven to 400°F. Roll out the pastry on a lightly floured surface to ⅛-inch thickness. Cut out 2 or 3 rounds, using a small saucer as a template. Carefully place the pastry rounds on a large, nonstick baking sheet and score the surface in a diamond pattern, using the tip of a small sharp knife.

5. Brush the pastry with the egg yolk glaze and bake for about 10 minutes until risen and golden. Bake for an additional 2 minutes with the oven door slightly ajar, to help crisp the pastry. Remove from the oven and slide onto a wire rack.

6. Meanwhile, add the chicken to the sauce and reheat until the meat is warmed through. Check the seasoning and divide the chicken mixture between your warmed serving plates. Top each pile with a pastry round and serve.

MOLASSES-GLAZED HAM

SERVES 8

I've always loved ham, not just hot with mashed potatoes and a cider gravy, but cold with salads and pickles. The sweet sticky glaze steals the glory here, but the poaching liquor has just as big a part to play. It's the chance to really inject extra flavor, especially when you replace most of the water with a couple of bottles of stout.

1 unsmoked, boneless ham roast, about
  4½ pounds, soaked overnight
1 large onion, peeled and roughly chopped
1 large carrot, peeled and roughly chopped
1 large leek, trimmed and roughly chopped
1 large cinnamon stick
2 bay leaves
1 tsp black peppercorns
Two 16-ounce bottles stout
Cloves, to stud

FOR THE GLAZE
¼ cup molasses
2 Tbsp Dijon mustard
1 Tbsp soy sauce
1 Tbsp Worcestershire sauce
⅓ cup light brown sugar

HOW TO STORE THE HAM
The boiled ham can be chilled for up to 2 days, and once roasted will keep in the fridge for a couple more days. If you aren't going to roast it right away, leave it to cool in the cooking liquor so that it absorbs even more flavor.

1. Drain the ham and place in a stockpot or large saucepan. Fill with enough cold water to cover and slowly bring to a boil, skimming off any foam that rises to the surface with a large metal spoon. Lower the heat and simmer for a few minutes, then carefully pour off the water along with any more foam.

2. Add the onion, carrot, leek, cinnamon stick, bay leaves, and peppercorns to the ham in the pot and pour in the stout. Top with enough cold water to make sure the ham is completely covered. Bring to a simmer and cook, partially covered, for 2½ hours over low heat. Skim off any foam during cooking and top off with boiling water as necessary.

3. Remove the ham from the pot and rest on a board until cool enough to handle. Preheat the oven to 375°F. Peel the skin off the ham, leaving behind an even layer of fat about ¼ inch thick. Using a sharp knife, score the fat in a crisscross diamond pattern at ½-inch intervals, then stud each diamond with a clove. Transfer the ham to a roasting pan.

4. Mix together all the ingredients for the glaze and brush half of it over the ham. Roast for 15 minutes, then pour over the rest of the glaze and continue to roast for an additional 10–15 minutes, basting every 5 minutes. Remove from the oven and give the meat a final basting with the pan juices. Leave to rest before carving into thin slices.

LEMON CURD TREACLE TART
SERVES 8–10

I love the tangy sharpness that lemon curd adds to a classic treacle tart. The recipe uses light treacle, generally known as golden syrup, a common British sweetener made from evaporating sugar cane juice until it's thick and syrupy. You can find golden syrup at British specialty shops or online; one source is www.britishfoodshop.com. Or you can substitute corn syrup or maple syrup. Do make sure the pastry base is well cooked before you add the curd or it will get soggy, and take the tart out of the oven while it still has a slight wobble. It will firm up more as it cools.

1½ cups golden syrup
4 Tbsp butter, melted
¼ cup heavy cream
Zest and juice of 1 lemon
1½ cups white breadcrumbs
3 large egg yolks
3 Tbsp lemon curd

FOR THE SWEET PASTRY
½ cup (1 stick) unsalted butter, softened
   to room temperature
7 Tbsp sugar
1 large egg
2 cups all-purpose flour

1. First make the sweet pastry. Place the butter and sugar in a food processor and process until just combined. Add the egg and process for 30 seconds.

2. Tip in the flour and process for a few seconds until the dough just comes together. (Do not overprocess or it will become tough.) Add a little ice-cold water (around a tablespoon) if the dough seems too dry.

3. Knead the dough lightly on a floured surface and shape into a flat disc. Wrap in plastic wrap and chill for 30 minutes before rolling out.

4. To make the tart, roll out the pastry on a lightly floured surface to a large round the thickness of ⅛ inch. Use to line a loose-bottomed tart pan (9–10 inches), leaving some excess pastry overhanging the rim. Chill for 30 minutes. Meanwhile, preheat the oven to 375°F.

5. Line the pastry case with parchment paper and ceramic baking beans or uncooked rice and bake "blind" for 15–20 minutes until the base is cooked through. Carefully remove the beans and paper and allow the pastry to cool a little. While still warm, cut off the excess pastry to level with the rim of the pan. Lower the oven setting to 300°F.

6. To make the filling, gently heat the golden syrup in a saucepan along with the butter. (Be careful not to boil this—just allow the butter to melt.)

7. When the butter has melted, stir in the cream, lemon zest and juice, and breadcrumbs, then add the egg yolks. Mix well.

8. Spread the lemon curd over the base of the baked pastry case, then pour in the filling.

9. Bake for 30–40 minutes until the top has just set but the center is slightly wobbly when you shake the pan gently. It should still feel slightly soft in the center.

10. Let the tart cool completely before slicing and serving.

HOW TO PREVENT PASTRY SHRINKAGE
Pastry tends to shrink when cooked—that's why leaving it overhanging the pan and trimming after baking is a good idea. Use a very sharp knife and you will be left with a lovely neat edge.

APPLE CRUMBLE

SERVES 4

Who doesn't love crumble? By combining both fruit purée and chunks, and sweet, chewy dried cranberries, I'm creating layers of texture and interest beneath a beautiful crunchy granola topping. Don't worry about peeling the fruit. Whether it's apples, pears, or peaches, the flavor is all in the skin.

6 Tbsp granulated sugar
Pinch of ground cinnamon
1 vanilla pod, seeds only
6 apples, cored but not peeled, 3 of them grated, 3 cut into chunks
3 Tbsp dried cranberries
Zest of 1 lemon, juice of ½

FOR THE CRUMBLE TOPPING
¾ cup all-purpose flour
2 Tbsp brown sugar
3½ Tbsp butter, chilled and cubed
Pinch of ground cinnamon
¼ cup nutty granola or muesli

1. Preheat the oven to 400°F.

2. Heat a small ovenproof baking dish, add the granulated sugar, and heat for about 5 minutes until it caramelizes. Add the cinnamon, vanilla seeds, and grated apples and cook for 1–2 minutes. Stir in the apple chunks, then mix in the cranberries and lemon zest and juice. Remove from the heat and set aside.

3. To make the topping, place the flour, sugar, butter, and cinnamon in a bowl and rub together with your fingertips until the mixture resembles breadcrumbs. Add the granola and mix until fully incorporated.

4. Scatter the crumble topping over the fruit and heat the dish again on the stovetop. Once the apple mixture is bubbling, transfer to the preheated oven and bake for 12–14 minutes until the topping is a deep golden color. Remove and serve warm.

HOW TO MAKE A CRUNCHY CRUMBLE
Brown sugar works best in a crumble mixture because it keeps the butter from melting into the flour, and adding one-third granola or muesli to two-thirds crumble opens out the texture to give a crunchier result. Finally, only ever sprinkle your topping over the fruit. Don't push it down or it will get soggy.

COCONUT PANCAKES WITH MANGO SLICES AND LIME SYRUP

MAKES ABOUT 16 SMALL PANCAKES

This makes the most brilliant breakfast or brunch, and gets you out of the rut of making the same old plain pancakes with maple syrup. It's important to leave the batter to relax for 15 minutes, as it will thicken slightly, making for fuller, fluffier pancakes.

1 cup unsweetened desiccated coconut
¾ cup all-purpose flour
1½ tsp baking powder
1 egg, beaten
1 cup coconut milk (shake the can before measuring to distribute the solids evenly)
1 Tbsp runny honey
Oil
1 ripe mango

FOR THE LIME SYRUP
⅔ cup sugar
Juice of 4 limes, finely grated zest of 1

1. To make the pancake batter, put the coconut into a blender and blend for 1 minute or until it becomes a coarse powder. Add the flour and baking powder and pulse for a couple of seconds to combine. Pour into a mixing bowl.

2. Make a well in the flour and add the egg. Stir into the flour, then whisk in the coconut milk and honey, whisking until a smooth batter forms. Cover and leave to rest for 15 minutes. Before cooking, add a little water or coconut milk if the batter is too thick.

3. Meanwhile, make the lime syrup. Put the sugar, ⅔ cup water, and the lime juice and zest into a small saucepan. Bring to a high simmer and stir until the sugar has dissolved. Continue to simmer briskly for 15 minutes until the liquid has reduced slightly and developed a syrupy consistency. Taste and add a little more lime zest if necessary. Leave to cool until just warm.

4. To cook the pancakes, heat a little oil in a large nonstick frying pan over medium-low heat, swirling it around to cover the bottom. Working in batches, place heaping tablespoons of batter in the pan and cook for 2–3 minutes until golden. Turn over with a pancake turner and repeat on the other side until golden and cooked through. Remove and set aside in a warm place while you cook the remaining batter, adding more oil to the pan as needed.

5. Peel the mango and cut the flesh into thin slices. Serve the pancakes with slices of mango and a drizzle of lime syrup on top.

HOW TO HANDLE HONEY
Sticky ingredients such as honey can be a mess to measure out, so rub the spoon first with a neutral oil, like grapeseed. The ingredient will slide off immediately.

RASPBERRY CHEESECAKE

SERVES 8

If there is one thing you Americans know how to do, it's how to make great cheesecakes. This is my take on dense, creamy, classic New York–style cheesecake.

Butter, for greasing
20 ounces (2½ cups) cream cheese, at room
   temperature
¾ cup sugar
3 eggs, lightly beaten
2 Tbsp all-purpose flour
Finely grated zest of 1 lemon
1½ cups raspberries

1. Preheat the oven to 350°F. Butter a 9-inch springform cake pan.

2. Beat together the cream cheese and sugar. Add the beaten eggs bit by bit until combined. Add the flour and lemon zest, then fold through the raspberries.

3. Spoon the mixture into the prepared cake pan, tapping it against the work surface to remove any bubbles and help the raspberries rise up from the bottom. Bake in the preheated oven for 35 minutes, or until set on the edges but wobbling slightly in the middle.

4. Once cooled, refrigerate until cold, at least 3 hours. Loosen the spring form and remove from the pan, running a knife around the edges to loosen if necessary, and serve.

HOW TO ZEST A LEMON
Place a four-sided grater on a plate. Using the side with the smallest holes, rub the lemon down it in long, sweeping strokes, turning the fruit a little after each stroke so you don't grate any of the bitter white pith.

FISH

GIVEN THAT FISH IS SO HEALTHY AND DELICIOUS, I'M ALWAYS SURPRISED WE DON'T EAT MORE OF IT, OR AT LEAST COOK MORE FISH AT HOME.

It seems that unless it comes covered in batter and in a sandwich, we have a deep mistrust of it. That's a great shame because, putting aside for a moment concerns about sustainability and dwindling stocks, fish is one of the simplest and most rewarding things to cook. It really doesn't need any adornment.

If you don't believe me, go out and get yourself a fillet of whitefish. It doesn't matter what—cod, haddock, sole, whatever. Now heat a tablespoon of olive oil in a pan and while you are waiting for that to get really hot, dredge the fish in some seasoned flour, shaking off any excess. Lay the fish down in the hot oil. Give it three to four minutes, depending on the thickness of the fillet, then turn it over and add a bit of butter to the pan. Now spoon the butter over the fish, infusing it with all that lovely fishy, nutty flavor as it cooks. Another couple of minutes and it should be done. Now slip it onto a plate, squeeze a little lemon juice over it, and have a taste. Amazing, isn't it? So simple, yet so utterly delicious. And ready within five or six minutes. If only more people realized how easy and versatile fish can be, we'd eat a lot more of it, so I hope the recipes in this chapter will give you the confidence to explore the world beyond the fish stick.

BUYING

As I mentioned, there is rightly much concern about sustainability. Overfishing has depleted a lot of stocks worldwide, with new species, from tuna to anchovy, being added to the endangered list all the time. There are frequent campaigns to encourage us to eat less overfished fish—Pacific cod rather than Atlantic cod, for example, or striped bass instead of Chilean sea bass—and while it's important to get these messages out, I don't think the occasional fish-eater should feel too guilty. Provided that the fish you are buying is certified by the Marine Stewardship Council, which works to ensure sustainability, or is on the Monterey Bay Aquarium Seafood Watch recommended list, you can eat fish with a clear conscience.

   Broadly speaking, fish can be divided according to six categories: freshwater or saltwater, flat or round, white or oily. All have their own distinct flavors and textures that suggest how they should be cooked, but they are often interchangeable. A recipe that calls for mackerel, for example, might work equally well with herring because they are both oily saltwater fish; similarly, tilapia will work in place of flounder. So don't be put off if your fishmonger doesn't have exactly what you are after. He is sure to be able to suggest an alternative.

I always like to buy my fish whole because it gives you more clues about its freshness, and that is very important when buying. Some fish, such as mackerel, will deteriorate very quickly, and can take on a muddy flavor. Look for bright, glossy eyes, fresh red gills, and firm flesh with a shiny, but not slimy, sheen. Contrary to popular belief, fish should not smell "fishy" but just faintly briny. Steer clear of anything tired-looking, especially with sunken or cloudy eyes or dry, soft skin that doesn't bounce back when you prod it with a finger.

Don't be put off if you see that fish has been previously frozen. It may well be "fresher" than the fresh fish. Deep-sea fishing boats are often out for weeks at a time, and better that it is frozen on board rather than merely kept on ice. Of course, this should never be the case with fish caught by day boats around our shores.

In an ideal world, we'd all buy our fish from the local fishmonger, who can tell us what has just come in, but sadly they are disappearing faster than independent butchers. If buying from the supermarket, it is often better to buy pre-packaged fillets that sit in a plastic tray rather than from the fish counter, as pre-packed fish is flushed with inert gas to preserve it better. There seems to be a fashion now to shrink-wrap fillets, which I think is the worst way to buy fish, as it marinates in its own juices and the flesh quickly becomes waterlogged and mushy.

Crabs, lobsters, mussels, oysters, and scallops all thrive in the cold waters of the northen states, producing sweet, juicy flesh. Lobsters are usually prohibitively expensive, though I often prefer the flavor of crab anyway, which can be a really good value, although the meat doesn't come out as easily as lobster meat does. For ease, you can buy them dressed, meaning cracked open, the flesh removed and picked over, then repacked into the empty shell. With a bit of practice, they are easy to dress yourself too. When buying a whole crab, look for one that feels heavy for its size.

Mussels are probably the most sustainable seafood on the planet. You'll find them in large net bags at supermarkets and they make a great quick lunch or supper, but for scallops and oysters you'll normally have to go to a fishmonger or buy online. Mollusks should always be cooked live, so as soon as you get them home, store them wrapped in a damp dish towel in the bottom of your fridge and eat within a day. Clean mussels only when you are about to eat them. Discard any with cracked shells or any open ones that fail to close when you give them a sharp tap. Then rinse them under running water, pulling away their stringy "beards" and using a knife to cut away any barnacles.

PREPARING

Fish and seafood sometimes need to be prepared before cooking. It's easiest, of course, to ask your fishmonger to do this job for you, but if you have a sharp, flexible knife, it's not that hard once you get the hang of it. Here are some of the techniques you may find most useful.

HOW TO FILLET, SKIN, AND PIN-BONE A FISH

1. Cut the fish's head off at a diagonal just behind the gills. Keeping the fish flat, with its tail toward you, and starting at head end, cut through skin along the length of the backbone, using long sweeping strokes. Arching the fish's back slightly with your free hand will make the skin tauter and therefore easier to cut.

2. Once you have reached beyond the ribcage, insert the knife fully and cut along the backbone to the tail, releasing the tail end completely.

3. Now go back to the head end and, using your free hand to pull the fillet away from the backbone, use short strokes of the knife to tease the flesh away from the ribcage. Work your way down the fish until the fillet is released.

4. Turn the fish over, with the tail away from you, and repeat the process, keeping the knife flat so that it stays as close as possible to the fish's backbone.

5. To remove the skin, place the fillet skin side down on your work surface. Grip the tail firmly with your free hand and cut down through the flesh, as low down the fish as you can, until you reach the skin. Now, pulling the fish taut and keeping the knife angled slightly downward, cut the flesh away from the skin using a long sawing motion.

6. To remove fine pin bones, use either tweezers or a swivel-bladed vegetable peeler. Catch the bones between the two blades and flick up, twisting as you do so, to pull out the bones. Pin bones in some larger fish, such as cod, can be difficult to remove without tearing the flesh. These are best removed once the fish is cooked.

HOW TO SHUCK AN OYSTER

Just before serving, scrub any dirt from the shell under running water. Holding the oyster level in a clean dish towel, insert a shucking knife through the hinge (tapered end) of the oyster and twist until the shell pops open. Run your knife around the inside of the top shell to release the oyster. Remove the top shell, being careful not to spill any of its precious juice.

HOW TO BUTTERFLY A MACKEREL FILLET

By removing the backbone from small fish but leaving the two fillets intact, you make them easier to stuff and much less fussy to eat. Remove the head, but leave the tail. Cut along the length of the belly and place the fish, belly down, on a work surface. Now push down on its backbone to flatten the fish out. Using your fingers and a sharp knife, you should be able to work the backbone free. Don't worry about any small bones as they will be soft enough to eat.

COOKING

Unlike meat, which doesn't generally require minute-precise cooking times, fish does require more accuracy. Overcooked fish will dry out and turn mushy. You want to bring your fish to the stage where the flesh has just turned white or opaque instead of translucent, and it divides easily into individual flakes. The thinner the fish, obviously, the quicker it will cook. Check by inserting a sharp knife. If it meets no resistance, it's done.

FRYING

This is probably the most common method for cooking filleted fish as you have total control and can easily see when it is cooked. There are a couple of rules. First, as with frying meat, make sure your pan is properly hot. I can't say often enough that overcoming the fear of a really hot pan will improve your cooking no end. This, along with confident seasoning, are the two things that most separate a professional chef from an amateur.

Add olive oil and once it is at the smoking point, lay your fish in. It should sizzle on contact with the oil. If it is a skinned fillet, especially of whitefish, which has more delicate flesh, you may need to dust it in flour or breadcrumbs first to protect it from the heat. However, I always like to cook my fish with the skin on because the skin does that job for you and also adds extra flavor. So cook it skin side down for 90 percent of the time, finishing it off only briefly on the other side. Don't worry if it looks like it is sticking. If you wait, it will release itself once it is cooked. The worst thing to do is to keep fiddling and shifting it around, or it will break up. During the last minute or so of cooking, add a bit of butter and baste the fish continuously to keep it moist and flavorful.

BROILING AND ROASTING

Both these methods work well for whole fish and large steaks, particularly oily types such as salmon or mackerel. Sometimes I will pan-fry thick fillets first to get some color on the skin, and then finish them off in a hot oven for about 10 minutes, this time with the skin on the top. Whitefish may need brushing with oil or melted butter to stop it from drying out.

POACHING

This is the gentlest way of cooking fish to enhance its delicate flavor and ensure that it stays perfectly moist. The fish is cooked in liquid, sometimes wine, sometimes stock, sometimes milk, to which you can add herbs, spices, and vegetables to infuse the fish. The key is to let the liquid barely simmer as a rolling boil will break up the fish. The stock you are left with can then be used to make a sauce to go with the fish.

STEAMING

Another very easy cooking method. You can, of course, use a fish kettle or steamer, but it is more interesting to steam fish *en papillote*, where you wrap the fish (normally a fillet) in a paper or foil parcel along with a splash of liquid, herbs, and other flavorings. The great thing about cooking this way is that all the flavor is trapped in the bag and it makes a great dinner dish because each guest can cut open their own parcel.

HOW TO COOK A CRAB

Yes, it is time-consuming and fussy to cook a crab, but it's also incredibly satisfying. The first thing to check in a crab is the weight: it should feel quite heavy for its size. A good live crab will also have extremely strong reflexes. A flaccid crab is a half-dead crab, and that's no good because the minute it begins to die, an enzyme is released that starts to break down the meat, making it wet and lackluster.

Every fisherman and cook seems to have different opinions on the correct way to kill and cook a crab (for the most humane way, consult the Humane Society website). I think the simplest solution is to place it in a large pan of salted, cold water and boil for five minutes per pound. Remove from the heat, allow it to cool, and prepare to pick.

Cover the table in plenty of old newspaper. Twist the claws to remove them from the body. Now hold the crab upside down by its shell and pull the abdomen away. Inside the shell you will find all the brown meat. You can now take this meat out with a teaspoon and set it aside for later. Next, remove the crab's gills, or dead man's fingers, from the abdomen and throw them away.

Now, using a sharp knife, dissect the abdomen. You will be able to see small tunnels, like a honeycomb, crammed with good, white crab meat. Here the real work begins. Use any small, sharp instrument, such as a skewer, to pick out the meat, keeping it separate from the dark meat.

Finally, gently crush the claws with a hammer or rolling pin and pick out more of the white meat. There will also be some meat in the legs, but you might feel they are not worth the trouble.

ROASTED COD WITH A WALNUT, LEMON, AND PARMESAN CRUST

SERVES 4

This dish makes a lovely fuss-free supper and is very quick to make. One large fillet makes an impressive centerpiece, but you can just as well use 4 separate fillets of about 6 ounces each. For a change from cod, try haddock, hake, or any other meaty whitefish.

1 whole skinless cod fillet, about 1½ pounds
Olive oil
Sea salt and freshly ground black pepper
Lemon wedges, to serve

FOR THE WALNUT, LEMON, AND PARMESAN CRUST
5½ Tbsp butter
⅔ cup walnut pieces
⅔ cup fresh breadcrumbs
Grated zest of 1 large lemon
¾ cup freshly grated Parmesan cheese
Sea salt and freshly ground black pepper

FOR THE PARSLEY AND CAPER SAUCE
2 cups fish stock
¾ cup crème fraîche
3 Tbsp capers
Small bunch of flat-leaf parsley, chopped
Sea salt and freshly ground black pepper

1. First make the walnut, lemon, and Parmesan crust. Chop the butter into small cubes and put into a food processor. Add the walnuts, breadcrumbs, lemon zest, two-thirds of the Parmesan, and some salt and pepper, then process everything until the mixture binds together.

2. Check the cod for pin bones, removing any you find with a pair of tweezers (see page 54, step 6). Lay the fillet on a lightly oiled nonstick roasting pan, skin side down, and season with salt and pepper. Spread the crust mixture in an even layer over the top of the fish. Chill for 20 minutes until the crust feels firm.

3. Preheat the oven to 400°F. Sprinkle the remaining Parmesan over the top of the crust, then roast the cod for 20–25 minutes until the crust turns golden and crisp and the fish is just cooked.

4. Meanwhile, prepare the sauce. Pour the stock into a small saucepan and bring to a boil. Cook over high heat for about 10 minutes until reduced by two-thirds. Off the heat, whisk the crème fraîche into the reduced stock. Return to low heat and simmer for 5–10 minutes until you have the consistency of a light cream.

5. Add the capers and parsley just before serving and adjust the seasoning, adding salt and pepper to taste. Transfer the cod to a serving platter and pour over the sauce. Serve with lemon wedges on the side.

PAN-SEARED SCALLOPS WITH CRUNCHY APPLE SALAD
SERVES 2

Scallops are cooked when the outside is golden brown and the center is just going from translucent to opaque. Any longer than 2 minutes on each side and they'll get tough, so it's essential that you stand over them and remember the order you put them in the pan. The simple salad goes equally well with crab or lobster.

Olive oil
6 large scallops, cleaned
Sea salt and freshly ground black pepper
Juice of ½ lemon

FOR THE SALAD
1 sharp apple, such as Granny Smith
2 handfuls of mâche
Sea salt and freshly ground black pepper
Juice and zest of ½ lemon
Olive oil

1. First make the salad. Peel, core, and cut the apple into julienne strips. Mix with the mâche and season with salt and pepper. Add some of the lemon zest (keeping a little back to garnish) and squeeze over the juice. Drizzle the salad with olive oil and mix well.

2. Heat a large nonstick frying pan over high heat until smoking hot, then add 1 tablespoon of olive oil. Lay the scallops out on a cutting board, pat dry with paper towels, and season one side with salt and pepper.

3. Think of the frying pan as a clock face and add the scallops, one by one, seasoned side down, in a clockwise order, then sear for 1–2 minutes until golden brown. Season the unseasoned side of the scallops, then flip them over in the same order you placed them in the pan and repeat the process. Squeeze the lemon juice over the scallops and give the pan a good shake.

4. When the scallops are cooked, tip the contents of the pan onto a plate lined with paper towels. This will instantly stop the cooking process, while the paper towels will absorb any excess oil.

5. Divide the salad between 2 serving plates and arrange the scallops around each pile. Garnish with the remaining lemon zest and serve immediately.

HOW TO CUT JULIENNE STRIPS
Julienne are fine strips about the size of matchsticks. To make them, peel and core your ingredient, then cut in half or into quarters. Place flat side down on a work surface and cut into slices about ⅛ inch thick. Cut these slices into matchstick-sized pieces.

CHILE AND SPICE WHITEBAIT

SERVES 4

Fresh whitebait, dusted in seasoned flour, quickly fried in oil, and sprinkled with lemon juice is very quick and simple but makes a great starter on a summer's evening. If you can't find whitebait—it's often hard to find in the States—try raw tiger shrimp, squid, or even crab claws.

1 tsp Sichuan peppercorns
1 tsp coriander seeds
1 tsp dried chile flakes
1½ pounds whitebait, defrosted if frozen
Flavorless oil, such as peanut, for deep-frying
¼ cup all-purpose flour
Sea salt and freshly ground black pepper
Lemon wedges, to serve

1. Toast the Sichuan peppercorns and the coriander seeds in a dry frying pan for 1–2 minutes until aromatic. Transfer to a mortar, add the chile flakes, and pound with a pestle until powdered, then set aside.

2. Gently wash the whitebait and pat dry with paper towels. Pour the oil into a deep-fat fryer and heat to 340°F, or fill a large saucepan one-third full of oil and heat until a cube of bread dropped into the hot oil sizzles and turns golden after 30 seconds.

3. Season the flour with salt and pepper and mix with the ground spices. Dust the whitebait in the spiced flour, shaking off any excess, and deep-fry in batches for 1–2 minutes on each side until golden and cooked through.

4. Remove and drain on paper towels. Taste and season with a little more salt if necessary. Repeat with the remaining batches.

5. Serve while still warm with wedges of lemon.

HOW TO PAN-FRY WHITEBAIT
You can pan-fry the whitebait if you prefer. Just cook smaller batches at a time in less oil.

PAN-GRILLED SEAFOOD
WITH SWEET PEPPER SAUCE
SERVES 4

I'm always happy eating grilled seafood with a garlicky mayonnaise, but sometimes it's good to change it up. The sauce, sometimes called romesco, originated in Catalonia in Spain, and is a blend of roasted peppers, tomatoes, nuts, vinegar, and olive oil. You can use it right away, but it benefits from a night in the fridge for the flavors to develop.

4 medium to large squid, prepared and cleaned
12 jumbo shrimp, shell on
Sea salt and freshly ground black pepper
2 Tbsp chopped parsley, to garnish

FOR THE SWEET PEPPER SAUCE
2 red peppers
1 thick slice of ciabatta or farmhouse white bread, crusts removed, torn into chunks
Olive oil

3 garlic cloves, peeled and roughly chopped
3 ripe tomatoes, such as plum tomatoes, on the vine
1 tsp smoked paprika
1 tsp dried chile flakes
½ cup blanched almonds, toasted and roughly chopped
Juice of ½ lemon
1–2 Tbsp sherry vinegar
Sea salt and freshly ground black pepper

1. First make the sauce. Heat a broiler until very hot. Put the peppers on a foil-lined baking sheet and place under the broiler. Cook for 5 minutes, turning regularly until the skin is blackened and blistered all over. Transfer to a bowl, cover with plastic wrap, and set aside to cool.

2. Cook the bread chunks for 2 minutes in a small frying pan with a dash of oil, then add the garlic and cook for an additional minute until the garlic is tender and the bread is toasted. By this stage the peppers should have cooled and it will be easy to peel and rub off the charred skins. Peel, seed, and roughly chop them, then place in a blender. Roughly chop the tomatoes and add to the peppers with the bread and garlic. Blend to form a rough paste.

3. Add the smoked paprika, chile flakes, almonds, lemon juice, vinegar, and a pinch of salt and pepper to the blender and blend until well mixed. Taste and adjust the seasoning. With the motor running, slowly pour in ½ cup olive oil. Taste and adjust the seasoning again if necessary. Allow to come to room temperature and stir well before serving.

4. Prepare the seafood. Heat a grill pan over high heat until hot. Lightly score one side of the squid in a diamond pattern before cutting into strips. Toss the shrimp and squid together in a little olive oil and season with salt and pepper. Place the shrimp on the hot grill pan and cook for 2½–3 minutes. Starting diamond side up, cook the squid for about 1 minute on each side. Leave it to curl up, and give it an additional minute until just cooked.

5. Serve the seafood hot, garnished with parsley, and with the sweet pepper sauce alongside.

ROASTED MACKEREL WITH GARLIC AND PAPRIKA
SERVES 4

I don't know why some people don't like mackerel and why it's not more widely served in the States. It's such a lovely fish, cheap and plentiful, and, served with this gently Spanish vinaigrette, an absolute winner. Make sure you dress the potatoes while they are still warm as they'll take on the dressing much better.

2 garlic cloves, peeled
2 tsp paprika
1 tsp sea salt, plus more to taste
Olive oil
8 mackerel fillets, skin on
1 pound new potatoes
2–3 scallions, trimmed and thinly sliced

FOR THE VINAIGRETTE
Pinch of saffron
1 Tbsp white wine vinegar
1 tsp Dijon mustard
¼ cup extra virgin olive oil
Sea salt and freshly ground black pepper

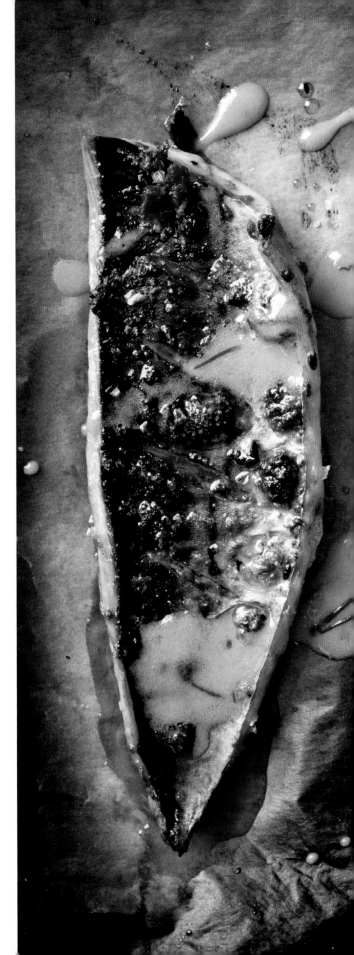

1. Preheat the oven to 400°F.

2. Put the garlic and paprika into a mortar, add the salt, and pound to a smooth paste. Add a few drops of olive oil, then rub the flesh side of the mackerel fillets with the paste and set aside.

3. Make the vinaigrette. Put all the ingredients into a small bowl and whisk together with a fork. Season with salt and pepper to taste.

4. Line a baking sheet with parchment paper and brush lightly with olive oil. Lay the mackerel fillets skin side up on the paper and season the skin with sea salt. Roast for 8–10 minutes until the skin is crisp and the fish is cooked through. Remove from the oven and leave to rest.

5. Meanwhile, boil the potatoes in a large pan of salted water for about 15 minutes until tender, then drain. Return to the pan with 1 tablespoon of olive oil. Crush lightly with the back of a fork, then add the scallions and stir to combine. Season with salt, then add a couple of tablespoons of the vinaigrette.

6. Serve the crushed potatoes topped with the mackerel and a drizzle of the remaining vinaigrette.

CRAB AND MASCARPONE CRÊPES

MAKES 6 CRÊPES

This is an unusual way of serving crab but makes a great change from a crab sandwich or crab with chile flakes, lemon, and linguini. The white crab meat looks pretty and has a lovely sweet flavor, but it's the brown meat that packs the real punch. I always use a combination of the two, but it is up to you.

½ cup mascarpone cheese
Pinch of cayenne pepper, or to taste
¼ cup chopped chives
Juice and zest of ¼ lemon, or to taste
Sea salt and freshly ground black pepper
10 ounces cooked white crab meat, or mixed white and brown meat
Olive oil
Lemon wedges, to serve (optional)

FOR THE CRÊPE BATTER
1 cup all-purpose flour
Good pinch of salt
1 egg, beaten
1–1¼ cups milk

1. First make the crêpe batter. Sift the flour and salt into a mixing bowl. Make a well in the middle and add the egg. Slowly pour in the milk, mixing with the flour as you add. Whisk to form a smooth batter with no lumps, the thickness of heavy cream. Cover and leave to rest for 15 minutes.

2. Mix together the mascarpone, cayenne pepper, half of the chives, and some lemon juice and zest. Add some salt and pepper, then fold in the crab meat. Taste and adjust the seasoning as necessary, adding more lemon juice and/or zest and another pinch of cayenne or salt and pepper, if needed.

3. To cook the crêpes, heat a dash of oil in a small to medium nonstick frying pan and swirl around to cover the bottom. When hot but not smoking, add a small ladleful of the batter, just enough to coat the bottom of the pan, and swirl to spread it out thinly.

4. Cook on one side for 1–1½ minutes until golden, then flip the crêpe and repeat on the other side. Transfer to a plate and keep warm while using the remaining batter in the same way.

5. To serve, place spoonfuls of the crab mascarpone mixture in the center of the warm crêpes, fold them over it, and garnish with a sprinkling of the remaining chopped chives. Serve with lemon wedges, if using.

GORDON'S KEDGEREE

SERVES 4–6

Kedgeree is wonderfully comforting, especially after a hard night, and very easy to make. To enrich it at the end and make a lighter dish, I've used plain yogurt instead of the more usual butter or cream. Hot-smoked trout or even mackerel work just as well as smoked haddock, but in these cases use plain water to cook the rice.

2 bay leaves
1½ pounds undyed smoked haddock fillets,
   pin-boned (see page 54, step 6)
½ cup (1 stick) butter or ghee
1 garlic clove, peeled and finely chopped
1 onion, peeled and finely chopped, or 1 bunch
   of scallions, trimmed and finely chopped
Thumb-sized piece of fresh ginger, peeled
   and grated
2 Tbsp curry powder
1 Tbsp mustard seeds

2 tomatoes, seeded and chopped
1 cup long-grain or basmati rice
Juice of 2 lemons
½ cup plain yogurt

TO SERVE
2 good handfuls of cilantro, leaves chopped
1 red chile, seeded and finely chopped
4 large eggs, boiled for about 5 minutes with
   yolks left soft, peeled and halved
Sea salt and freshly ground pepper

1. Heat 3 cups water and the bay leaves in a large frying pan and bring to a simmer. Put in the haddock, skin side up, and simmer for 5 minutes until the fish feels flaky and is cooked through. Remove with a fish spatula and drain on a plate. Reserve the cooking liquid.

2. In a second pan, melt the butter, add the garlic and onion, and gently sauté for a couple of minutes. Add the ginger, curry powder, mustard seeds, and tomatoes and cook for an additional 3 minutes until the onions have softened.

3. Add the rice, stir a couple of times to coat it in the butter, then gradually add the lemon juice and cooking liquid from the fish, stirring well after each addition. (This should take about 20 minutes.)

4. Carefully pull the skin off the haddock and flake the flesh, checking for any bones, then stir into the rice along with the yogurt.

5. To serve, divide the kedgeree among 4–6 warmed serving plates, sprinkle on the cilantro and chile, top with the eggs, and season with salt and pepper.

PORGY WITH TOMATO AND HERB SALSA

SERVES 2

This is a beautiful way of serving all kinds of fish fillets, from porgy to sea bass or even cod.
The salsa is effectively a warm vinaigrette, so don't heat it too vigorously. The idea is just to encourage the flavors to mingle so they cut through the fish.

Olive oil
2 porgy fillets, about 5 ounces each
Sea salt and freshly ground black pepper

FOR THE TOMATO AND HERB SALSA
Olive oil
8 ounces cherry tomatoes
½ cup pitted black olives (Kalamata if possible), drained
Sea salt and freshly ground black pepper
Small bunch of cilantro
Small bunch of basil
1 lemon

HOW TO CHOP HERBS
Soft herbs, such as basil, parsley, cilantro, and mint, can bruise very easily, so try to make sure you cut them only once. The easiest way to do this is to roll them gently into a ball or cigar shape, and slice along their length. Don't be tempted to go back over them—unlike rosemary, say, they never have to be cut that fine.

1. First make the salsa. Place a small saucepan over low heat and add 3 tablespoons of olive oil. Chop the tomatoes in half and add to the oil. Add the olives, season with salt and pepper, and stir over low heat for 1–2 minutes. Set aside.

2. Hold the cilantro and basil stalks together and slice down with a sharp knife to shave off the leaves. Discard the stalks, then gently roll the cilantro and basil leaves into a ball and chop. Reserving a little for garnish, add the cilantro and basil to the salsa and stir to combine.

3. Roll the lemon on a cutting board to soften it and release the juices, then cut in half. Add the juice of one half to the pan, stir, and set the salsa aside to allow the flavors to infuse.

4. To cook the porgy, heat a heavy-bottomed frying pan over high heat. Meanwhile, slash the skin of the fillets in 2 or 3 places. Add a dash of oil to the pan and, when really hot, add the porgy fillets skin side down. Season with salt and pepper and cook for 2–3 minutes until the fish is dark golden and the skin is crisp. (The flesh should be opaque two-thirds of the way up the fillet.)

5. Turn the fillets and cook on the other side for 1 minute, basting with the oil in the pan, until just cooked through.

6. To serve, sit the fish fillets on top of the tomato and herb salsa and sprinkle with the reserved cilantro and basil.

SEA BASS WITH FENNEL, LEMON, AND CAPERS

SERVES 4

Cooking fish in individual foil packets, or *en papillote*, as they say in France, is a great way of sealing in all the flavors. The smell that hits you when you open them up is just phenomenal, so let everyone do their own at the table. Feel free to change the fish and aromatics, but make sure you include a little liquid so the fish steams. Serve with crushed new potatoes and zucchini ribbons.

2 sea bass, 3 pounds in total (or use 4 small ones, about 10 ounces each), scaled and cleaned
Sea salt and freshly ground black pepper
2 small fennel bulbs, fronds reserved
3 Tbsp small capers, drained and rinsed

1 lemon, sliced
2 dill sprigs
2 Tbsp butter
Olive oil
½ cup white wine

1. Preheat the oven to 400°F.

2. Season the fish with salt and pepper really well inside and out. Thinly slice the fennel and place, along with some fronds, inside the sea bass stomach cavity. Sprinkle in the capers and line the lemon slices on top of the fennel inside the cavity. Top with the dill and dot over the butter in small pieces.

3. Drizzle the fish with a little olive oil and then wrap in foil. Pour the wine into the parcel just before you close up the last corner and make sure the parcel is well sealed, wrapping it in a second piece of foil if necessary.

4. Place the parcel on a roasting sheet and bake in the oven—about 20 minutes for the 2 larger fish, or 8–10 minutes if using the smaller ones—until the fish is just cooked through with the flesh flaking away from the bone.

5. Remove from the oven and leave to rest for a few minutes before serving (be careful of the hot steam when you unwrap the foil). Serve sprinkled with the reserved fennel fronds.

RED MULLET WITH SWEET CHILE SAUCE

SERVES 4

What I love about the Asian style of food is that it has made my cooking so much lighter, and taken me away from using too much butter and cream. Red mullet is a sweet, robust fish that needs a lot of help with flavors (if you can't find red mullet, striped mullet or sea bass are good substitutes), and the chiles, fish sauce, lime, and cilantro really give it a wake-up call. The peanuts are there to add crunch—don't crush them too much or they will burn. Serve with fragrant rice and stir-fried broccoli.

4 red mullet fillets, about 5 ounces each, scaled
Olive oil
1 lime

FOR THE CRUST
5 ounces skinless peanuts
1 tsp dried chile flakes
Sea salt
Small handful of cilantro, leaves chopped
2 eggs, beaten
Dash of fish sauce

FOR THE SWEET CHILE SAUCE
2 red chiles, seeded and finely chopped
2 garlic cloves, peeled and sliced
Pinch of sea salt
1 Tbsp sugar, plus more if needed
2 Tbsp fish sauce
1 Tbsp rice vinegar
3 Tbsp olive oil
3 scallions, trimmed and chopped
Handful of cilantro, leaves chopped
Juice of 1 lime

1. First make the sweet chile sauce. Place the chiles in a mortar with the garlic, salt, and sugar. Pound until smooth. Add the fish sauce, rice vinegar, and olive oil, and mix with a spoon. Stir in the scallions, cilantro leaves, and lime juice. Taste and adjust the seasoning, adding more sugar if necessary. Pour into a serving bowl.

2. To make a crust for the fish, place the peanuts, chile flakes, and a good pinch of salt in a mortar. Pound until they look finely chopped but not powdered, then mix in the cilantro leaves. Scatter onto a plate or into a shallow bowl, and place the beaten eggs on a separate plate or in a shallow bowl. Season the eggs with a dash of fish sauce and a pinch of salt.

3. Dip the fish skin side down into the egg. Shake off any excess egg wash, then dip into the peanut mixture, coating the skin with a layer of peanuts. Repeat until all the fillets are coated on one side.

4. Add a little oil to a hot frying pan and fry the seasoned fillets over medium heat, crust side down, for 2–3 minutes until the crust is golden and the fish is half cooked. Turn and cook for an additional 1–2 minutes, basting as you cook. Remove from the heat and finish with a fresh squeeze of lime juice over each fillet.

5. Spoon the chile sauce over the fish to serve.

FISH PIE
SERVES 4–6

I can never understand why most fish pie recipes require you to precook the fish in milk, then subject it to 30 minutes in the oven. No wonder the fish is often chewy or turned into mush. A nicer—and much quicker—way is to bake it from raw ingredients. Invest in a bottle of Noilly Prat—that, rather than the type of stock, is what gives the sauce its flavor.

2 large shallots or 1 onion, peeled and chopped
2 Tbsp olive oil
3 Tbsp butter
1 large thyme sprig, leaves only
¼ cup Noilly Prat or dry vermouth
2 tsp Pernod (optional)
¼ cup all-purpose flour
1 cup fish, chicken, or vegetable stock
  (a stock cube is fine)
¾ cup milk
Sea salt and freshly ground black pepper
¼ cup heavy cream
3 Tbsp chopped fresh parsley
6 ounces skinless salmon fillets
9 ounces skinless cod or haddock fillets
7 ounces medium scallops
8 ounces large shrimp
1 Tbsp fresh lemon juice

FOR THE MASHED POTATO TOPPING
1¾ pounds red-skinned potatoes, peeled
5 Tbsp butter, cubed
¼ cup hot milk
2 large egg yolks
Sea salt and freshly ground black pepper
3 ounces medium Cheddar cheese, grated

1. Preheat the oven to 400°F. Grease a shallow (about 2-quart capacity) baking dish.

2. Start by making the mashed potato for the topping. Chop the potatoes into 2-inch chunks and cook in boiling salted water until tender, about 15 minutes. Drain well and push through a potato ricer, or mash until smooth. Add the butter and hot milk and mix until well incorporated. Allow to cool slightly, then stir in the egg yolks. Season well with salt and pepper and set aside.

3. Sauté the shallots or onion in the oil and butter with the thyme leaves for about 5 minutes until softened. Add the Noilly Prat and Pernod (if using), then cook for 4–5 minutes until reduced right down.

4. Stir in the flour and cook for a minute or so. Heat the stock in a small pan or a pitcher in the microwave. Gradually whisk it into the shallot mixture then stir with a wooden spoon until smooth, and boil for about 5 minutes until the mixture turns a shade darker. Mix in the milk, lower the heat, and simmer for a few minutes. Season well with salt and pepper, then add the cream and parsley.

5. Meanwhile, cut the salmon and cod into bite-sized chunks and scatter in the baking dish with the scallops and shrimp. Sprinkle with the lemon juice and season with salt and pepper. Put the dish on a baking sheet.

6. Pour over the sauce and mix well with a fork. Spread the mashed potatoes on top and fluff up with a fork. Scatter with the grated cheese and put the pie immediately in the oven. Bake for 10 minutes, then turn the oven down to 350°F and bake for another 20 minutes, turning if it browns unevenly. Allow to stand for 10 minutes before serving.

MUSSELS WITH CELERY AND CHILES

SERVES 2

If you are worried about sustainability, the one seafood you can eat with a totally clear conscience is mussels. This recipe is a reworking of a classic moules marinières. Be sure to eat it with some good bread to soak up all those fantastic juices.

2 pounds fresh mussels
Olive oil
3 scallions, trimmed and chopped
1 shallot, peeled and thinly sliced
1 celery stalk, trimmed and finely diced
2 garlic cloves, peeled and thinly sliced
1 fresh red chile, seeded and finely chopped
4 thyme sprigs, leaves only
1 bay leaf
1–2 Tbsp vermouth
⅔ cup dry white wine
2 Tbsp crème fraîche
Small bunch of flat-leaf parsley, roughly chopped
Sea salt and freshly ground black pepper
Crusty bread, to serve

1. To test that the mussels are okay to eat, place them in a sink or large bowl of cold water. Throw away any that do not close when tapped against a hard surface. Drain the mussels and remove the beards.

2. Heat a large, heavy-bottomed sauté pan or shallow saucepan over high heat. Add a good glug of oil and sauté the scallions, shallot, celery, garlic, chile, thyme, and bay leaf together. Cook for 2 minutes, shaking the pan, until the shallot and celery start to become tender.

3. Add the mussels to the pan and shake over very high heat for about 30 seconds. Cover tightly with a lid and leave to steam for 1–2 minutes, shaking the pan now and again. When the mussels begin to open add the vermouth and wine and continue to cook, uncovered, for an additional 1–2 minutes to reduce the liquid. Cover and cook for a final 30–60 seconds until the mussels have completely opened. Discard any that remain shut at the end of cooking.

4. Add the crème fraîche and parsley to the pan, then taste and season with salt and pepper as needed. Cover the pan and shake to combine the flavors. Remove the lid, stir, and serve immediately with plenty of crusty bread.

MEAT

FOR LOTS OF PEOPLE, A MEAL ISN'T A MEAL WITHOUT A PIECE OF MEAT AS ITS CENTERPIECE.

My generation was brought up on "meat and two veg," and it's a tradition that lives on in houses up and down the world. I still remember the Sunday roasts I sat down to as a child, but the rest of the week would be punctuated by meat of some sort, too, whether it was a piece of ham, a cottage pie, or the occasional steak as a treat.

What has changed is our understanding of what constitutes good meat. In the old days, in the absence of chemical fertilizers and growth-promoting hormones, all meat was by definition slow-reared and organic. But things went a bit off in the second half of the last century, when speed and efficiency took priority over compassion and taste. In a world with a fast-expanding population and ever more mouths to feed, I can see how that happened, but I'm pleased that many farmers have started once again to value slow-growing traditional breeds over their factory-farmed cousins. The rewards in terms of animal welfare and taste are amazing. There's a price implication in that, of course: free-range and organic animals will always cost a premium, but it's fantastic that we once again have the choice.

I don't want to get on my high horse and tell you to buy only this or that type of meat because we all have budgets we have to live by. What I will say is that personally I'd rather eat meat less often, but buy better-quality meat when I do, than eat cheap meat every day. Everything in an animal's life, from the moment it is born to the way it is slaughtered, will have an effect not just on its well-being but on its flavor. If a producer is having to cut corners to keep the price down, the end result is bound to suffer, and as a chef I know my cooking can only ever be as good as the raw ingredients I start with.

Does that mean I always buy organic? Not at all. Organic is a useful label that suggests more careful husbandry, but it can only ever be a guide. You can get good organic farmers and you can get bad organic farmers. What is far more important is to find a supplier you can trust, someone who knows all his

animals and wants to do his best by them, who really cares what you think of his produce. That way you are sure to end up with better-quality meat. I remember visiting my chicken supplier and asking if he had thought of upgrading from free-range to organic. "Why would I want to do that?" he asked. "I already treat my birds the best I possibly can, and I don't need a certificate to prove it. You can taste it in every mouthful." Plus, he wanted to know that if one of his birds did get sick, he'd be able to give her antibiotics to make her better. That's what you want. The very definition of compassionate farming.

BUYING

CHICKEN

is far and away the most popular meat, the staple of countless fast-food takeout places and sandwich fillings. As a result, it is one of the most open to abuse. At its best it can be the Rolls-Royce of meats—rich, dense, and versatile—but equally it can be produced as cheap protein fodder devoid of all flavor. That's why of all meats, I think the difference here between free-range and factory-farmed is the most obvious in both appearance and flavor. A factory-farmed bird killed at six to seven weeks, with its pumped-up breasts and legs weak from all that sitting around, is never going to have the personality of one that's lived a little. Naturally reared birds aren't killed until they are about 12 weeks old. That means an extra six weeks of scratching in the dirt, pecking at seeds and grains, and working those leg muscles to build up a rich depth of flavor.

If you are struggling to find a bird with real flavor, look for guinea fowl instead, which has a slightly gamier taste but can be cooked in exactly the same way. A lot of people say it tastes the way they remember chicken used to taste in the old days.

PORK

has also had a bad time of it recently, with many pigs kept in atrocious conditions—hemmed into concrete-floored pens too small for them to turn around in. As ever, happy animals make for happier eating, and slow-growing rare breeds that have been allowed to do what pigs do best, rooting around in the mud, are what we should be buying. Whatever recipe you are making, be it a spiced slow-roast belly, a rack of chops, or smoked back bacon, you'll always notice the difference.

LAMB

is a less controversial meat because sheep are naturally less intensively reared as they are happy grazing on scraggy hillsides that can't be put to any other agricultural use.

Spring lamb (from animals born before Christmas but slaughtered in March or April) is the most prized, but the flavor's better later in the summer, once it's had time to mature and be fed not just on its mother's milk but on that mineral-rich grass as well. Older animals need slower cooking as they will be tougher, but they can be more rewarding in terms of flavor.

We use a lot of the presentation cuts in my restaurants, such as loin, saddle, and best end (or rack), which cook very quickly. At home, I love things like leg, shoulder, and shanks, from the lower rear legs, which all need longer in the oven. Breast is another lovely cut, but is quite fatty, so benefits from slow roasting.

BEEF

is the meat that throws up the biggest divide in opinion, mainly because the same cut can taste so different depending on how it has been produced. Again, I favor slow-growing rare breeds that have a good marbling of fat throughout their meat. People are scared of fat these days, but it is so important to flavor and texture. Not only does it protect the meat from the heat of the oven or the pan and stop it from burning, but it melts as the muscle fiber cooks, adding flavor at the same time as keeping the meat moist. You'll find less marbling in young animals, and in cuts from muscles that aren't used as much, such as tenderloin. That's why these cuts need more careful cooking, as they can get dry and tough if overdone.

Hanging beef for anywhere up to 35 days is important as it gives time for enzymes to start to break down the muscle fiber, making it more tender and allowing the flavor to develop. Your butcher should be able to tell you how long his meat has been hung, but color can also be a clue. Well-hung beef should be a dark ruby color, rather than a bright, bloody red. You should know that supermarkets are less likely to age their meat, not only because the delay in getting it to the shop floor costs them money, but also because meat loses moisture as it hangs, thereby reducing its final selling weight. Farm shops, farmers' markets, and traditional butchers are the best places to buy.

If you are buying for a traditional Sunday roast, I'd always recommend a sirloin or rib roast, from the middle of the cow's back. You'll often see topside and silverside, from the top of the thigh, dressed up as roasts, sometimes with an extra layer of fat stitched on top like a poor man's hairpiece. These cuts are never as flavorful and can be very tough. They are better suited to slower pot-roasting, with a bit of liquid in the pan to keep them moist.

STORING

Once you get your meat home, you need to keep it correctly. Meat needs to breathe, so remove any plastic wrapping right away. This is particularly important with vacuum-packed cuts, which will otherwise marinate in their own blood and take on a nasty metallic taste. Put the meat on a plate loosely covered with paper or plastic wrap pierced with a few holes and place it at the bottom of the fridge so it can't drip onto any other foods.

    If you choose to freeze meat, wrap it up tightly in plastic wrap to keep water crystals from forming on the surface and chill it as quickly as possible. Always defrost meat slowly, ideally in the fridge or at room temperature. Never defrost raw meat in the microwave or the juices will seep out and the meat will toughen.

PREPARING

The meat that's likely to need the most fussy preparation prior to cooking is chicken. I always buy my chickens whole and then cut them up myself. It works out so much cheaper and you'll be amazed how far they go. The method described below will produce six pieces of dark brown meat (wings, thighs, and drumsticks) and two beautiful plump breasts. I've also given instructions for deboning, but this is altogether a more complicated affair, and, unless you're brimming with confidence, is probably best done by your butcher.

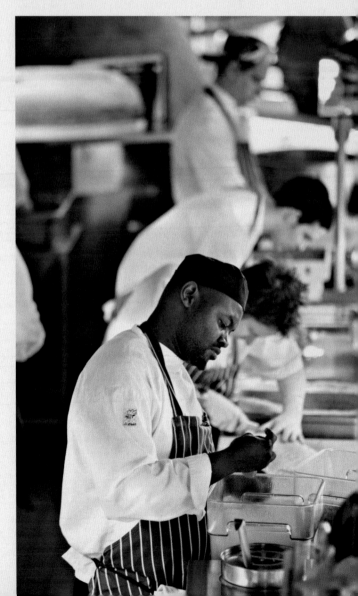

HOW TO CUT UP A CHICKEN

1. Open up the chicken legs and pierce the skin where the thigh joins the body. Holding the bird steady, pull the leg out and down until the thighbone pops out of its socket. Cut through the skin and sinew with a sharp knife until you can pull the thigh and drumstick off in one piece. Turn the bird around and repeat with the other side.

2. With your thumb, feel where the knuckle is between the thigh and the drumstick and slice through, letting the weight of the knife do the work. The thigh is great for roasting or barbecuing, but the drumstick is the most difficult part to cook evenly. A trick is to slice through to the bone about halfway down the drumstick, where the meat gives way to skin and sinew. Scrape away the tendons until you expose a length of bare bone. Now cut off the end of the knuckle by placing your left hand on top of the knife blade and banging down hard to cut through the bone. Keep the knuckle for making stock.

3. Pull out the wing and feel with your thumb for where the bone joins the body. Slice through and take off the wing. You can also slice off the wing tips for stock if you like.

4. Place the chicken on a cutting board with its neck end toward you. With a nice dry knife to keep it from slipping, slice down one side of the breastbone, starting at the leg end and keeping the blade as close to the bone as possible. When you reach the wishbone, pull the knife out slightly, tilt it slightly upward, and, using your other hand to guide the blade, push it through the wishbone. You should now be able to work the breast free of the breastbones. Turn the carcass round, and repeat with the other breast, again cutting through the wishbone and keeping the knife as close to the carcass as possible so as not to leave any meat behind. Keep the carcass for making stock.

HOW TO DEBONE A CHICKEN

Place the chicken on its front, and cut down through the skin to expose the whole length of its backbone. Using your knife to loosen the meat from the bones, pull the chicken flesh away, as though ripping open a shirt, to expose its ribcage. Cut through the thighbone at its joint and, using your fingers, pull the bone out of the thighs, pulling the thigh meat inside out as you do so. Repeat on the other side. Now continue to work around the ribcage, releasing the wing bones as you do so, until you have released the breastbone from the breast. Cut the two tendons at either end of the ribcage and you should now be able to remove the carcass, leaving a single piece of meat, all of uniform thickness.

COOKING

Meat lends itself to every type of cooking, from roasting, grilling, or frying to poaching and braising. As a rule, the leaner and more delicate the cut of meat, the quicker you want to cook it, or else it will toughen up and dry out. Fattier cuts need slower cooking so that the fat can melt into the meat and imbue it with flavor.

Unless you are poaching your meat (a wonderful, healthy way of cooking chicken breasts), the key is to get a good searing of color on the outside. This is what will give your finished dish that lovely richness and is essential for everything from a pork loin to a sirloin steak or a lamb casserole. Chefs used to talk about this as searing in the juices, but it's not about keeping the meat moist—it's about kick-starting that flavor-building process.

There are two ways to do this: either to start your meat in a hot oven, and then turn it down after an initial sizzle (this is the way many people cook roasts); or to cook it over high heat on the stovetop, and then transfer to the oven as necessary. If doing the latter, the key thing is to get your pan good and hot so that it drives off the moisture in the meat instantly and starts browning it. If the pan is not hot enough, the meat will start to boil in its juices and then it will never brown. And without color, you'll have no flavor.

So start with dry meat (patted dry with paper towels if necessary) and a very hot pan. Put in a swirl of oil—peanut, canola, or light olive oil are all good, but not butter as it will burn (unless the meat is very thin and will cook in seconds)—and once it is almost smoking, add the meat. It should sizzle as soon as it hits the pan. If it doesn't, take it out and wait a bit. Don't crowd the pan as this will cause the temperature to drop. It's better to brown meat in batches than to try to rush it. Also, avoid the temptation to move it. People often feel they are being better cooks if they are constantly prodding or stirring, but sometimes you need the confidence to leave things alone. If you keep the meat moving around the pan, it won't caramelize. Don't worry about it sticking; once it is browned, the meat will release itself. That's the time to turn it over to make sure all the sides are seared.

Your meat is now ready for the next stage, be it roasting in the oven, bubbling away in a casserole, or, in the case of a steak or pork chop, for eating.

HOW TO COOK A SIRLOIN STEAK

1. Bring your steak to room temperature 20 minutes before cooking; otherwise, the outside will be cooked before the middle has had a chance to warm through. Meat at room temperature will also absorb the seasoning better.

2. Get the pan really hot, hotter than you'd normally dare. If it's not hot, it won't color the meat; and without any color, there'll be no flavor. Season your steak well with lots of salt and pepper.

3. Pour some peanut or other neutral-flavored oil into the pan. Canola is also good as it has a high burning point, which means you can get more color onto the steak. Wait until the oil is almost smoking, then lay in the steak, with the fat to the back of the pan.

4. Leave it to cook for 2½–3 minutes on one side, then turn it over. Don't keep moving the meat or it won't take on a caramelized crust. About 1½ minutes before it is ready, add a bit of butter and spoon it over the steak as it cooks, giving it a rich, nutty brown finish. Finally, use your tongs to hold the steak up and cook the fat.

5. The best way to tell if a steak is cooked is by feel. A rare steak will have the same texture as the fleshy base of your thumb when the hand is open. Now move your thumb so it touches your middle finger, and feel the fleshy base again. It will feel slightly firmer and is equivalent to a medium steak. If you move your thumb over to touch your little finger, the fleshy base feels very firm and is equivalent to well done.

6. Now leave the steak to rest in a warm place for up to 5 minutes. This will allow the muscle fibers to relax and redistribute the moisture throughout the meat. Slice the steak at an angle—not too thinly or it will cool down too quickly—and serve.

PORK CHOPS WITH PEPPERS
SERVES 2

You'll be amazed at how two such simple things can taste so good together. The sweet and sour peppers cut through the richness of the beautifully sautéed chops and make for a really good, quick supper dish. As always when cooking chops, leave them to rest as long as you cooked them so that they can tenderize and reabsorb their juices.

2 pork chops, about 7 ounces each
Sea salt and freshly ground black pepper
Olive oil
2 garlic cloves, skin on, crushed
Small bunch of thyme
Butter

FOR THE SWEET AND SOUR PEPPERS
Olive oil
1 red onion, peeled and sliced
2 red peppers, seeded and thinly sliced
Sea salt and freshly ground black pepper
1 Tbsp sugar
3 Tbsp red wine vinegar
1 Tbsp extra virgin olive oil
Small bunch of basil, leaves shredded

1. First prepare the peppers. Heat a little olive oil in a large frying pan, then add the onion and peppers. Season with salt and pepper, add the sugar, and sauté over high heat for 4–5 minutes until soft and colored. (Make sure you can hear the vegetables hissing in the pan. If not, the pan isn't hot enough and you're in danger of boiling the vegetables instead of sautéing them.)

2. Add the vinegar and let it bubble for a minute or two until it has reduced and the peppers are soft. Turn down the heat, add the tablespoon of extra virgin olive oil, and cook for an additional 2–3 minutes. Stir in the shredded basil and continue to cook for 30 seconds, then turn off the heat. Transfer to a bowl and set aside to infuse. Wipe the pan clean, ready to cook the pork.

3. Using a sharp knife, make cuts into the fat of the chops, about ¼ inch deep and at 1½-inch intervals, making sure you don't cut into the meat. (This will stop the meat from curling up during cooking and will make it cook more evenly.) Season the chops with salt and pepper really well on both sides, pushing the seasoning into the meat.

4. Place the cleaned-out frying pan over high heat until hot and add a dash of oil. Add the chops, garlic, and thyme and cook for 2–3 minutes until colored. Turn and cook for another 2–3 minutes on the other side, pushing the thyme under the chops and breaking up the garlic a little.

5. Toward the end of cooking time, add 3 chunks of butter and baste the chops with it as they are cooking, to speed up the cooking process and keep the chops moist. (Push the fatty edge of the chops toward the back of the pan to help render the fat.) Squeeze the garlic out of its skin and place with the herbs on top of the chops.

6. Transfer the chops to a plate, and let rest for 5–10 minutes, spooning over the basting butter now and again.

7. Serve the chops on top of the peppers with the resting juices and a little juice from the peppers.

HOW TO SLICE PEPPERS
Chop off the green stalk and stand the flat end on your cutting board. Now slice down from the top, almost like peeling an orange, working your way around the pepper, to leave a tree of seeds. Now place the pepper slices down on the worktop, and holding them down with your three middle fingers, cut them into slices. Don't try to rush: speed will come with practice.

SICHUAN CHICKEN THIGHS

SERVES 4

Chicken thigh is the best part of the bird for me because its rich meat is tastier and stands up to robust flavors. This dish shows just how good it can be, cooked in a wonderfully sticky marinade. Shaoxing is a Chinese rice wine. You can find it in most supermarkets nowadays, but you could use medium-dry sherry instead. Serve with rice or noodles.

8 skinless, boneless chicken thighs
Sunflower or peanut oil, for frying
3 garlic cloves, peeled and sliced
1½-inch piece of fresh ginger, peeled and grated
1 red chile, seeded and finely chopped
1 tsp Sichuan peppercorns, toasted and
   roughly ground
Zest of ½ orange
Pinch of sugar

FOR THE MARINADE
¼ cup light soy sauce
2 Tbsp Shaoxing rice wine
1 Tbsp rice vinegar
Sea salt and freshly ground black pepper to taste

TO SERVE
3 scallions, trimmed and roughly chopped
Soy sauce
Toasted sesame oil

1. Cut each chicken thigh into three pieces, then mix together all the marinade ingredients with 2 tablespoons of water. Use to coat the chicken. Season and mix well, then leave in the fridge to marinate for up to 2 hours.

2. Heat a heavy-bottomed frying pan or a wok over high heat, add a little oil, and saute the garlic, ginger, and chile for 3 minutes until tender and aromatic. Add the Sichuan peppercorns and orange zest and stir over the heat for 30 seconds.

3. Add the chicken and the marinade. Sprinkle in the sugar and stir well. Cover the pan and cook the chicken over medium heat for 20–25 minutes until colored on all sides and the marinade has reduced to a sticky sauce.

4. To serve, add the scallions and a drizzle each of soy sauce and sesame oil.

HOW TO PEEL GINGER
The easiest way to peel ginger, getting neatly around all those knobbly bits, is to use a teaspoon rather than a knife.

PAN-FRIED DUCK BREASTS WITH BLACK CURRANT SAUCE

SERVES 2

Duck with orange or cherries is such a classic, but there is no reason why you can't pair it with other fruit or vegetables, such as rhubarb, cranberries, or, as here, with black currants—anything with a little acidity to cut through the meat's richness. You'll find black currant jam in specialty shops or stores specializing in British products. Baby new potatoes and chopped greens would make ideal accompaniments.

2 duck breasts, skin on
Sea salt and freshly ground black pepper

FOR THE SAUCE
⅔ cup dry red wine
2 garlic cloves, skin on and lightly crushed
A few thyme sprigs
⅔ cup duck or chicken stock
3 Tbsp black currant jam or conserves
2 Tbsp butter, cut into cubes
Sea salt and freshly ground black pepper

1. Preheat the oven to 350°F.

2. Score the skin of the duck breasts in a crisscross pattern, then rub with salt and pepper. Place them skin side down in a dry ovenproof roasting pan and cook over very low heat to render most of the fat. This may take 10–15 minutes.

3. Meanwhile, make the sauce. Place the red wine in a pan with the garlic and thyme and boil for 7–8 minutes until reduced by half. Pour in the stock and reduce again by half. Stir the black currant jam into the sauce and add a few chunks of butter to give it a shine. Taste and adjust the seasoning, then strain through a fine sieve and discard the solids.

4. Turn up the heat under the duck breasts and cook for about 5 minutes until the skin is crisp. Turn them over and cook on the other side for 1–2 minutes until cooked through. Place the pan in the hot oven for 8–10 minutes until the duck is slightly springy when pressed.

5. Rest the duck breasts on a warm plate for 5 minutes, then cut into slices on the diagonal. Place on warmed serving plates. Spoon over the black currant sauce and serve.

HOW TO MINIMIZE FATTINESS IN DUCK MEAT
Normally, meat should be added to a hot pan and sizzle the moment it goes in. Duck breast, however, should be added to a cold pan and slowly brought up to temperature. This is because the breast skin is very fatty and needs time for the fat to run out into the pan, or render. If you added the breast to a hot pan, it would seal the fat in.

SMOKY PORK SLIDERS WITH BARBECUE SAUCE

SERVES 2–4

These mini burgers are absolutely stunning, all smoky from the bacon and paprika and with the sweet and sour hit from the homemade barbecue sauce. People often add too much to their burgers, thinking it will enrich the flavor, but let me tell you, when it comes to burgers, less is more. Trust me.

4 strips of rindless smoked bacon,
  finely chopped
Olive oil
1 shallot, peeled and finely chopped
1 tsp smoked paprika
1 pound ground pork
Sea salt and freshly ground black pepper

FOR THE BARBECUE SAUCE
Olive oil
1 small onion, peeled and finely diced
2–3 garlic cloves, finely chopped
Sea salt and freshly ground black pepper

1 Tbsp brown sugar
1 tsp smoked paprika
1 Tbsp cider vinegar
2 tsp Worcestershire sauce
6 Tbsp tomato ketchup

TO SERVE
Mini burger buns/bread rolls
Baby Boston lettuce leaves, shredded
Slices of smoked Cheddar cheese
Slices of tomato

1. First make the barbecue sauce. Heat the oil in a frying pan, add the onion and garlic with some salt and pepper and the sugar, and cook for 5 minutes until softened. Add the paprika and stir to combine. Cook for 10–15 minutes until the onion is caramelizing, then add the vinegar and let it cook for a couple of minutes. Add the Worcestershire sauce and tomato ketchup, mix well, and continue to cook for about 8 minutes until the sauce has reduced to a dropping consistency. Taste and adjust the seasoning as necessary. Remove from the heat and set aside.

2. While the barbecue sauce is reducing, start preparing the burgers. Cook the bacon in an oiled pan for about 5 minutes until almost cooked through. Add the shallot and continue to cook for 5 minutes until the shallot is tender and the bacon is crisp. Sprinkle in the smoked paprika and mix well. Continue to cook for 1–2 minutes, then remove from the heat, draining off any excess fat on paper towels, and cool.

3. Season the ground pork with salt and pepper and mix well with the cooked shallots and bacon. Shape into balls the size of golf balls and flatten into patties.

4. Heat a large, heavy-bottomed frying pan with a little oil. Season the patties and cook them for 1–2 minutes on each side, basting with the juices until cooked through and colored. Turn off the heat and leave them to rest in the pan. Top each patty with a slice of cheese, allowing it to melt slightly.

5. Assemble your sliders in mini buns, layered with the barbecue sauce, lettuce, and slices of tomato. Any remaining barbecue sauce will keep in the fridge very well. Serve immediately.

CHICKEN WITH GARLIC AND CHESTNUT STUFFING
SERVES 6

This is an all-in-one dish, where the deboned chicken encases a stuffing of rice and chestnuts. It will slice very easily and the sweetness of the chestnuts is set off with a simple parsley vinaigrette. Deboning a chicken is a complicated job, so unless you are very confident, it is best to ask your butcher to do it for you. If you're feeling brave, see page 85.

1 large deboned free-range chicken, wings removed
Sea salt and freshly ground black pepper
Olive oil

FOR THE STUFFING
Olive oil
½ onion, peeled and diced
1 garlic clove, peeled and chopped
1 celery stalk, trimmed and diced
⅓ cup pine nuts
3 ounces peeled cooked chestnuts, broken into pieces
Sea salt and freshly ground black pepper
½ cup cooked mixed rice, such as basmati or wild rice
2 Tbsp chopped parsley

FOR THE PARSLEY DRESSING
Leaves from small bunch of flat-leaf parsley
1 garlic clove, peeled
½ Tbsp grainy mustard
1–1½ Tbsp red wine vinegar
5 Tbsp olive oil

1. Preheat the oven to 350°F.

2. First prepare the stuffing. Heat a large frying pan over medium heat and add a glug of oil. Sauté the onion for 4 minutes, then add the garlic and continue to cook for another 1–2 minutes until softened. Add the celery, then stir in the pine nuts and chestnuts, taste, and season well with salt and pepper. Add the cooked rice and parsley, stir again, then taste and adjust the seasoning as necessary.

3. Place the deboned chicken skin side down on a work surface. Season with salt and pepper inside. Place the stuffing in the center of the chicken and fold the sides around it. Tie the chicken at regular intervals with string, then turn the parcel over so that the breast faces upward.

4. Drizzle olive oil over the outside of the chicken and season with salt and pepper. Place in a roasting pan and roast for 1 hour, basting now and again, then turn the oven up to 400°F and roast for an additional 15–20 minutes until the chicken is cooked through and the skin is golden and crisp. Remove and let rest for 15 minutes before serving.

5. Meanwhile, make the parsley dressing. Finely chop the parsley and garlic. Mix with the mustard and vinegar, then add the olive oil bit by bit, whisking continuously to thicken.

6. Serve the stuffed chicken in slices with the dressing spooned on top.

STEAK SANDWICHES

SERVES 4–6

These are effectively very posh burgers. You take a rare beef tenderloin, add homemade relish and mustard mayonnaise, and sandwich it between two pieces of toasted ciabatta. Heaven! It's very important to start the beef on the stovetop because meat that goes straight in the oven looks boiled rather than beautifully caramelized.

Olive oil
Sea salt and freshly ground black pepper
1½ pounds beef tenderloin
1 whole head of garlic, cut in half horizontally
3–4 thyme sprigs
Butter
1 head baby Boston lettuce, to serve

FOR THE SPICY TOMATO RELISH
Olive oil
½ red onion, peeled and finely chopped
2 red chiles, seeded and chopped
8 ounces mixed red and yellow cherry
    tomatoes, halved
Sea salt and freshly ground black pepper
1–2 tsp sherry vinegar, to taste
Small handful of shredded basil leaves

FOR THE MUSTARD MAYONNAISE
3 Tbsp good-quality mayonnaise
1 Tbsp grainy mustard
Sea salt and freshly ground black pepper to taste

FOR THE TOASTED CIABATTA
8–12 slices of ciabatta, about ½ inch thick
2–3 Tbsp olive oil
Salt and freshly ground black pepper

1. Preheat the oven to 400°F.

2. Heat a large ovenproof frying pan until hot and add a glug of oil. Grind a generous amount of salt and pepper onto a board and roll the tenderloin in the seasoning. Cook over high heat for 1–2 minutes on each side until gently colored all over, including the ends. Add the garlic and thyme sprigs, heat for a minute, then sit the beef on top of them. Add a couple of chunks of butter, spooning it over the steak to baste.

3. Place the beef in the preheated oven and roast for 15–17 minutes until rare or medium-rare. It should feel springy when pressed. Remove from the oven, cover loosely with foil, and leave to rest for 15 minutes, basting now and again with the juices from the pan.

4. Meanwhile, make the relish. Heat the olive oil in a large frying pan, add the onion and chiles, and cook over medium heat for about 5 minutes until softened. Stir in the tomatoes, then season with salt and pepper and cook for 6–8 minutes until the tomatoes are beginning to collapse. Add the vinegar and stew down over medium heat for about 6 minutes until reduced to a rough relish consistency. Remove from the heat, stir in the basil, and season well with salt and pepper. Tip into a serving bowl and set aside.

5. Combine the ingredients for the mustard mayonnaise. Spoon into a serving bowl and set aside.

6. To make the toast, heat a grill pan until smoking hot. Drizzle the sliced ciabatta with the olive oil, season with salt and pepper, and then grill for 1–2 minutes until golden on both sides. Repeat until all the bread is toasted and then place on a serving platter.

7. To serve, thickly slice the rested beef, place on a platter, and put on the table with the toast, mayonnaise, relish, and lettuce leaves to be assembled by your guests.

PORK STUFFED WITH MANCHEGO AND MEMBRILLO

SERVES 4

Membrillo is a sweetened quince jelly, which, given that quince is related to the pear and apple, goes brilliantly with pork. You can find it in international and gourmet food stores, or order it online at igourmet.com. The Spanish normally eat it with cheese, so I've paired it here with Manchego, a hard sheep's milk cheese. You could equally use a hard pecorino instead. Serve with roasted potatoes and sautéed carrots.

2-pound pork loin, skin scored
Sea salt and freshly ground black pepper
6 ounces Manchego cheese, thinly sliced
5 ounces membrillo
2 sage sprigs
Olive oil
1 thyme sprig
1 head of garlic, cut in half horizontally
¾ cup medium-dry sherry

1. Preheat the oven to 425°F.

2. Lay the pork loin, skin side down, on a cutting board and cut three-quarters of the way into the flesh lengthwise from top to bottom. Open the meat out to form a long rectangle and season with salt and pepper.

3. Arrange the slices of cheese and the membrillo along the center of the meat. Scatter the leaves from 1 sage sprig on top, and roll the meat up to enclose the stuffing. Tie at 1-inch intervals along the length of the meat with string.

4. Place the thyme and remaining sage in an oven-proof roasting pan with the garlic. Lay the pork on top, skin side up. Drizzle with olive oil and season generously with salt and pepper.

5. Transfer the roasting pan to the preheated oven and cook for 20 minutes until the skin is crisp and golden. Turn the oven down to 350°F and cook for an additional 50 minutes until the pork is just cooked through. Remove the pork from the pan and set aside on a serving dish to rest.

6. Put the roasting pan on the stovetop. Pour in the sherry and bring to a boil, scraping up any bits stuck in the bottom of the pan. Lower the heat, crush the garlic, and remove the herbs. Add any resting juices from the meat.

7. To serve, carve the pork into thick slices, strain the sauce, and pour it over the meat.

EASY BOLLITO MISTO

SERVES 4

This sausage casserole is traditionally served in Italy on Christmas Day with salsa verde, a dressing of garlic, anchovies, mustard, vinegar, oil, and lots of chopped herbs. I've added lentils to make a more self-contained meal, but simplified the dressing—just a scattering of fresh parsley.

Olive oil
6 Italian fennel sausages
8 ounces chorizo sausages, halved lengthwise
3 garlic cloves, peeled and sliced
2 celery stalks, trimmed and thickly sliced diagonally
2 carrots, peeled and sliced diagonally

7 ounces Puy lentils
1 bay leaf
2 thyme sprigs
3 cups chicken stock
Sea salt and freshly ground black pepper
Chopped flat-leaf parsley, to garnish

1. Heat a large saucepan over medium heat and add a little oil. Cook the fennel sausages for 3–4 minutes until colored on all sides. Remove and set aside. Add the chorizo pieces, cut side down, and cook for 2–3 minutes until they start to release their colored oil and begin to crisp up. Turn over and color on the other side for a minute or two. Remove and set aside with the sausages.

2. Add the garlic, celery, and carrots to the pan and stir for 2 minutes until the garlic is tender. Stir in the lentils, then return the sausages and chorizo to the pan with the bay leaf and thyme sprigs. Stir well.

3. Add 2½ cups of the stock, then taste and season with salt and pepper. Bring to a boil, then lower the heat and simmer gently for 25–30 minutes until the sausages are cooked through, the lentils are tender, and the stock is well flavored. If the stock level drops too low while the lentils are cooking, top up with a little of the remaining stock.

4. Discard the bay leaf and thyme sprigs and serve the bollito misto in shallow bowls, garnished with the chopped parsley.

SLOW-BRAISED
STUFFED LAMB BREAST

SERVES 6

Breast of lamb is a fatty cut that needs slow cooking, but it can be just as rewarding as the more expensive choice cuts. Here I'm stuffing it with anchovies, garlic, and olives, which all go so well with lamb, and braising it in canned tomatoes instead of stock. Try to stuff the breasts a day ahead as it helps to tenderize the meat even more. Serve with mashed potatoes and buttered kale.

3 lamb breasts, bones and skin removed
Sea salt and freshly ground black pepper
1½ Tbsp dried oregano, plus a pinch for later
1½ Tbsp dried chile flakes, plus a pinch for later
Zest of 2 lemons
Two 3-ounce jars anchovies, drained
Olive oil

1 onion, peeled and sliced
3 garlic cloves, peeled and crushed
1 Tbsp capers
¾ cup pitted black olives, such as Kalamata, drained
One 750-ml bottle dry white wine
One 14-ounce can whole peeled plum tomatoes

1. Preheat the oven to 350°F.

2. Open out the lamb breasts and place them on a cutting board. Season each one on both sides with salt and pepper. Scatter the oregano, chile flakes, and three-quarters of the lemon zest evenly over the fleshy side of the meat. Arrange the anchovies equally over each breast.

3. Starting at the smaller end of the meat, roll each breast into a tight sausage shape and tie at intervals with string.

4. Cook the rolled breasts in a large hot, oiled casserole dish for about 3 minutes until lightly browned all over. Remove the lamb and set aside, then add the onion and garlic to the pan. Cook over medium heat for 5 minutes until soft and colored. Add the pinches of chile flakes and oregano, the remaining lemon zest, then the capers and olives.

5. Add the wine to deglaze the pan, scraping up any bits from the bottom. Boil for 5 minutes, then add the tomatoes and gently bring back to a boil. Return the lamb breasts to the pan, basting them in the sauce.

6. Cover the pan with a lid and cook in the preheated oven for 2–2½ hours until the meat is tender. Baste and turn the meat often.

7. Remove the meat from the oven and let it rest for a couple of minutes before slicing thickly. Skim any excess fat from the pan, then spoon the sauce over the lamb.

HOW TO USE DRIED HERBS
Many people assume these days that you should always use fresh herbs. While some, such as basil and parsley, don't dry well, others, such as marjoram, bay leaves, and oregano, do. I wouldn't use them to finish a dish, but they can work well in a slow braise, where they will naturally rehydrate and flavor the meat. Never use as much as you would fresh, though, as the flavor can be very concentrated.

CHICKEN AND CHICORY IN MARSALA SAUCE
SERVES 2

Chicken breasts make for a quick and easy main course, but because chicken is such a lean meat, it can easily dry out. Here it is colored in a pan and then braised in chicken stock, butter, and Marsala. Marsala is a fortified wine from Sicily, and can be substituted with Madeira or medium-sweet sherry.

Olive oil
2 chicken breasts, skin on
Sea salt and freshly ground black pepper
2 heads of chicory, trimmed and cut in
    half lengthwise
4 thyme sprigs
1 garlic clove, peeled and lightly crushed
3 Tbsp Marsala wine
⅔ cup chicken stock
Butter

1. Heat a heavy-bottomed pan over medium heat and add a little oil. Season the chicken with salt and pepper on both sides, and place it, skin side down, in the hot pan. Add the chicory, cut side down, 2 thyme sprigs, and the garlic and cook for 3–4 minutes until the chicken skin is dark golden.

2. Turn the chicken and chicory over. Pour in the Marsala to deglaze the pan, scraping up the bits from the bottom, then add the chicken stock and a couple of chunks of butter. Cook over medium heat for 10 minutes, occasionally spooning over the sauce, until the chicken is just cooked through.

3. Serve the chicken and chicory topped with spoonfuls of sauce and garnished with the remaining thyme sprigs.

BEEF BRISKET WITH ENGLISH NEW POTATO RELISH

SERVES 6

Brisket is a cut of beef from the cow's lower chest and is traditionally used to make salt beef and pastrami. However, I'm not brining it here, but instead poaching it in aromatics, sautéed off first to boost their flavor.

4½ pounds beef brisket, boned, rolled, and tied
Sea salt and freshly ground black pepper
Olive oil
1 carrot, peeled and roughly chopped
2 celery stalks, trimmed and roughly chopped
1 head of garlic, cut in half horizontally
1 tsp black peppercorns
1 tsp cloves
1 tsp freshly grated nutmeg

FOR THE NEW POTATO RELISH

1 pound new potatoes of a similar size
1 small cauliflower, cut into florets
10 ounces green beans, topped and tailed
1 carrot, peeled and grated
1 small shallot, peeled and thinly sliced
3 scallions, trimmed and finely chopped
Pinch of ground turmeric
1–2 tsp English mustard powder, to taste
1 Tbsp grainy mustard
1–2 tsp honey, to taste
3 Tbsp white wine vinegar
½ cup olive oil
Sea salt and freshly ground black pepper

1. Preheat the oven to 275°F.

2. Season the brisket all over with salt and pepper. Heat a large flameproof casserole dish or high-sided roasting pan on the stovetop. Add a glug of oil and brown the meat in the hot pan for about 5 minutes until colored on all sides. Turn the heat down to medium, add the carrot, celery, garlic, and spices and stir them through the oil at the bottom of the pan.

3. Pour in enough water to almost cover the brisket. Bring to a boil, then cover tightly. Transfer the dish to the preheated oven and leave to cook for 3–4 hours, turning the meat halfway through, until it is very tender. Remove the meat from the cooking liquor and allow to rest for 20 minutes.

4. Meanwhile, make the salad. Boil the new potatoes in salted water for about 15 minutes until tender and cooked through. Blanch the cauliflower and green beans by dropping them into boiling salted water for 2 minutes until their rawness has been removed but they are still crunchy. Refresh immediately in cold water.

5. Mix together the carrot, shallot, scallions, and turmeric and add the potatoes, cauliflower, and green beans. To make the dressing, stir the mustard powder into the grainy mustard, making sure there are no lumps. Add the honey and vinegar, mix well, then slowly pour in the oil, stirring as you do so to thicken. Dress the salad and season with salt and pepper to taste.

6. Slice the rested brisket and serve with the salad.

ROAST GUINEA FOWL WITH APPLES

SERVES 4

Guinea fowl is a great alternative to chicken, with a slightly deeper flavor, but like a lot of game birds it needs careful cooking to prevent the breast from drying out. In the restaurant we remove the legs and wings, and poach the crown in flavored stock before quickly roasting it at a high temperature. I've simplified the recipe for the home, where you may prefer to serve the whole bird.

1 guinea fowl, about 2 pounds
Sea salt and freshly ground black pepper
6–8 strips of smoked bacon
5 Tbsp butter
4 sweet apples, cored and sliced
¾ cup heavy cream
½ cup Calvados or apple brandy

1. Preheat the oven to 400°F.

2. Season the guinea fowl with salt and pepper, cover the breast with the bacon, and place in a roasting pan.

3. Melt the butter in a cast-iron frying pan and carefully lay the apple slices in the butter. They need to be kept in a single layer, so cook in batches if necessary. Sauté the apples for 3–4 minutes until they are nicely caramelized, then arrange them around the guinea fowl. Brush the breast of the bird with the remaining melted butter and season with salt and pepper again. Pour over half the cream, then place in the preheated oven and cook for 20 minutes.

4. Remove the bacon and set aside. Lower the temperature to 350°F, then baste the bird and cook for an additional 20–25 minutes.

5. Remove the guinea fowl from the oven and transfer to a warm plate with the bacon. Leave to rest for 15 minutes.

6. Add the brandy and the remaining cream to the pan and bring to a boil. Taste and adjust the seasoning. Pour the sauce over the guinea fowl and serve immediately, with the reserved bacon on the side.

SPICES

SPICES NEVER PLAYED A HUGE PART IN THE FOOD I GREW UP ON. I DON'T THINK THEY DID FOR ANYONE OF MY GENERATION.

There was the occasional curry or chili con carne, of course, but they'd have been made with generic mixes that did little to excite my palate beyond the initial hit of heat. Once I started cooking professionally, though, I slowly came to see how exciting spices could be, how they could take dishes in a totally new direction. We're all familiar with cloves in a roasted ham, or grated nutmeg on a rice pudding, but the time I first tried star anise in a lamb stew it blew my mind. I couldn't believe what a difference it made to a dish I thought I knew. From then on I was hooked and have loved experimenting with unusual combinations, but always within the context of classic French and British cooking.

It wasn't until I went to India a couple of years ago that I was exposed to spices in all their glorious colors and varieties. I remember visiting a market in Cochin and seeing all the ginger, turmeric, cinnamon, cardamom, and saffron piled up and knowing I had to learn the art of spicing. We still tend to view it in a one-dimensional way in the West, as a way of delivering an addictive heat, but it's so much about fragrance, flavor, and subtlety too. If you learn to use spices confidently they can add a new dimension to your cooking. The trick is to find the balance of flavors that really suits you.

Let's start closer to home, though, with the two most common forms of seasoning: salt and pepper. These are like the cement that holds your cooking together. They help to meld all the other flavors and make them stronger for it, and provide the backbone on which the other ingredients will rest. By seasoning confidently, and early on in the cooking process, you lock in the flavors and allow them to permeate the whole dish.

People are sometimes shocked at how much seasoning professional chefs use. When we say a pinch, we sometimes mean a handful. But as I say, this is what helps to develop a depth of flavor, and although it

looks like a lot, you probably end up using less than you would if you had to add salt at the table. There was a rumor that I had CCTV installed in my restaurant at Claridge's in order to see who was adding salt to their food so I could have them thrown out. It wasn't true, of course—we did have cameras, but they were to see when customers were finishing their dishes so we could time their next course—but I do think that if the kitchen is doing its job properly, by the time food leaves the kitchen it should be perfectly seasoned.

SALT

I never have refined table salt in my house, not even for salting vegetable water. I always use sea salt—fleur de sel from Brittany out of preference, but Maldon salt is very good too. I find the minerals in it give it a more complex flavor, and again you need less of it. If you watch Italians cooking pasta, you'll see them actually taste the boiling water to make sure it is seasoned properly. They will use 2 teaspoons for every quart of water. It should be a similar ratio for boiling vegetables.

PEPPER

All pepper is not the same either, although the three types—black, green, and white—all come from the same bush. Black peppercorns are fully mature and have the strongest flavor. Green peppercorns are immature berries that are either dried or brined. They are milder and much used in Asian cooking. White peppercorns are black ones with the husk removed. They tend to have a more nose-prickling quality but lack the brute strength of black ones. They are generally used for aesthetic purposes— in a white sauce, for example, where you might not want to have black specks. You certainly don't need to worry about stocking both, but, as with all spices, it is better to keep them whole and grind them as and when you need them. The recipe for Sichuan Dan Dan Noodles (page 127) uses Sichuan pepper, which is not actually pepper at all, but the pod of an Asian berry. It has a mild lemony flavor and causes a slight tingling around the mouth when you eat it.

BASIC SPICE KIT

We're probably all guilty of having a few jars of spice festering at the back of our cabinets, but you should really have a clear-out at least every 12 months. Spices deteriorate very quickly, and after six months they'll have lost most of their flavor, especially if they are already ground. So the first rule is not to buy in bulk. Only purchase what you think you will need within the next six months or so. Keep them in an airtight container, away from direct sunlight and heat (a tin is better than a jar for this reason). Whole spices will stay fresh longer than ground ones, so, where possible, buy whole and grind as and when you need them. Listed opposite are the basic spices I keep on hand. They'll allow you to make your own Madras powder for the Curry-Spiced Corn Soup (page 115), for example, or a Moroccan-style ras el hanout mix for the Roasted Squash Hummus (page 121).

CARDAMOM

A versatile spice with a warm, sweet flavor. You can either add the pod whole, or crush it to extract the seeds, which can then be ground if you like.

CHILI POWDER

Made of ground dried chiles, the powder can vary in potency, so treat with caution. Cayenne pepper is specifically from the cayenne chile.

CINNAMON

The rolled bark of a Sri Lankan tree, cinnamon goes particularly well with sugar. It's also used a lot in meaty savory dishes such as Moroccan tagines.

CLOVES

These dried flower buds, with their medicinal flavor, are essential in dishes as diverse as roasted ham, apple crumble, and mulled wine. Go easy with them, as they can easily overpower.

CORIANDER

These dried berries have a sweet aromatic flavor that bears no similarity to the herb that produces them. Great with cumin in homemade burgers or poaching liquor for fish.

CUMIN

These small seeds have a strong, pungent aroma that lends a familiar backnote to many Indian and Mexican dishes. A little goes a long way.

FENNEL SEEDS

The seeds of the fennel plant have a more pronounced anise flavor than the bulbs and go particularly well with pork.

FENUGREEK

A bitter Mediterranean seed used in curry powders, with an aroma similar to celery. An essential part of homemade ras el hanout, a Moroccan spice mix also containing cinnamon, cloves, coriander, and cumin.

GINGER

I use fresh ginger where possible because it has a much more lively, zingy flavor. But ground ginger is also useful, particularly in baking.

MUSTARD SEEDS

We are used to seeing these in grainy mustard. Their natural fieriness is tempered when they are roasted and they become nuttier in flavor. Essential in Indian cooking.

NUTMEG AND MACE

Both these spices come from the nutmeg tree, mace being the outer lattice covering of the nutmeg seed. Both have a warm, earthy, aromatic flavor, but mace is slightly stronger and sweeter; it works particularly well in custard-based desserts. Nutmeg is essential in a traditional white sauce or rice pudding.

PAPRIKA

A bright red powder made from dried peppers. It can be sweet or hot, smoked or unsmoked, and is a characteristic feature of Spanish and Hungarian cooking.

STAR ANISE

I love star anise more than any other spice. It has a fragrant, slightly sweet anise flavor and is a key ingredient in Chinese five-spice powder. It lends itself to everything from lamb casserole to tarte tatin.

SUMAC

A dark reddish spice, sumac is widely used in Middle Eastern cooking, imparting a tangy, lemony flavor.

TURMERIC

A bright yellow spice that comes from a dried root. It gives curry powder its hallmark color and has an earthy, mustardy flavor.

HOW TO USE SPICES

Toasting spices before cooking with them releases their oils and aromas, making them much more fragrant and easier to grind. Place them in a dry pan over medium heat and shake the pan until the spices give off a warm, nutty aroma—about a minute. Take them off the heat and allow them to cool before crushing them with a mortar and pestle.

Alternatively, if the recipe calls for leaving the spices whole, you can cook them gently in oil. The oil will then take on all the spices' flavors and pass them on to anything else that is now added to the pan, such as chopped onions or tomatoes. Be careful, though, as spices can quickly burn, so you need to keep stirring them. Add more oil or a little water if they start to stick.

CHILES

As with most ingredients, we are really spoiled with the range of chiles we can buy now. Not so long ago, you'd be lucky to find a choice between red and green. Nowadays most supermarkets stock a choice of varieties and there are lots of chile farms that will do mail order. The best chiles deliver a wonderful fruitiness alongside a liberal dose of heat.

Which chiles you use in your cooking depends on how spicy you like your food. The heat comes from an alkaloid called capsaicin and is measured in units known as Scovilles. The bird's eye chile—the small red one used in a lot of Thai cooking—measures 225,000 Scovilles, while the Scotch bonnet, which I use in Jerk Chicken (page 128), comes in at 350,000. If that all sounds too much, the green jalapeño is just 5,000, although the heat does develop the longer it cooks. When smoked and dried, the jalapeño becomes the chipotle. Sold dried, or in a sweet adobo sauce, it adds a rich spiciness to braised meats and sauces.

If you want to reduce the heat of a chile, remove the seeds before cooking as these are the fieriest part. To do this, hold the chile between the palms of your hands and rub them together backward and forward. This will break the membrane holding the seeds. Then cut the top off and shake the chile to release all the seeds. To chop chiles finely, see page 212.

CURRY-SPICED CORN SOUP
SERVES 4

One of the first things I learned on my travels to India was that there is no such thing as curry powder. Every household would have its own favorite blend of spices, with subtle distinctions. Below is my version of a spicy Madras mix, which takes a simple corn soup into another league. Pan-toasting and grinding up the spices fresh and to order make a world of difference to recipes.

Olive oil
1 onion, peeled and finely diced
1 large potato, peeled and cubed
1 quart vegetable or chicken stock
Sea salt and freshly ground black pepper
One 15-ounce can creamed corn
One 15-ounce can corn kernels

FOR THE MADRAS CURRY PASTE
1 Tbsp coriander seeds
1 Tbsp cumin seeds
2 garlic cloves, peeled and crushed
1 tsp chili powder
1 tsp ground turmeric
2 tsp peeled and chopped fresh ginger
½ tsp sea salt
Olive oil

1. First make the curry paste. Toast the coriander and cumin seeds in a dry, medium-hot frying pan for about 1 minute until aromatic. Grind in a mortar to a fine powder, then add the garlic and grind to form a smooth paste. Add the chili powder, turmeric, ginger, and salt and mix well. Loosen by adding a little oil.

2. To make the soup, heat a large oiled saucepan over medium heat. Sweat the onion for 5 minutes until soft but not colored. Add the curry paste and cook with the onion for about 2 minutes until aromatic. Add the potato and stir around in the curry paste. Pour in the stock, season with salt and pepper, and bring to a boil. Lower the heat and simmer gently for about 7 minutes until the potato is soft and cooked through.

3. Add the creamed corn, then add half the can of corn kernels and half the liquid they are stored in. Heat through, then remove from the heat and blend with a stick blender until the chunks of potatoes have been fully broken down and the soup is smooth. Add the remaining canned corn and its liquid. Heat, taste, and adjust the seasoning as necessary. Serve warm.

SPICY PANCAKES
MAKES 6 PANCAKES

These spicy pancakes are traditionally served for breakfast in India. I know some people might balk at so much spice for breakfast, but they are strangely addictive. There's no reason why you shouldn't have them for lunch or supper instead, washed down with beer instead of chai.

1–2 tsp cumin seeds
Olive oil
½–1 green chile, seeded and finely chopped, to taste
2 garlic cloves, peeled and thinly sliced
1-inch piece of fresh ginger, peeled and finely chopped or grated
1 cup all-purpose flour
Sea salt and freshly ground black pepper
1 large egg
1 cup whole milk, plus an extra 1–2 Tbsp

FOR THE SPICED POTATO FILLING
Olive oil
1 tsp black mustard seeds
½ onion, peeled and thinly sliced
½ tsp ground turmeric
Sea salt and freshly ground black pepper
4 cold, peeled boiled potatoes, roughly chopped

TO SERVE
6 Tbsp plain yogurt
2 Tbsp chopped cilantro
Sea salt and freshly ground black pepper

1. Toast the cumin seeds with a pinch of salt in a dry, medium-hot pan for about 1 minute until aromatic. Add a dash of oil and sauté the chile, garlic, and ginger for an additional 2 minutes until softened. Remove from the heat.

2. Put the spice/garlic mixture into a bowl. Sift in the flour, season with salt and pepper, and make a well in the middle, then break in the egg and add half of the milk. Whisk the flour into the egg slowly until well incorporated, then gradually add the remaining milk. Continue whisking until the mixture is smooth and has the consistency of heavy cream. Whisk in 1 teaspoon of oil and leave the batter to rest for 10 minutes.

3. Meanwhile, make the spiced potato filling. Heat a little oil in a large frying pan over medium heat, add the mustard seeds, and cook for 1–2 minutes until the seeds begin to pop. Add the onion and cook for 5 minutes until soft and golden brown. Stir in the turmeric and cooked potatoes and season with salt and pepper, adding a dash of olive oil if necessary to aid cooking. Cook over medium heat for 3–4 minutes until softened and heated through. Set aside while you cook the pancakes.

4. Heat a large, wide frying pan, then add a little oil. If the batter has thickened too much, add a tablespoon or two of milk. Pour in a generous ¼ cup of batter and tilt the pan to spread the batter out. Cook for about a minute on one side until golden and crisp, then flip the pancake and continue to cook for another minute until cooked through. Keep warm while repeating with the remaining batter.

5. Mix the yogurt and cilantro together and season with salt and pepper to taste.

6. To serve, place a large spoonful of the potato filling in the middle of each pancake, adding a dollop of the yogurt, then roll up into a sausage shape.

STOVETOP GRILLED CORN WITH CHIPOTLE CHILE BUTTER

SERVES 4

We're switching continents here and going to Mexico, where you'll find street vendors selling grilled corn on every corner. Chipotles are smoked and dried jalapeño peppers with a sweet, earthy flavor, and dry Monterey Jack cheese has just the right milkiness to tame the mild heat.

Olive oil
4 ears corn on the cob, husks removed
5½ Tbsp butter, softened
1–2 dried chipotle chiles, rehydrated
  and finely chopped
2 Tbsp chopped cilantro leaves
Sea salt and freshly ground black pepper
4 Tbsp crumbled dry Monterey Jack cheese
Lime wedges, to serve

1. Heat a large, heavy-bottomed frying pan over medium heat. Add a little oil and gently cook the corn in the pan for about 5 minutes until colored and lightly charred all over. Add 3–4 tablespoons of water to the pan and continue to cook over medium heat for about 8 minutes until the liquid has evaporated and the corn is cooked through (turn down the heat if it starts to color too much).

2. Meanwhile, mix together the butter, chiles, cilantro, and a little salt and pepper.

3. Once the corn is cooked, remove and slather with the chipotle butter, allowing it to melt over the corn. Sprinkle over the cheese and serve with wedges of lime.

ROASTED SQUASH HUMMUS

SERVES 8–10

Just as there's no universal curry powder, nor is there a universal ras el hanout. It is Arabic for "head of the shop" and is traditionally a blend of the best spices a merchant has to offer. Combined with chickpeas, roasted squash, and tahini, and served with pita, it makes a lovely dip to accompany drinks or, with a salad, a nice light lunch.

1 butternut squash, about 2 pounds, peeled, seeded, and cubed
2 garlic cloves, smashed
1-inch piece of fresh ginger, peeled and finely chopped
Olive oil
Sea salt and freshly ground black pepper
1 Tbsp tahini
One 14-ounce can chickpeas, drained and rinsed
Juice of ½ lemon
Warmed or grilled pita bread or flatbread, to serve

FOR THE RAS EL HANOUT SPICE BLEND
1 cinnamon stick
1 tsp cloves
1 Tbsp coriander seeds
½ Tbsp fenugreek seeds
½ Tbsp fennel seeds
1 Tbsp mustard seeds
½ Tbsp cumin seeds
1 tsp paprika

1. First make the spice blend. Break the cinnamon stick into pieces. Place in a dry pan with the cloves and seeds, and toast over medium heat for about 1 minute until aromatic and the seeds are popping (shake the spices in the pan as you heat them to prevent them from burning).

2. Once toasted, remove from the heat and add the paprika. Place in a spice grinder, blender, or mortar and grind until the mixture is a powder—sift it if necessary. This spice blend will keep for up to 3 months if stored in an airtight container.

3. Preheat the oven to 350°F.

4. Make the hummus. In a large bowl mix the cubed squash, garlic cloves, and ginger with 2 tablespoons of olive oil and 1 tablespoon of the spice mix. Season with salt and pepper and scatter in a single layer in a roasting pan. Place in the preheated oven and cook for 30 minutes until tender all the way through.

5. Once the squash is soft, add the contents of the pan to a blender, discarding the garlic skins. Add the tahini, chickpeas, and a squeeze of lemon juice along with 2 tablespoons of olive oil. Blend until smooth. Taste and adjust the seasoning as necessary—you might need some extra lemon juice.

6. Transfer the hummus to a bowl and sprinkle with a little of the spice mix. Drizzle with olive oil and serve with warmed or grilled pita bread on the side.

NOODLES WITH CHILES, GINGER, AND LEMONGRASS

SERVES 2

The best noodles to use for this dish are those fine ones dried into flattened nests sold in Asian supermarkets. They are packed slightly less tightly than the ones that come in round nests or sticks in other supermarkets, meaning that they will be even better at expanding and puffing up. If you prefer not to fry the noodles, you can simply rehydrate them according to the package instructions.

Olive oil
1 small onion, peeled and finely diced
2 garlic cloves, peeled and finely chopped
1 red chile, seeded and finely chopped
1-inch piece of fresh ginger, peeled and grated
1 lemongrass stalk, crushed and cut in half
1 kaffir lime leaf
1 tsp ground cumin
½ tsp ground coriander
½ tsp ground turmeric
2 cups vegetable or chicken stock
⅔ cup coconut cream
Fish sauce, to taste
Sea salt and freshly ground black pepper
1 cup vegetable or peanut oil, for deep-frying
5 ounces rice vermicelli noodles
Cilantro leaves and sliced red chiles, to garnish

1. Heat a saucepan over medium heat and add a little oil. Sauté the onion for 3–4 minutes until soft, then add the garlic, chile, and ginger and sauté for an additional 2 minutes until the garlic is soft.

2. Stir in the lemongrass and lime leaf. Sprinkle in the spices, being careful not to burn them, and immediately add the stock and coconut cream. Season with fish sauce, salt, and pepper. Bring to a boil, then lower the heat and simmer gently for 10–15 minutes until the sauce is slightly thickened, aromatic, and flavorful. Taste and adjust the seasoning as necessary, adding more fish sauce if needed.

3. To make the noodles, heat the vegetable oil in a large wok or wide, high-sided frying pan until it reaches 340°F or a cube of bread dropped into the oil sizzles and turns brown after 30 seconds. Drop small handfuls of the noodles into the hot oil (stand back as they will expand rapidly as soon as they hit the heat). As soon as they puff out, turn them over with kitchen tongs, and cook on the other side for 1 minute. Do not allow them to color at all. Remove, drain on paper towels, and repeat with the remaining batches of noodles.

4. Place the noodle nests in 2 wide serving bowls. Remove the lemongrass and lime leaves from the sauce, then spoon the sauce around the noodles. The underside of them will absorb some of the sauce, but the top will remain crisp and crunchy. Serve garnished with cilantro leaves and chiles.

SPICY BEEF SALAD
SERVES 4

I fell in love with this simple dressing of garlic, chile, fish sauce, sugar, and lime in Vietnam and Cambodia. It's the perfect blend of sweet, sour, salty, and bitter, and works with most seafood and meat, but is particularly good with steak.

2 sirloin steaks, 7–9 ounces each
Sea salt and freshly ground black pepper
Olive oil
2 carrots, trimmed and peeled
6 radishes, trimmed and thinly sliced
8 ounces cherry tomatoes, sliced in half
Bunch of mint, leaves only, shredded
1 small shallot, peeled and thinly sliced
3 scallions, trimmed and shredded
½ large cucumber, trimmed, peeled, seeded, and sliced
2 baby Boston lettuces, shredded
¼ cup skinless peanuts, to garnish

FOR THE THAI-STYLE DRESSING
1 garlic clove, peeled and roughly chopped
1 red chile, seeded and chopped
Sea salt
2 tsp grated palm sugar or palm sugar paste (available in Asian markets; if unavailable, use brown sugar)
2–3 Tbsp fish sauce, or to taste
Juice of 1–2 limes

1. Season the steaks with salt and pepper generously on both sides, pushing the seasoning into the meat. Add a dash of oil to a hot pan and cook the steaks over high heat on either side for 2–3 minutes (medium-rare). Hold the fat side of the steaks against the pan to render the fat. When cooked to your liking, remove the steaks from the heat and leave to rest, pouring any cooking juices on top.

2. To make the dressing, put the garlic and chile in a mortar with a pinch of salt and grind to a paste. Add the sugar, fish sauce, and lime juice and stir with a spoon. Taste, add a little more lime juice if needed, and set aside.

3. Meanwhile, using a vegetable peeler, cut the carrots into ribbons. Place in a bowl with the radishes, tomatoes, mint, shallot, scallions, cucumber, and lettuce. Add about 4–6 tablespoons of the dressing and mix well to combine.

4. Thickly slice the steak at an angle. Toast the peanuts with a pinch of salt for a few minutes in a clean dry pan and roughly chop. Place the steak on top of the salad and scatter over the chopped peanuts. Drizzle over the remaining dressing and serve immediately.

HOW TO CHOOSE SALAD ONIONS
Shallots are particularly good used raw in salads. They are sweet and flavorful and have none of the acridness of Spanish onions.

VIETNAMESE-STYLE BEEF BAGUETTE

SERVES 2

France and Vietnam have an association going back to the nineteenth century, so mixing their cuisines isn't as odd as it might sound. The ingredients used here—baguettes on the one hand and a Vietnamese marinade and dressing on the other—work really well together, proving that sometimes cooking is all about combining the unexpected.

1 Tbsp soy sauce
1 Tbsp runny honey
2 thin sirloin steaks, trimmed
  of fat, each cut into ½-inch strips
1 carrot, peeled and grated
1½ tsp rice vinegar
1 baguette
Olive oil
½ cucumber, seeded and julienned
  (see page 58)
Sea salt and freshly ground black pepper
2 Tbsp chopped cilantro, to taste

FOR THE DRESSING
1 Tbsp fish sauce
Juice of ½–1 lime, to taste
1 tsp sugar
½ red chile, seeded and finely chopped

1. Mix the soy sauce and honey together in a bowl. Once combined, add the strips of steak and toss well. Leave to marinate in the fridge for up to 2 hours.

2. Meanwhile, mix the dressing ingredients together, stirring to dissolve the sugar. Taste and adjust the flavors as necessary, adding a little more lime juice if needed.

3. Mix the grated carrot with the rice vinegar and set aside to marinate.

4. Cut off the ends of the baguette and cut the loaf in half. Slice the two halves open and push down the bread inside.

5. Thread the strips of steak onto skewers (if using bamboo skewers, soak them in water for 20 minutes beforehand), reserving any leftover marinade. Heat a frying pan over high heat, add a dash of oil, and cook the skewered meat on each side for 1 minute, pouring over any reserved marinade.

6. Remove the steaks from the skewers and press into the opened baguette so that any meat juices run into the bread. Drain the carrot and divide between the sandwiches. Top with the cucumber and season with salt and pepper to taste.

7. Drizzle the dressing over the filling. Garnish with cilantro, close the sandwiches, and serve.

SICHUAN DAN DAN NOODLES

SERVES 2

Dan dan noodles is a classic Chinese dish from Sichuan, which is noted for its spicy food. The heat here comes not from fresh chiles, but from chile bean paste. If you can't find any, replace it with ½–1 tablespoon of Chinese chile oil instead.

8 ounces ground pork
½ Tbsp Shaoxing rice wine
½ Tbsp soy sauce, plus extra to taste
½ Tbsp toasted sesame oil, plus extra to garnish
Olive oil
2 garlic cloves, peeled and crushed
¾-inch piece of fresh ginger, peeled and chopped
1 tsp Sichuan peppercorns
½–1 Tbsp Chinese chili bean paste, to taste
Rice vinegar, to taste
8 ounces dried Chinese egg noodles
Sea salt and freshly ground black pepper

TO SERVE
2 scallions, trimmed and shredded
1 Tbsp toasted sesame seeds

1. Marinate the ground pork in the Shaoxing wine, soy sauce, and sesame oil. Leave for at least 10 minutes.

2. Heat a wok over medium-high heat and add a dash of oil. Add the garlic and ginger to the pan and cook for 30 seconds to soften their raw flavor. Add the ground pork, along with any marinade, and the Sichuan peppercorns. Cook for 5 minutes, breaking up the pork until it's colored on all sides. Taste and season with a little extra soy sauce if needed. Add the chile bean paste and a couple of drops of rice vinegar.

3. Cook the pork mixture for an additional 2 minutes to allow the flavors to develop. Add a couple of tablespoons of water and mix over low heat to create a sauce.

4. Meanwhile, cook the noodles following the package instructions. Drain, then stir into the pork in the wok. Taste and season with salt and pepper if needed. Serve garnished with drops of sesame oil, the scallions, and toasted sesame seeds.

JERK CHICKEN
SERVES 4

This is real feel-good carnival food. There's nothing demanding about it, but the warmth of the spices, punctuated by the fierce heat of the Scotch bonnet chiles, always puts a smile on my face. If you don't like too much heat, use less chile, of course, or even a milder variety, such as the jalapeño.

4 large chicken legs, skin on, cut into
  drumsticks and thighs and scored
Olive oil
2 Tbsp Worcestershire sauce
Rice, to serve
4–5 thyme sprigs, to garnish (optional)

FOR THE MARINADE
1–2 Scotch bonnet chiles, seeded
  and finely chopped
2 garlic cloves, peeled and crushed
1 tsp ground cloves
1 tsp ground cinnamon
1 tsp ground nutmeg
2 tsp ground allspice
5–7 thyme sprigs, leaves only (you will need
  about 2 Tbsp)
Freshly ground black pepper
Olive oil

1. Preheat the oven to 425°F.

2. First prepare the marinade by combining all the ingredients with a good grinding of black pepper and a dash of oil. Rub the marinade into the chicken pieces, massaging it into the scored meat. Leave to marinate for at least 1 hour (or, better still, overnight).

3. Heat a large ovenproof pan over medium–high heat and add a dash of oil. Cook the chicken pieces for about 10 minutes until golden brown on all sides. Add the Worcestershire sauce and cook for 2 minutes.

4. Cover with an ovenproof lid or foil and place in the preheated oven for 20 minutes until cooked through (if your pan isn't ovenproof, simply transfer the chicken to a roasting pan). Remove the foil for the last 5 minutes if the chicken needs coloring a little more.

5. Serve the chicken hot with rice and thyme sprigs, if using.

SHAWARMA SPICED CHICKEN WRAPS
SERVES 2

Shawarma is the name of the vertical spits of meat you see in Middle Eastern restaurants, normally eaten in pita bread with tabbouleh, cucumber, and tomato and topped with hummus or tahini. It's the Middle Eastern take on fast food, and just as good made at home.

4 boneless, skinless chicken thighs
2–4 tortilla wraps
Olive oil
2 scallions, trimmed and finely shredded
¼ head of cabbage, finely shredded

FOR THE MARINADE
½ tsp ground cinnamon
½ tsp ground ginger
½ tsp ground coriander
Seeds from 3 cardamom pods, ground in a mortar
Pinch of freshly grated nutmeg
2 garlic cloves, peeled
Juice of ¼ lemon
Small bunch of cilantro, leaves chopped
Olive oil
Sea salt and freshly ground black pepper

TO SERVE
Mayonnaise
Chile sauce or sauce of your choice

1. First make the marinade. Place the spices, garlic, lemon juice, and cilantro in a small blender or mortar and grind until smooth. Add 5 tablespoons of olive oil, along with a generous pinch of salt and pepper, and blend again to mix well. Transfer the marinade to a large dish. Add the chicken and rub in the marinade, making sure that all of the chicken is covered. Leave to marinate for up to 2 hours.

2. Preheat the oven to 400°F.

3. Heat a grill pan over medium heat. Remove the chicken from the marinade, shaking off any excess, and cook on the hot grill for 3–4 minutes on each side until slightly charred but not burnt. Transfer to a roasting pan and finish cooking in the oven for 5–8 minutes. Leave the chicken to rest.

4. Meanwhile, cook the tortillas in batches in a single layer on the cleaned, slightly oiled grill pan. Toast on each side for 2 minutes or until they are hot all the way through but still pliable. Keep warm.

5. Remove the chicken from the oven and slice into bite-sized chunks. Place some chicken on each warm wrap and sprinkle with scallions and shredded cabbage. Add mayonnaise and chile sauce to taste, then roll up the wraps and serve.

CHILE BEEF
LETTUCE WRAPS
SERVES 4

Great food doesn't have to be complex, as these simple beef wraps show. They are really quick to make and are perfect with a few beers at the start of the evening. It's really important to get a good color on the ground beef. Be bold and take it further than you've ever dared before.

Olive oil
8 ounces lean ground beef
8 ounces ground pork
Sea salt and freshly ground black pepper
Toasted sesame oil
2 garlic cloves, peeled and finely chopped
2-inch piece of fresh ginger, peeled
  and finely chopped
1–2 red chiles, seeded and chopped
1 Tbsp light brown sugar
1 Tbsp fish sauce
Zest of 1 lime, juice of ⅓
3 scallions, trimmed and chopped
2 little Boston lettuces, separated into leaves,
  to serve

FOR THE DRESSING
1 Tbsp soy sauce
Juice of ½ lime
1 tsp toasted sesame oil
½ red chile, thinly sliced
Small bunch of cilantro leaves, chopped
1–2 tsp fish sauce, to taste
1 tsp light brown sugar
1 Tbsp olive oil

1. Heat a large frying pan and add a little oil. Mix the ground beef and pork together. Season with salt and pepper and mix well to make sure the seasoning is evenly distributed. Cook the meat in the hot pan for 5–7 minutes until crisp and brown and broken down to a fine consistency. Drain the crisped meat in a sieve—this will help it stay crisp. Set aside.

2. Wipe out the pan and add a tablespoon of toasted sesame oil. Add the garlic, ginger, and chiles. Cook with a pinch of salt and the sugar for 2 minutes. Add the drained meat and stir to mix.

3. Add the fish sauce and heat through. Stir in the lime zest and juice, then add the scallions, stirring for 30 seconds. Turn off the heat.

4. Mix all the dressing ingredients together and adjust the seasonings to taste.

5. To serve, spoon some of the meat mixture into the lettuce leaves, drizzle with a little dressing, and serve.

PORK NECK CURRY WITH MANGO SALSA

SERVES 4–6

This has got to be my favorite curry in the world: all those zingy Thai flavors with one of the most overlooked cuts of pork, and topped off with a really fresh, light mango salsa. Don't be put off by the long list of ingredients: this is one of those dishes that takes a bit of setting up, but then bubbles away on its own.

Olive oil
2 pounds pork neck, cut into 1-inch chunks
1 onion, peeled and thinly sliced
One 14-ounce can coconut milk
3 cups chicken stock
1 Tbsp palm sugar or brown sugar
1½ Tbsp soy sauce, to taste
1½ Tbsp fish sauce, to taste
Sea salt and freshly ground black pepper
Rice, to serve

FOR THE CURRY PASTE

1 lemongrass stalk, crushed and finely chopped
2 kaffir lime leaves, shredded
1–2 red chiles, seeded and finely chopped,
   to taste
1½-inch piece of fresh ginger, peeled and grated
3 garlic cloves, peeled and roughly chopped
1 tsp ground cinnamon
2 tsp ground coriander
Sea salt and freshly ground black pepper
2 Tbsp olive oil

FOR THE MANGO SALSA

1 mango, not too ripe, peeled and finely diced
1 small red onion, peeled and finely diced
Small bunch of cilantro, leaves roughly chopped
2 Tbsp chopped toasted peanuts
Juice of 1 lime
1 red chile, seeded and finely chopped
Sea salt and freshly ground black pepper

1. First make the curry paste. Combine the lemongrass, shredded lime leaves, chiles, ginger, garlic, cinnamon, and coriander with a good pinch of salt and a generous grinding of pepper in a small food processor. Process to a smooth paste, then add the oil to thin it slightly.

2. Heat a glug of oil in a heavy-bottomed pan over medium heat and brown the pork neck (you may have to do this in batches, depending on the size of your pan) for about 5 minutes until colored all over. Remove and set aside. Add a little more oil to the pan, then add the onion and cook for 3–4 minutes until tender and beginning to color on the edges.

3. Add the curry paste, stirring it around until aromatic and well mixed into the onions. Return the pork to the pan, stir to coat in the curry paste, then add the coconut milk. Stir thoroughly, scraping up any bits stuck to the bottom of the pan.

4. Add the chicken stock, mixing well, then stir in the sugar, whole lime leaves, soy sauce, and fish sauce. Taste and adjust the flavors as necessary, adding more soy, and/or fish sauce along with salt and pepper if needed. Bring to a boil, then simmer gently for 1 hour, stirring occasionally until the sauce is thick and flavorful and the pork is tender.

5. Meanwhile, mix together the salsa ingredients and season with salt and pepper to taste. Serve the curry with rice topped with the mango salsa.

CHOCOLATE MOUSSE
WITH CHILES AND MANGO
SERVES 4–6

Chocolate and chile is one of those combinations made in heaven, and the mango just takes it to another dimension. As always, make sure you use a good-quality chocolate, and if you can get from an Indian market a sweet, perfumed Alphonso mango, in season from April to May, so much the better.

3½ Tbsp unsalted butter
2–3 mild red chiles, seeded and chopped
5 ounces dark chocolate (70 percent cocoa solids)
2 large egg yolks
¼ cup sugar
¾ cup heavy cream
1 small ripe mango

1. Melt the butter in a small pan with the chopped chiles over low heat. Remove from the heat, leave to infuse for 30 minutes, then strain and discard the chiles.

2. Chop the chocolate into pieces and place in a large heatproof bowl. Add the infused butter and set the bowl over a pan of gently simmering water. Heat the chocolate for about 5 minutes, stirring frequently, until it melts, then remove and cool to room temperature.

3. Meanwhile, put the egg yolks, sugar, and 2 tablespoons of cold water in a large bowl. Place the bowl over a pan of gently simmering water. Using an electric mixer, beat the egg yolks and sugar for 5–10 minutes, until you are left with a pale, thick foam that holds a trail when the beaters are lifted up. Remove the bowl from the heat and gently fold into the cooled chocolate mixture using a large metal spoon. Let cool to room temperature.

4. Using a balloon whisk, softly whip the cream in a separate bowl. Using a figure-eight motion, fold the whipped cream quickly and gently into the cooled chocolate–egg yolk mixture.

5. Divide the mixture among 4–6 small glasses, cover with plastic wrap, and chill for at least 2 hours. When you are ready to serve, cut the mango on both sides of the pit, then peel and slice the flesh into thin wedges. Place a couple of mango slices delicately on top of each mousse and serve.

HOW TO WHIP CREAM
It is very easy to overwhip cream and cause it to go grainy if you are using an electric mixer. Whisking cream by hand is tiring but gives you more control and allows you to achieve the perfect, soft billowy texture you're looking for.

FRAGRANT SPICED RICE PUDDING

SERVES 6–8

I really got into the fragrance of chai when I was in India, and transferring the same spices of cardamom, cloves, vanilla, and cinnamon to rice pudding transforms it from a plain Jane into something spectacular. Don't wash the rice first, as you would for a savory dish, because the starch helps the pudding.

2 cardamom pods, lightly crushed
1 vanilla pod, split open and seeds scraped out
3 cloves
½ cinnamon stick, snapped in half
One 14-ounce can coconut milk
¼ cup sugar
2½ cups whole milk
2 Tbsp heavy cream
Zest of 1½ limes
1 cup short-grain white rice
2 egg yolks
2 heaping Tbsp mascarpone cheese

1. Preheat the oven to 400°F.

2. Put the cardamom pods and vanilla pod and seeds in a 9-inch ovenproof baking pan with the cloves and cinnamon stick. Place over medium heat and toast for 2 minutes until aromatic.

3. Add the coconut milk, sugar, milk, and heavy cream and bring slowly to a boil, stirring gently as you do so. Add the zest of 1 lime, then taste, adding more if you like. Pour in the rice and mix well. Bring to a boil, reduce to a simmer, and cook gently for 20 minutes, stirring constantly, until most of the milk mixture is absorbed and the rice is softened.

4. Mix together the egg yolks and mascarpone and add to the rice mixture off the heat, making sure it is well combined. Wipe the sides of the pan of any liquid (so it doesn't burn while in the oven). Sprinkle the remaining lime zest over the top of the dish and place in the preheated oven for 20–25 minutes until golden brown on top and the rice is cooked through.

HOW TO TOAST SPICES

Toasting spices in a dry pan for even just a few seconds enhances and draws out their fragrance. Be careful not to burn them or they will turn bitter and you'll taste it in the final dish.

GOOD
FOOD
FOR
LESS

WE'VE ALL SEEN HOW OUR FOOD BILLS HAVE ROCKETED OVER THE PAST FEW YEARS.

We're feeling it at home and in restaurants, too, and the signs are that it's only going to get worse. We've grown used to a period when the cost of food has actually been very low as a percentage of our income, so now we're all having to readjust. That's why it's such an important skill in the kitchen to be able to conjure up great meals from cheap ingredients.

What would a Michelin-starred chef know about economy, you might ask? Don't we just buy the best ingredients, the most expensive cuts, and then charge our customers accordingly? Well, best ingredients, yes; but most expensive, no. Of course customers will expect a piece of salmon, scallops, and steak on the menu of a smart restaurant, but you always have to balance this out with cheaper ingredients. The secret is knowing how to make those cheaper ingredients sing.

When I opened Aubergine in the early 1990s, money was incredibly tight, so I took two approaches. The first was to make sure that absolutely nothing was wasted. Every meat carcass, every vegetable peeling, every scrap of leftover bread had to be reused, whether for a stock or just a staff meal. I swear we had the emptiest garbage cans in London.

Second, I used all the less fashionable, cheaper cuts of meat, the ones the other smart restaurants would turn up their noses at—things like pork belly, oxtail, and lamb shanks. I knew that through my skill as a chef, I'd be able to add value to those humble cuts, to wrestle maximum flavor out of them. Any fool (well, almost any fool) can make a meal out of beef tenderloin or a piece of wild salmon—you just add heat and serve—but to produce something magical out of lamb breast or the humble sardine is so much more rewarding. It may take a little more work, a little more imagination, but it means you can eat well for considerably less.

The first task is to identify the best-value ingredients. Your main source of protein, typically meat or fish, is normally the most expensive thing on your plate, so if you want to keep costs down, this is the place to start. You have two choices: either, as I say, to use cheaper cuts or less popular fish, or to eat less of them.

When I say cheaper cuts, I don't of course mean poorer quality. Cheap meat won't cook as well, it won't taste as good, and in the long run it is always a false economy. But cheaper cuts from a quality animal are another matter. It's a shame we don't eat as much liver or kidney as we used to, because they still represent great value and can be cooked very quickly in a pan. Otherwise, cheaper cuts tend to lend themselves to slow cooking—something I'll cover in the next chapter, where you'll find recipes for economical braises of all sorts of unfashionable cuts, such as lamb neck, beef short ribs, or oxtail.

Similarly with fish, we tend to turn out of habit to the prime pieces—fillets of salmon or cod, whole sea bass—when less fashionable and cheaper fish, such as sardines or mackerel, have a superb flavor and can be dressed up to become just as exciting. Try my Spaghetti with Chiles, Sardines, and Oregano (page 154) if you don't believe me.

Cooking with more vegetables, rice, and beans is probably the best way to save money, though. They are fantastic for bulking out a dish if you want to make your meat or fish go further—in risotto, for example, or a shrimp jambalaya—but they can just as easily be the star of the show in their own right. The trick is to give them a bit of attitude, to perk them up with spices and build up layers of flavor.

Vegetables are always cheaper than meat, even more so if you shop seasonally. We talk endlessly about the provenance of food, where it is sourced, how far it's traveled, carbon footprint this, food miles that, and the debate will rumble on for years. But the best argument for buying in season is that it's how to get produce at its best and its cheapest. Asparagus flown in from Peru in November? No thanks. I'll wait for the local asparagus to arrive in April, when it will have more flavor and be half the price. Apples shipped in from New Zealand? Well, yes, but I won't cook with them with such abandon as I will when the native crop is coming in and the shops and markets are full of them.

Always make the most of these seasonal gluts. Visit pick-your-own farms for strawberries in June or blackberries in August, freezing what you don't use immediately, and you'll never have to reach for another overpriced pint of summer fruits again. Thinking ahead is always essential. It's not just about planning what you will eat in two or three days' time (important though that is to make sure you don't waste food), but what you might eat in the months ahead.

I've been inspired to cook with more vegetables and grains and beans from my travels around the world. To see the way the Indians can make a whole meal out of lentils, the Mexicans their black beans, and the Thais a stir-fry of rice noodles shows how much they have to teach us. Developing countries like these have had to invent healthy, nourishing, and cheap meals out of necessity, and now it's a lesson we'll do well to learn in the West.

With all of these dishes—with cooking in general but even more so here—the key is to make your ingredients work for you. If you are using fewer ingredients, or less of them, you must get the maximum flavor out of what you do have. You need to lock every last inch of flavor into the pan. Never rush an onion, for example. Let it sweat slowly and gently in butter or oil and you will be rewarded with a sweetness you could never imagine. Crumble a sausage out of its skin and you will be harnessing far more of its flavor. You'll be able to spread it around the pan and it will lend more of its herbs and spices to the other ingredients in there.

Finally, remember what every shrewd cook has always known: embrace your leftovers and throw nothing away. Stale bread makes a great bread pudding, but also turn it into breadcrumbs so you can make the meat in a burger stretch further. Leftover baked potatoes aren't just for home fries: bound with ricotta in Homemade Gnocchi (page 150), they make a fantastic alternative to pasta. If you can get into the habit of incorporating your leftovers into the next day's meal, you'll not only eat better, but you'll save a fortune too.

SPICY BLACK BEANS WITH FETA AND AVOCADO

SERVES 4

This is Mexican street food at its best, and shows that you don't need meat to make a tasty dish. Black beans are a staple of Mexican cooking because they are so robust and filling, and the spices, feta, and squeeze of lime juice really bring them to life. When enclosed in crisp tortillas, known as tostadas, the beans make a great starter or snack to go with beer.

1 small onion, peeled and finely chopped
1 Tbsp olive oil
1 red chile, seeded and finely chopped
2 garlic cloves, peeled and crushed
1 tsp ground cumin
½ tsp ground cinnamon
Two 14-ounce cans black beans, drained, liquid reserved
Sea salt and freshly ground black pepper

FOR THE TOSTADAS (OPTIONAL)
Vegetable oil
8 small tortillas

TO SERVE
4 ounces feta cheese, crumbled
2 avocados, peeled, pitted, and roughly chopped
Leaves from 1 small bunch of cilantro, roughly chopped
Lime wedges

1. Sauté the onion in the olive oil for about 5 minutes until soft, then add the chile and garlic and cook for an additional 2–3 minutes. Add the cumin and cinnamon and cook for an additional minute until aromatic. Add the beans and a couple of tablespoons of the reserved liquid.

2. Cover the beans and cook gently for 10 minutes until they start to break down, then remove from the heat and leave to cool slightly. Mash about three-quarters of the beans roughly with a fork or the back of a spoon, leaving some whole. Alternatively, if it's a less rustic-looking effect you're after, pour the beans into a blender and blend until smooth. Heat through gently—if the mixture is too thick, add a little more of the reserved liquid from the beans. Season with salt and pepper to taste.

3. The beans can be served as is, scattered with the feta, avocado, cilantro, and lime wedges. If making the tostadas, pour vegetable oil into a large frying pan to a depth of 1 inch and set over medium-high heat. When hot, fry the tortillas in batches for 1–2 minutes on each side until golden and crisp. Remove with a slotted spoon and drain on paper towels.

4. The crisp tortillas should be assembled just before serving so that they don't get soggy: spread them with the black bean mixture and garnish with crumbled feta, avocado, and cilantro. Serve with wedges of lime.

NORTH AFRICAN EGGS

SERVES 2–4

Eggs poached in tomato, pepper, chiles, and onions is a typical breakfast dish throughout the Middle East and makes a great start to the day, or a late-morning brunch. The roll call of spices varies from country to country and can include anything from fennel seeds to caraway or ginger, but cumin is generally a constant. To make a more substantial meal, you could always add some herb sausages. Prick their skins first and poach them in the tomato sauce for 20 minutes.

Olive oil
1 onion, peeled and diced
1 red pepper, seeded and diced
1 green pepper, seeded and diced
2 garlic cloves, peeled and sliced
1 red chile, seeded and chopped
1 tsp cumin seeds
5 ripe tomatoes, roughly chopped (add a pinch
    of sugar if the tomatoes aren't quite ripe)
Sea salt and freshly ground black pepper
4 eggs

TO SERVE
1 Tbsp chopped cilantro leaves
1 scallion, trimmed and finely chopped
Crusty bread

1. Heat a heavy-bottomed frying pan over medium heat. Add a dash of oil and sweat the onion for 5 minutes until soft. Add the peppers and continue to sweat for 5 minutes, then add the garlic and chile and cook for 1–2 minutes until soft and tender.

2. Add the cumin and cook for 1 minute, then add the tomatoes, season with salt and pepper, and cook for 15–20 minutes until the tomatoes have completely collapsed (add 3–4 tablespoons of water to the mixture if the tomatoes aren't that moist). The mixture should be the consistency of a thick sauce. Stir to mix well, taste, and adjust the seasoning.

3. Make 4 wells in the tomato mixture and break an egg into each well. Cover the pan and cook gently over medium-low heat for 5–6 minutes, or until the egg white is set and the yolk is still a little runny.

4. Serve sprinkled with cilantro leaves and chopped scallions, plus plenty of crusty bread on the side to mop up any juices.

CHICKEN STIR-FRY WITH RICE NOODLES
SERVES 2

You'll find versions of this recipe all across Asia, and it shows how good fast food can be. Because you are cooking over high heat, it's important to work quickly and keep everything moving around the wok, especially once the garlic has been added, as it will burn easily and taste bitter. Flattening the chicken not only means it will cook more quickly, but helps to tenderize it too.

8 ounces flat, wide rice noodles
8 ounces chicken breast
Flavorless oil, such as peanut
Sea salt and freshly ground black pepper
2 garlic cloves, peeled and thinly sliced

8 ounces baby broccoli, cut in half lengthwise
About 2 Tbsp soy sauce, to taste
2 eggs, beaten
Wedges of lime, to serve

1. If using dried noodles, soak them in warm water until softened, according to the package instructions. (This will take about 10 minutes, depending on the brand.)

2. Meanwhile, butterfly the chicken by slicing through it horizontally, but leaving it joined down one side, then open it out. Flatten it with a rolling pin, then cut it diagonally into strips.

3. Heat a wok over high heat and add a dash of oil. Season the chicken with salt and pepper, and stir-fry for about 3 minutes until golden brown all over but not quite cooked through.

4. Add the garlic and stir-fry for 30 seconds, then add the broccoli and continue to stir-fry for a few minutes until tender; add the soy sauce to season. When the broccoli is tender, remove the contents of the wok and set them aside. Wipe out the wok, add a dash of oil, and heat through.

5. Drain the soaked noodles. Add the eggs to the hot wok, season with salt and pepper, and stir over the heat, allowing the bottom of the egg to cook. Add the noodles and toss well, breaking up the egg as you do so. Return the chicken and broccoli mixture to the wok and heat through, stir-frying over medium heat.

6. Serve the noodles immediately with wedges of lime to squeeze on top.

HOW TO STIR-FRY
Tossing the contents of a pan with a smooth flick of the wrist doesn't just look good—it means you can stay in control and keep things cooking evenly. The secret is to push the pan away from you and sharply pull it back. Push away, pull back, push away, pull back. It will take a little practice, but it's a skill definitely worth perfecting.

HOMEMADE GNOCCHI
SERVES 4

This is a great way to use up baked or boiled potatoes. You can make gnocchi with just flour and eggs, but potato gives it a beautiful, light, fluffy texture, while the ricotta adds a rich creaminess. When you see what a beautiful meal this makes, you won't believe it all started with leftover potatoes.

2 large russet potatoes
¼ cup ricotta cheese
Sea salt and freshly ground white pepper
¾ cup all-purpose flour
1 free-range egg, beaten
1 thyme sprig, leaves only
Grated Parmesan cheese, to serve

FOR THE SAUCE
Olive oil
Sea salt and freshly ground black pepper
1 cup peas, shelled if fresh, defrosted if frozen
Butter
1 thyme sprig, leaves only
Zest of 1 lemon

1. Preheat the oven to 400°F.

2. Bake the potatoes in their skins for 1–1¼ hours until tender all the way through. Remove the flesh from the skins (ideally while still warm) and mash until smooth—a potato ricer works best here. Mix in the ricotta, a pinch of salt and white pepper, and the flour. Make a well in the middle, add the beaten egg, and begin to combine the mixture with floured hands. Work in the thyme leaves and continue until a smooth dough has formed. (Be careful not to overwork it or the dough will end up too dense and won't expand when it goes into the water.)

3. Cut the dough in half and shape each piece into a long cigar shape about ½ inch thick. Using the back of a floured table knife, cut each length of dough into ¾-inch pieces to make "pillows" or individual gnocchi. Gently press each one in the center using your floured finger. The dent will hold more sauce and allow the gnocchi to take on more flavor.

4. Bring a large pan of water to a boil. Add the gnocchi, tilting the pan from side to side briefly to keep them from sticking together, then simmer for about 1½–2 minutes until they start to float. Drain the gnocchi and leave them to steam-dry for 1–2 minutes.

5. Meanwhile, start to make the sauce. Heat a frying pan over medium-high heat and add a little olive oil. Add the gnocchi to the hot pan with a pinch of salt and black pepper and sauté for 1–2 minutes on each side until nicely colored.

6. Add the peas to the pan with a chunk of butter and the thyme leaves. Toss to heat through, then add the lemon zest. Serve with grated Parmesan cheese.

LEEK AND GRUYÈRE ROSTI WITH FRIED EGGS

SERVES 2

Every good cook has a few ideas up their sleeve for using leftover potatoes, and this Alpine dish is another one of my favorites. The Swiss will sometimes flavor their rostis with bacon, onion, or even apple, but I like to add leeks, to make a kind of cheesy take on the classic British bubble and squeak. This would make a light supper with a green salad, or, molded into separate patties, goes really well with roast chicken or grilled chops.

1 pound boiling potatoes, of a similar size
3 Tbsp olive oil, plus a little extra for the eggs
About 3 Tbsp butter
1 leek, trimmed and finely shredded
Sea salt and freshly ground black pepper

2 ounces Gruyère cheese, grated
2 eggs
Tarragon leaves, to garnish

1. Parboil the potatoes in boiling salted water until turning tender but not soft (about 10 minutes if using 2 medium potatoes). Remove, drain thoroughly, and leave to cool (you can leave until completely cooled and chill overnight if you have time).

2. Meanwhile, heat a tablespoon of the oil and 1 tablespoon of the butter in a pan. Sauté the leeks for 3–4 minutes until soft but not colored; season with salt and pepper to taste.

3. When the potatoes are cool enough to handle, peel off the skin and coarsely grate the flesh. Pat dry with paper towels or a clean dish towel.

4. Gently mix the grated potato with the leeks and cheese. Season with salt and pepper and mix again.

5. Heat a frying pan over medium heat. Add another tablespoon of the oil and 1 tablespoon of the butter. When the butter has melted, add the potato mixture, shaking the pan to form an even layer of potato. Leave to cook for 10 minutes over medium heat until golden brown (turn the heat down if the potato is browning too quickly).

6. Place a plate over the frying pan and invert both plate and pan so that the browned side of the rosti is facing upward on the plate. Add the final tablespoon of oil and butter to the pan and, once melted, slide the rosti back into the pan, browned side up. Continue to cook for 10 minutes or until golden brown underneath and cooked through.

7. Meanwhile, fry the eggs in a separate oiled hot frying pan until cooked to your liking.

8. Serve the rosti with the egg on top and garnish with tarragon leaves.

HOW TO FRY WITH BUTTER
Frying with butter gives a richer flavor, but you have to be careful it doesn't burn. By adding a splash of oil to the butter as you cook the potato cake, you raise the butter's burning point, meaning you can get a better color on the potato without compromising the flavor.

SPAGHETTI WITH CHILES, SARDINES, AND OREGANO
SERVES 2

Never be snobby about canned fish—as every student knows, it can be the secret behind plenty a quick and cheap meal. I've used sardines in this Italian standby, but mackerel would work just as well. The secret is to get the breadcrumbs beautifully golden, garlicky, and crunchy so they add a bit of texture to the pasta and fish.

Olive oil (or use the oil from the canned
   sardines if you wish)
2 garlic cloves, peeled and finely chopped
½ cup rough breadcrumbs, made from stale bread
Sea salt and freshly ground black pepper
8 ounces dried spaghetti
1 red chile, seeded and finely chopped

One 4-ounce can good-quality boneless sardines
   in olive oil or water, drained
5 oregano sprigs, leaves only, or ½ tsp
   dried oregano
2 ounces arugula leaves

1. Heat a small frying pan over medium heat. Add a glug of oil and, when hot, add half the chopped garlic along with the breadcrumbs. Cook over medium heat for about 3 minutes until the breadcrumbs are golden and toasted and the garlic is tender and lightly browned. Season with salt and pepper and toss together. Drain on paper towels.

2. Cook the pasta in boiling salted water until al dente, according to the package instructions.

3. Meanwhile, heat a frying pan over medium heat and add a little oil. Sauté the remaining garlic and the chile for 1–2 minutes. Flake the sardines into small pieces, then toss in the pan with the garlic and chile.

4. Drain the cooked pasta and add to the pan with the sardines. Toss to mix well. Add the oregano, taste, and adjust the seasoning as necessary.

5. When ready to serve, stir the arugula leaves into the pasta and divide between serving plates. Garnish with the crisp garlic breadcrumbs and serve immediately.

HOW TO USE UP STALE BREAD
While stale bread is perfect for making breadcrumbs, it's also great for croutons, and for making the classic Tuscan salad panzanella, based on stale bread, tomatoes, olives, peppers, and capers.

EASY FRAGRANT FRIED RICE

SERVES 4

Most of us are familiar with egg-fried rice from our local Chinese, but here I take it one step further by adding extra broccoli and greens to make it the original one-pot meal. Tasty, cheap, and nutritious, it's a great way of using up any leftover rice.

Flavorless oil, such as peanut, for frying
1 red chile, seeded and chopped
2 garlic cloves, peeled and finely chopped
1-inch piece of fresh ginger, peeled and finely chopped
8 ounces broccoli, cut into small florets
2 big handfuls of shredded greens, such as Chinese cabbage
3 cups day-old cooked jasmine rice

2 eggs, beaten
2 scallions, trimmed and finely chopped
Fish sauce, to taste
Pinch of sugar, to taste

TO SERVE
2 scallions, trimmed and shredded
Lime wedges

1. Heat a large, high-sided frying pan or wok over medium heat. Add a glug of oil and cook the chile, garlic, and ginger for 30 seconds until aromatic.

2. Add the broccoli and greens to the pan with 1–2 tablespoons of hot water to create a bit of steam. Cook over high heat for about a minute until the water has evaporated and the vegetables are becoming tender.

3. Add the rice and stir-fry in the pan, mixing it into all the ingredients. Cook for 1–2 minutes until the rice is hot all the way through.

4. Make a well in the middle of the pan and add the beaten eggs. Sprinkle over the scallions and a couple of drops of fish sauce. Scramble the eggs over medium-high heat until cooked through and separating into clumps, then mix the eggs into the rice.

5. When the eggs are cooked and mixed into the rice, taste the dish. Add a pinch of sugar and season with fish sauce.

6. Serve the fried rice garnished with shredded scallions, and lime wedges on the side to squeeze over.

HOW TO ACHIEVE FLUFFY COOKED RICE
To get fluffy grains of rice that don't stick together, you should always wash rice in a sieve under a running tap to rinse away the starch. Once cooked, if you are not serving it right away, the rice should be cooled down as quickly as possible by spreading it out on a baking sheet and placing it in the fridge. When stir-frying rice, it is essential to use cooked rice that has spent at least a few hours in the fridge, as this helps to dry it. Otherwise, you will end up with a mushy mess.

CHEAT'S SOUFFLÉ WITH THREE CHEESES
SERVES 6

This is either a giant eggy pancake or a giant doughy omelette, depending how you look at it. You can play with the cheeses as much as you want, but I like to keep things light by always including cottage cheese.

2 Tbsp butter, plus extra for greasing
½ cup all-purpose flour
1 tsp sugar
1 tsp baking powder
6 eggs, beaten
1 cup whole milk (see tip below)
Sea salt and freshly ground black pepper
¾ cup cottage cheese
12 ounces Monterey Jack cheese, grated
⅓ cup cream cheese

1. Preheat the oven to 350°F. Butter a 12 x 8-inch baking dish.

2. Mix together the flour, sugar, and baking powder in a bowl. Make a well in the middle and add the beaten eggs, milk, and a pinch of salt and pepper. Beat well.

3. Stir in the cottage cheese and grated cheese. Dot small lumps of the cream cheese and butter over the egg mixture, then fold in with a spoon.

4. Pour into the greased baking dish and bake in the preheated oven for 30–40 minutes until golden and set all the way through. This is ideal served with a light tomato and watercress salad.

HOW TO MAKE A LOWER-FAT BAKE
This bake is deliciously creamy, but if you're worried about the fat content, use low-fat milk and low-fat versions of the cottage cheese and cream cheese.

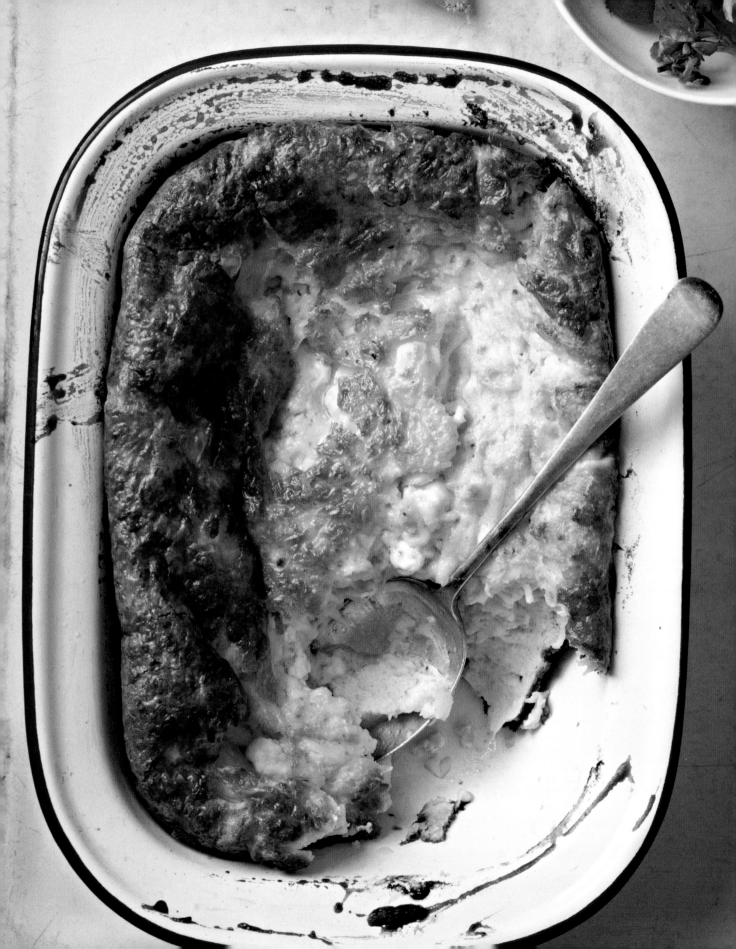

EASY ARANCINI

MAKES 18 ARANCINI

You might like to double up the ingredients here, because this is effectively two meals in one. You start by making a wonderful, rich mushroom risotto, which you could serve warm one night (perhaps finished with a drizzle of olive oil), and then you could make these rice balls for the following evening. They are perfect with a glass of prosecco (or champagne if you haven't really gotten the hang of this economizing business).

1 ounce mixed dried wild mushrooms
Butter
Flavorless oil, such as peanut
1 small onion or large shallot, peeled and
    finely diced
1 garlic clove, peeled and crushed
1⅓ cups risotto rice
½ cup dry white wine
2 cups vegetable or chicken stock
1 ounce Parmesan cheese, grated
Sea salt and freshly ground black pepper
9 mini mozzarella cheese balls or ½ large ball
2 eggs, beaten
About ¾ cup all-purpose flour
1 cup panko breadcrumbs or regular breadcrumbs
Lemon wedges, to serve (optional)

1. Soak the mushrooms in 1 cup hot water for 20 minutes.

2. Heat a heavy-based, high-sided frying pan or saucepan over medium heat. Add a generous chunk of butter and a glug of oil and sauté the onion and garlic for about 5 minutes until soft but not colored.

3. Add the rice and stir vigorously around the pan for a couple of minutes until the grains start to turn slightly translucent at the edges. Deglaze the pan by pouring in the wine and scraping up the bits at the bottom. Bring to a boil, then lower the heat and simmer for a minute or two to burn off the alcohol.

4. Meanwhile, heat the stock and add the soaking liquor from the mushrooms. Add a ladleful of the hot stock mixture to the rice and stir over medium heat until absorbed, then add another ladleful. Repeat until all the stock is used up or the rice is tender but still al dente. Make sure to stir regularly to create a creamy risotto. (This should take about 20 minutes.)

CONTINUED ON PAGE 160

CONTINUED FROM PAGE 159

5. Chop the rehydrated mushrooms into small pieces and gently stir into the cooked risotto. Add a chunk of butter and the Parmesan, then stir to mix well. Taste and adjust the seasoning if necessary, then leave the risotto to cool (it will do this more quickly if you spread it onto a baking sheet).

6. If using mini mozzarella balls, halve them; if using part of a large ball, cut it into ¾-inch cubes.

7. Lay out 3 plates or shallow bowls. Put the beaten eggs in one, the flour (seasoned with a pinch of salt and pepper) in another, and the breadcrumbs in the final one.

8. Once the risotto is cooled (it doesn't matter if it is still a little warm, as long as it has stiffened up a bit and is cool enough to handle), roll it into balls the size of golf balls. Push a piece of mozzarella into the middle of each ball, making sure that the cheese is completely enclosed. Leave to set in the fridge for at least 30 minutes or overnight.

9. Heat a deep-fat fryer to 340°F or fill a large saucepan one-third full of flavorless oil and heat until a cube of bread dropped into the hot oil sizzles and turns golden brown in 30 seconds.

10. Dip a rice ball into the flour, shake off any excess, then dip into the egg, allowing any excess to drip off. Finish by coating completely in the breadcrumbs. Repeat with the remaining balls.

11. Deep-fry the balls in batches for 2–3 minutes until golden brown all over. Remove with a slotted spoon and drain on paper towels. Serve immediately while the middles are still melting. Drizzle with lemon juice, if using.

HOW TO PAN-FRY ARANCINI
You can make arancini with leftover risotto, if you happen to have some on hand. They can also be pan-fried rather than deep-fried. Cook them over medium heat and make sure you turn them frequently, basting with the oil.

LAMB WITH FRIED BREAD

SERVES 2

Lamb steak is cut from the upper part of the leg, and the bone running through it is full of flavorful marrow. Because it's a cheap cut, it does need lots of color on it to impart flavor, so although you can grill it, it will never be the same as sealing it in a pan and basting it to keep it moist. With the anchovy dressing and croutons, the lamb just needs a green salad or some green beans to make it into a complete meal. Who'd have thought you could make something so delicious out of a cheap cut plus a stale loaf of bread?

2 lamb leg steaks
Sea salt and freshly ground black pepper
Olive oil
12 garlic cloves, skin on, crushed
8 ounces crusty white bread roll, cut into chunks
3–4 Tbsp milk

FOR THE ANCHOVY DRESSING
1 ounce anchovies preserved in olive oil
1 Tbsp capers
1½ tsp Dijon mustard
2 Tbsp red wine vinegar, or to taste
Extra virgin olive oil
Small bunch of parsley, leaves roughly chopped

1. Make small cuts into each edge of the lamb steaks to prevent them from curling up while cooking. Season well with salt and pepper (lamb needs a lot of pepper), pushing the seasoning into the meat. (This will be much easier if the meat has been taken out of the fridge earlier and allowed to come up to room temperature.)

2. Heat a frying pan until hot and add a little oil. When it's hot, add the lamb and the garlic. Color the lamb for 2½–3 minutes on each side until golden brown, basting with the oil as you cook and turning the garlic regularly to make sure that it doesn't burn. Remove the meat from the pan and leave to rest, pouring over any pan juices and reserving the garlic.

CONTINUED ON PAGE 162

CONTINUED FROM PAGE 161

3. Meanwhile, season the chunks of bread with salt and pepper. Soak in the milk, tossing the bread to help it soak evenly. (The milk will give it a rich creamy texture, almost like French toast.) Set aside.

4. Make the dressing by placing the reserved garlic in a mortar with the anchovies and capers, grinding until smooth. Stir in the mustard, vinegar, and enough oil to bring it to a thick dressing consistency. Add the parsley to the mortar and mix well with a spoon. Taste and adjust the seasoning as necessary.

5. Heat a little olive oil in a clean frying pan over medium heat. Squeeze out any excess milk from the bread, then cook it with some extra salt and pepper for 4–5 minutes, turning it regularly until it's golden on all sides. Remove and drain on paper towels.

6. To serve, spoon the dressing onto serving plates, scatter over half the croutons, and place the lamb steaks on top. Finish with the remaining croutons and a little extra dressing. Serve immediately.

HOW TO PAN-FRY MEAT PROPERLY

When pan-frying any meat, you want to be able to hear a sizzling sound as the meat cooks to show that the pan and oil are hot enough. If you can't hear it, take the meat out and bring the oil up to temperature. Cuts such as rib-eye or leg steak have a fatty rind on them that needs to be cooked until golden. To do this, lay the fatty part away from you in the pan and tilt the pan so that the rendered fat pools at the bottom edge and cooks as it does so.

SPICY SAUSAGE RICE

SERVES 4

This is like an old-fashioned jambalaya—a mixture of rice, vegetables, and meat, a bit like risotto but without the need for stirring. Sausage is cheap but packed with flavor, and taking it out of the casing first flavors the rice beautifully. You can use any sausage you want—chorizo, merguez, pork, or beef, depending on how spicy you want it.

Olive oil
1 red onion, peeled and sliced
1 red pepper, seeded and chopped
2 garlic cloves, peeled and thinly sliced
5 spiced sausages, such as spicy Italian
1 heaping tsp smoked paprika
Sea salt and freshly ground black pepper
1 cup long-grain rice

⅓ cup white wine
2 cups chicken stock
4 scallions, trimmed and chopped
1 tomato, chopped
Small bunch of flat-leaf parsley, leaves roughly chopped

1. Add a glug of oil to a heavy-bottomed casserole dish and sauté the onion for 5 minutes until soft but not colored. Add the pepper and garlic and cook for 2 minutes. Slit the sausage skins and crumble the sausage meat into the pan, then cook over medium heat for 4–5 minutes until colored. Add the smoked paprika and mix. Season with salt and pepper to taste.

2. Add the rice and stir well to mix thoroughly and absorb the flavor. Deglaze the pan by pouring in the white wine and scraping any bits stuck to the bottom. Add the stock and bring to a simmer. Cook gently for 15–20 minutes until the rice is tender and the liquid is almost entirely absorbed.

3. Remove from the heat, gently fold in the scallions, tomato, and parsley, and serve.

HOW TO SAUTÉ ONIONS
When sautéing onions, don't slice them too thinly or they will burn before they have a chance to caramelize. Never rush cooking an onion. Always give it 5 or 6 minutes in the pan on its own.

PORK AND SHRIMP MEATBALLS IN AROMATIC BROTH

SERVES 2

I've always been a fan of that surf 'n' turf combination, seafood and meat, and these simple pork and shrimp meatballs in a comforting broth make a great light lunch or supper dish. As always, it's important to taste as you go along so that you can control the depth of flavor of the stock. The longer you cook it, the more potent it will become.

4 ounces raw shrimp, peeled and deveined
  (see tip below)
8 ounces ground pork
1½ Tbsp finely chopped chives
½-inch piece of fresh ginger, peeled and diced
Sea salt and freshly ground black pepper
Flavorless oil, such as peanut
2 big handfuls of spinach
1 scallion, trimmed and thinly sliced,
  to garnish

FOR THE BROTH BASE
1 quart chicken or fish stock, homemade
  or from stock cubes
2 whole star anise
1–2 tsp oyster sauce, to taste
1–2 tsp soy sauce, to taste
¾-inch piece of fresh ginger, peeled
  and chopped

1. Finely chop the shrimp until almost ground. Place in a bowl with the pork, chives, and ginger, season with a good pinch of salt and pepper, and mix until the ingredients are well combined and sticking together. Roll the mixture into small balls about 1 inch wide. Transfer to a plate, cover, and chill until needed.

2. Meanwhile, make the broth base. Heat the stock in a saucepan, add the other ingredients, and mix well. Bring to a boil, lower the heat, and gently simmer for 10 minutes to infuse, then taste and adjust the seasoning as necessary. (For a strong broth base, leave the mixture to simmer for longer.)

3. Heat a heavy-based frying pan over medium heat and add a dash of oil. Cook the pork and shrimp balls, turning frequently, for 6–7 minutes until golden brown all over. Transfer into the gently simmering pan of broth and leave to cook for 5 minutes until the balls are cooked through. Add the spinach and cook for 1 minute until just wilted.

4. Taste the dish and adjust the seasoning if necessary. Serve garnished with scallions.

HOW TO PREPARE SHRIMP
First, twist off the head, then peel off all the shell, and pull off the tail. With the tip of a sharp knife, score the shrimp along the back and lift out the black vein. Rinse the prepared shrimp before using.

CHICKPEA, CUMIN, AND SPINACH KOFTAS WITH TAHINI DRESSING

MAKES ABOUT 20 KOFTAS

Chickpeas can be very bland on their own, but they take on spicy flavors really well. Because of their texture, they make a great substitute for ground beef—in a burger, say, or in these classic koftas. It's important to let them rest in the fridge so that they hold their shape when you pan-fry them.

8 ounces spinach
Olive oil
1 Tbsp cumin seeds
Two 14-ounce cans chickpeas, drained
1 tsp paprika
½ tsp ground turmeric
Sea salt and freshly ground black pepper
2 Tbsp chickpea (gram) flour, plus extra for dusting

FOR THE DRESSING
½ cup plain yogurt
1–2 Tbsp tahini paste, to taste
Juice of ½ lemon
2 Tbsp chopped cilantro leaves
Sea salt and freshly ground black pepper
Olive oil (optional)

1. Wash the spinach, then place in a medium-hot oiled pan and stir until wilted. Drain thoroughly, squeezing out any excess water, then finely chop.

2. Toast the cumin seeds in a dry hot pan for about 1 minute until aromatic and golden, then grind in a mortar with a pestle.

3. Place the chickpeas, cumin, and spices, along with a good pinch of salt and pepper, in a blender and blend to a fine paste. (If the mixture looks too dry to hold together, add 2–3 tablespoons of water and blend again.) Add the spinach, sprinkle in the flour, and mix well to combine.

4. Dust your hands with flour, then take a tablespoon of the mixture and mold it into an egg shape. (If this is too tricky, simply roll it into a ball.) Repeat until all the mixture has been used, then place on a plate or baking sheet dusted with flour. Chill for at least 1 hour until you are ready to cook.

5. Preheat the oven to 250°F.

6. Heat some oil in a pan and pan-fry the koftas in batches over medium heat for 2–3 minutes until golden brown on all sides and hot all the way through. Drain after frying, and keep them warm in the oven.

7. Combine all the dressing ingredients and season with salt and pepper to taste. Add a little olive oil if you want a looser consistency.

8. Serve the koftas warm with the dressing on the side.

CANTALOUPE SOUP AND CRÈME FRAÎCHE

SERVES 4

When you buy fruit at the peak of its season, not only is it cheaper, but you don't have to do much to it to bring out its best. This recipe shows how simple a fruit dish can be—just melon, sugar syrup, and grapes. To check if a melon is ripe, sniff it near the stalk: a ripe melon will smell sweet.

1 ripe cantaloupe
1 Tbsp lemon juice
¾ cup simple syrup (see tip below)
¼ cup crème fraîche
A few small seedless grapes, halved
8 mint sprigs, to garnish

1. Cut the melon in half, scoop out the seeds, then cut the fruit away from the rind in chunks. Place in a food processor with the lemon juice and simple syrup, and process until smooth. Chill for 3–4 hours.

2. Spoon the soup into 4 chilled glass bowls, top with the crème fraîche and grapes, garnish with the mint, and serve.

HOW TO MAKE SIMPLE SYRUP
Boil ¾ cup water with ¼ cup sugar for 5 minutes, stirring to dissolve the sugar, then allow to cool. You can add any flavors you like during cooking—a strip of lemon rind, a chunk of ginger, or a star anise would all work beautifully here.

BREAD AND BUTTER PUDDING

SERVES 6–8

Bread and butter pudding was absolutely my favorite when I was growing up. My mother always made it with cheap white sliced bread, but I've experimented with all sorts since: baguette, panettone, brioche, croissants. Pain au chocolat is my current favorite, as the nuggets of chocolate give it that extra dimension.

3½ Tbsp softened butter, plus extra to grease
2–3 Tbsp apricot jam
6 pains au chocolat, cut into slices ½ inch thick
1–2 Tbsp ground cinnamon
¼ cup brown sugar

¼ cup golden raisins
2 cups whole milk
½ cup heavy cream
6 eggs
2 vanilla pods, seeds scraped out

1. Preheat the oven to 350°F. Lightly butter 9 x 7-inch baking dish.

2. Heat the jam in a pan over low heat for a couple of minutes until melted. Remove and set aside.

3. Butter the slices of pain au chocolat on one side, place them in a large bowl, and set aside. Now sprinkle about 2 teaspoons of the cinnamon into the buttered serving dish along with 2 tablespoons of the sugar and all of the raisins. Pour over most of the melted jam, reserving a small amount for glazing at the end.

4. Whisk together the milk, cream, eggs, vanilla seeds, and 1 teaspoon of the cinnamon and pour half of this mixture all over the bread. When it has soaked in slightly, arrange the bread in the baking dish so the pieces are overlapping. Continue layering the bread until all the pieces have been used, then pour over the rest of the egg mixture and scatter the surface with the remaining sugar and a light dusting of cinnamon.

5. Place in the preheated oven and bake for 35–40 minutes until golden.

6. To serve, brush the pudding with the reserved melted jam and serve immediately.

COOKING IN ADVANCE

AN ORGANIZED COOK IS A RELAXED COOK, AND ONE OF THE BEST WAYS OF BEING ORGANIZED IS TO DO AS MUCH WORK IN ADVANCE AS YOU CAN.

That doesn't just mean putting out your ingredients before you start cooking, or prepping all your vegetables before you turn on the gas—important as these things are—sometimes it also means fully preparing dishes ahead of time. Not only will the meal be less stressful if you know one of the courses is already taken care of, but a lot of dishes actually taste better if cooked in advance. It's what you might call a win-win, and it's why advance planning is so important in the kitchen.

With some things you have no choice: they have to be made beforehand anyway. A jar of chutney, for example, is a great way to add flavor to a simple supper, but you're hardly going to look in your fridge at 7 p.m., see some ham, and think, "I know, I'll make a quick chutney to go with that." These are things to make in batches and have sitting in the fridge or pantry. With all that vinegar and sugar, they can keep for years if you sterilize the jars properly—something our grandparents knew only too well. (To sterilize jars, and their lids, wash them thoroughly and allow to dry on a clean dish towel. Preheat the oven to its lowest setting, then place the jars and lids on a baking sheet and heat in the oven for 30 minutes.)

The freezer can be another life-saver when it comes to cooking in bulk. We've been turning up our noses at frozen foods over the past decade or so, I think, because we've been encouraged to see chilled foods as somehow being fresher. In fact frozen is often best (I'll take frozen peas over the so-called fresh pods you see in supermarkets anytime; likewise with a lot of fish). When it comes to your own cooking, there's no question that making in bulk and then freezing some of it makes sense. I've always got things like chicken stock, tomato sauce, and meatballs in handy sizes in the freezer, ready to be taken out when needed. Meatballs are a good example as they freeze really well and are so versatile that you can take them in any direction you like once they've defrosted: in a Mexican soup, a pasta bake, a melted cheese sandwich...

Other things are best served at room temperature anyway, so it's a good idea to make them during a quiet time in the day. That doesn't just mean cakes, cookies, and the like, but also delicately flavored dishes, such as quiche. When food is too hot we tend to gulp it down without savoring it; too cold and the flavors almost hibernate. That's why you should always allow foods you've kept in the fridge, like cheese or cold meats, to come to room temperature before you serve them, to give the flavors a chance to wake up. Similarly, there is no shame in serving a main course like poached salmon at room temperature. Again, less stress for the cook.

Then there are dishes where the flavor genuinely improves with time. Marinades and casseroles are the most obvious examples. So much of cooking is about maximizing flavors, making the ingredients work for you, and the easiest way to do that is to leave them in contact with each other for longer to meld together. If you marinate a piece of meat in herbs and wine for a couple of hours, it's going to take on some of the flavors and become more tender. Marinate it for 24 hours, though, and your patience will be rewarded a hundred times over. Make a casserole the day before, and as the meat sits in all those lovely juices, it almost acts like a sponge and soaks up all that flavor, making it moister and tastier when you gently reheat it the next day. It's a trick we use so often in my restaurants.

I'm also including in this chapter a lot of slow-cooked dishes, such as Slow-Roasted Pork Belly with Fennel and Slow-Cooked Beef Short Ribs (see pages 189 and 194). You're not necessarily making them in advance (although with the short ribs there's no reason why you shouldn't), but what you are doing is putting in the work much earlier on and then just leaving them to their own devices. Slow cooking works best on the fattier, tougher, less fashionable cuts of meat, such as cheek, neck, and belly. This is gutsy, robust cooking at its best. Ten minutes spent really caramelizing the meat, cooking out the wine, and packing in the flavors will result, a couple of hours later, in a meltingly tender and flavorful dish worthy of any dinner table. And the great thing is that because it's all self-contained in one pan or casserole dish, you've got almost no cleanup.

SPICY MEATBALL SOUP

SERVES 4–6

This is real comfort food, meatballs in a richly spicy soup. It adds hugely to the flavor if you can find chipotles in adobo—jalapeño chiles in a smoky, sweet and sour purée—but if you can't, you could try regular chiles with a teaspoon or two of smoked paprika.

1 onion, peeled and diced
2 garlic cloves, peeled and thinly sliced
Sea salt and freshly ground black pepper
1 tsp cumin seeds
½–1 Tbsp chipotle chile paste or chipotles in adobo
One 14-ounce can chopped tomatoes
1 tsp dried oregano
1 quart beef or chicken stock
One 12-ounce can corn, drained
2 zucchini, trimmed and diced into ¾-inch pieces

FOR THE MEATBALLS

1 small onion, peeled and finely diced
2 garlic cloves, peeled and finely sliced
Sea salt and freshly ground black pepper
1 tsp dried chile flakes
1 pound ground beef
⅔ cup fresh breadcrumbs
3–4 Tbsp milk
Olive oil

TO SERVE

1 large handful of tortilla chips, roughly chopped
¼ cup chopped cilantro
2 Tbsp jalapeño peppers, seeded and chopped

HOW TO FREEZE MEATBALLS

The meatballs in this recipe freeze brilliantly and can be used in many different ways. Just remember to let the onion and garlic mixture cool completely before combining it with the beef and rolling into balls. Freeze right away and allow to defrost completely before cooking.

1. First prepare the meatballs. Sauté the onion and garlic with salt and pepper to taste in a hot oiled frying pan for about 5 minutes until soft and lightly colored, adding the chile flakes after a minute or two. Place the beef in a large bowl and season with salt and pepper. Put the breadcrumbs in a separate bowl and moisten with the milk. Add salt and pepper, then stir the breadcrumbs and onion mixture into the beef and combine well. With wet hands, shape the beef mixture into balls just smaller than a golf ball (about 1¼ inches wide). Transfer to a lightly greased plate or baking sheet and chill for 30 minutes until firm.

2. Heat a little oil in a large saucepan and sauté the onion and garlic for the soup base with a pinch of salt and pepper for 4–5 minutes until softened. Add the cumin seeds and meatballs and cook over high heat to toast the cumin seeds and color the meatballs on all sides.

3. Add the chipotle chile paste and stir over high heat. Add the canned tomatoes, oregano, and stock, bring to a boil, then lower the heat. Season with salt and pepper and gently simmer for 20 minutes until the meatballs are cooked through and the soup has thickened a little. (This can be done in advance, then left overnight for the flavors to develop if you prefer.)

4. Before serving, add the corn and zucchini and cook for 3–4 minutes until both are tender. Serve the soup garnished with crushed tortilla chips, cilantro, and jalapeño peppers.

BEEF MEATBALLS WITH ORECCHIETTE, KALE, AND PINE NUTS

SERVES 4

Orecchiette means "little ears," and refers to the ear-shaped pasta traditionally used in a Puglian dish of broccoli, anchovies, and chiles. This dish is similar in feel, with kale instead of broccoli, and the meatballs replacing the anchovies and chiles.

1 pound dried orecchiette pasta
2 garlic cloves, peeled and sliced
8 ounces kale, shredded
Sea salt and freshly ground black pepper
¼ cup pine nuts, toasted
Freshly grated Parmesan cheese, to taste

FOR THE MEATBALLS
1 small onion, peeled and finely diced
2 garlic cloves, peeled and thinly sliced
Sea salt and freshly ground black pepper
Olive oil
1 tsp dried chile flakes
1 pound ground beef
⅔ cup fresh breadcrumbs
3–4 Tbsp milk

1. First prepare the meatballs. Sauté the onion and garlic with salt and pepper to taste in a hot oiled frying pan for about 5 minutes until soft and lightly colored, adding the chile flakes after a minute or two. Place the beef in a large bowl and add salt and pepper. Put the breadcrumbs in a separate bowl and moisten with the milk. Add salt and pepper, then stir the breadcrumbs and onion mixture into the beef and combine well. With wet hands, shape the beef mixture into small balls about ¾ inch wide. Transfer to a lightly greased plate or baking sheet and chill for 30 minutes until firm.

2. Cook the pasta in boiling salted water until al dente, according to the package instructions.

3. Meanwhile, heat a large frying pan over medium heat and add a little olive oil. Brown the meatballs for 6 minutes until colored on all sides. Add the garlic to the pan and cook for 2 minutes until tender, then add the kale and season with salt and pepper. Sweat the kale over medium heat for 5 minutes with a couple of tablespoons of the cooking water from the pasta. Taste and adjust the seasoning as necessary, then stir in the pine nuts.

4. Drain the pasta, reserving a few tablespoons of cooking water. Tip the pasta into the pan with the meatballs and stir over medium-low heat until well mixed. Add a good handful of finely grated Parmesan, and mix well with a little cooking water to help coat the pasta. Taste and adjust the seasoning as necessary.

5. Serve garnished with another grating of Parmesan.

HOW TO SWEAT VEGETABLES
The aim of sweating vegetables is to soften them without coloring. Start by heating a heavy-bottomed pan over medium heat. When hot, add a little oil (or water, as called for opposite) and your vegetable, and cook, stirring frequently, for 5–10 minutes. It is important that the vegetable doesn't brown or it will develop a bitter flavor.

MEATBALLS IN FRAGRANT COCONUT BROTH

SERVES 2–4

To me, a meatball is all about softness and texture and the way it melts in your mouth. Adding milk to the breadcrumbs lightens the meatballs and means that you shouldn't need to bind them with eggs. Don't make them too small or they'll dry out—about golf ball size is just right. This is a classic way of making meatballs, but cooking them in this beautiful aromatic broth means they really soak up the fresh, spicy flavors. Asian cuisine uses coconut milk to enrich a sauce, in much the same way as classic French cooking uses cream, but of course it isn't as heavy.

2 tsp coriander seeds
4 cardamom pods, lightly crushed
1 tsp ground turmeric
½ tsp ground cinnamon
1–2 tsp dried chile flakes, to taste
2 lemongrass stalks, trimmed, smashed, and
    cut into small sticks
2-inch piece of fresh ginger, peeled and sliced
1½ cups chicken stock
One 14-ounce can coconut milk
Zest and juice of 1 lime

FOR THE MEATBALLS

1 small onion, peeled and finely diced
2 garlic cloves, peeled and thinly sliced
Sea salt and freshly ground black pepper
Olive oil
1 tsp dried chile flakes
1 pound ground beef
⅔ cup fresh breadcrumbs
3–4 Tbsp milk

1. First prepare the meatballs. Sauté the onion and garlic with salt and pepper to taste in a hot oiled frying pan for about 5 minutes until soft and lightly colored, adding the chile flakes after a minute or two. Place the beef in a large bowl and season with salt and pepper. Put the breadcrumbs in a separate bowl and moisten with the milk. Season with salt and pepper, then stir the breadcrumbs and onion mixture into the beef and combine well. With wet hands, shape the beef mixture into balls about the size of a golf ball. Transfer to a lightly greased plate or baking sheet and chill for 30 minutes until firm.

2. Brown the meatballs in a cleaned oiled pan for 4–5 minutes, turning frequently until nicely colored on all sides.

3. Add the coriander seeds, cardamom, turmeric, cinnamon, chile flakes, lemongrass, and ginger. Heat through, stirring, until aromatic, then add the stock and coconut milk and bring to a gentle simmer. Taste and adjust the seasoning as necessary. Simmer for 8–12 minutes until the sauce is flavorful and thickened and the meatballs are cooked through.

4. Add the lime zest and juice and serve hot.

HOW TO STORE COCONUT MILK
Leftover coconut milk can be stored in the fridge for about five days before it sours. If you don't plan to use it that quickly, simply freeze it in ice-cube trays or small plastic pots. After freezing, the milk will look curdled, but the flavor will be fine.

BEEF MEATBALL SANDWICH WITH MELTING MOZZARELLA AND TOMATO SALSA

SERVES 4

A simple variation on the beef burger, with mozzarella instead of Swiss cheese and a tomato, onion, and cilantro salsa as a fresher take on ketchup.

1 small onion, peeled and finely diced
2 garlic cloves, peeled and thinly sliced
Sea salt and freshly ground black pepper
Olive oil
1 tsp dried chile flakes
1 pound ground beef
⅔ cup fresh breadcrumbs
3–4 Tbsp milk
4 submarine or hot dog rolls
2 balls of mozzarella cheese, torn

FOR THE SALSA
3 tomatoes, finely chopped
½ red onion, peeled and finely chopped
1 Tbsp chopped cilantro
1 tsp white wine vinegar
Pinch of sugar

1. First prepare the meatballs. Sauté the onion and garlic with salt and pepper in a hot oiled frying pan for about 5 minutes until soft and lightly colored, adding the chile flakes after a minute or two. Place the beef in a large bowl and season with salt and pepper. Put the breadcrumbs in a separate bowl and moisten with the milk. Season with salt and pepper, then stir the breadcrumbs and onion mixture into the beef and combine well. With wet hands, shape the beef mixture into large balls about 1½ inches wide. Transfer to a lightly greased plate or baking sheet and chill for 30 minutes until firm.

2. Put a little oil in a frying pan and cook the meatballs over medium-low heat with a dash of oil for about 10 minutes until colored on the outside and cooked all the way through. Set aside to rest.

3. Meanwhile, combine all the salsa ingredients and mix well. Set aside.

4. Heat a broiler to medium. Slice the bread rolls in half and toast the insides for a couple of minutes until golden. Remove from the broiler and set the meatballs on half the sliced rolls, pressing them down into the bread. Spoon over any cooking juices from the meatball pan. Top the meatballs with mozzarella and place under the broiler to melt the cheese. Once melted, spoon the salsa on top and sandwich together with the remaining halves of the toasted rolls.

5. Serve while still warm with any extra salsa on the side.

SPICY CHUTNEY

MAKES 3 CUPS

Spicing is the light and shade of a good chutney, the element that gives it depth and personality, but don't go overboard on the chiles as the heat will increase the longer you keep it. Tamarind is a tropical fruit that tastes a little like sour dates and is used in vegetable curries and chutneys. You'll find it in paste form in most supermarkets.

6 dried curry leaves
1 tsp cumin seeds
1–2 Tbsp mustard seeds
1 tsp coriander seeds
Sea salt
3 dried red chiles
Olive oil
1 onion, peeled and grated

3 garlic cloves, peeled and thinly sliced
4–6 Tbsp tamarind paste or watered-down
    tamarind block (see tip below)
3 Tbsp sugar
4 heaping Tbsp desiccated coconut
2 large carrots, peeled and coarsely grated
Sea salt and freshly ground black pepper

1. Toast the curry leaves and cumin, mustard, and coriander seeds in a dry pan over low heat for about 2 minutes until aromatic (be careful not to burn them). Add a pinch of salt and the dried chiles. Add a little oil, then sweat the onion in it for 2 minutes. Add the garlic and cook over low heat for 1–2 minutes until soft.

2. Add the tamarind paste and sugar and cook over medium heat for about 2 minutes until the sugar has dissolved. Stir in the coconut.

3. Add the carrots and mix well. Bring to a boil, then lower the heat and simmer gently for 5–6 minutes, adding 2–3 tablespoons of water if necessary to loosen. Taste and adjust the seasoning and sweetness as needed. Remove from the heat.

4. Pour the chutney into sterilized jars (see page 175) right away and seal. You can eat this chutney immediately or store it in the fridge for up to a month. Serve with cold meats or cheese.

HOW TO PREPARE TAMARIND
To water down a block of tamarind, soak it in a little hot water, remove the seeds, and mash it well to create a thick juice.

SLOW-COOKED EGGPLANT

SERVES 4–6 AS A STARTER

This vegetable stew is such a simple combination of ingredients, but they undergo this amazing transformation during cooking to become more than the sum of their parts. Another dish that just gets better and better the longer you allow the flavors to mingle.

Olive oil
2 eggplants, trimmed and cut into 1-inch chunks
3 garlic cloves, peeled and chopped
1 red onion, peeled and diced
One 14-ounce can lima beans, drained and rinsed
2 Tbsp pomegranate molasses (see page 205)
Sea salt and freshly ground black pepper
One 14-ounce can chopped tomatoes
Pinch of sugar

TO SERVE
1 loaf of crusty white bread, such as sourdough or country bread
Small bunch of mint, leaves roughly chopped
3 ounces feta cheese, crumbled

1. Heat a heavy-bottomed casserole dish over high heat. Add a glug of oil and cook the eggplant for 3–4 minutes until colored on all sides. Add the garlic and onion and cook for another 5 minutes until the onion is tender.

2. Stir in the lima beans and pomegranate molasses with a generous pinch of salt and grinding of pepper. Add the tomatoes and sugar. Bring to a boil, then lower the heat and simmer, uncovered, for 40–45 minutes until the eggplant is tender and collapsed and the stew is reduced and flavorful. (If you find the mixture is drying out too much, add a couple of tablespoons of water.)

3. To serve, slice the bread and toast on each side until golden. Stir the mint through the eggplant, spoon onto the slices of toast, and scatter over the crumbled feta. Serve warm.

HOW TO SALT EGGPLANT
Although it's not essential to salt eggplant before you cook it, doing so draws out the moisture and makes it absorb less oil. Simply chop or dice the eggplant as instructed, place in a colander, and sprinkle with about 1 teaspoon of sea salt. Leave for 30 minutes, then rinse well, pat dry on paper towels, and cook as you like.

SLOW-ROASTED PORK BELLY WITH FENNEL

SERVES 4

Pork is a very sweet meat, so it's nice to add the vibrant anise flavor of fennel. You've got to take your time cooking pork belly, making sure the crackling on top is beautifully roasted while the meat beneath braises gently in the pan's juices. Cutting diamonds in the skin allows the seasoning to really penetrate, and although it may seem odd, adding more salt after you've seared it really helps the skin to crisp up. Serve with scalloped potatoes and broccoli.

2 pounds pork belly
Sea salt and freshly ground black pepper
1 fennel bulb, trimmed and roughly sliced
4 fresh bay leaves
3 garlic cloves, peeled and crushed
1 tsp cardamom pods, crushed
4 star anise

1 Tbsp fennel seeds
Olive oil
1½ cups white wine
2–3 cups chicken stock (depending on the size of your pan)
1 Tbsp grainy mustard

1. Preheat the oven to 350°F.

2. Score the pork belly skin diagonally in a diamond pattern at ½-inch intervals. Season generously with salt and pepper, rubbing it well into the skin.

3. Put the fennel, bay leaves, garlic, cardamom, star anise, and half the fennel seeds into a hot roasting pan on the stovetop with a little oil and heat for about 2 minutes until aromatic. Push to the side of the pan, then add the pork, skin side down, and cook for at least 5 minutes until turning golden brown. Turn the pork over, season the skin again with salt, and sprinkle with the remaining fennel seeds. Pour in the wine to deglaze the pan, scraping up the bits from the bottom (be careful not to get the skin of the pork wet). Bring to a boil, then pour in enough stock to come up to a layer of fat just below the skin and allow to boil again.

4. Transfer the pan to the preheated oven and cook for 2½ hours.

5. Transfer the meat to a warm plate and set aside to rest. Meanwhile, spoon off any excess fat in the roasting pan or drag a slice of bread along the surface of the cooking juices to absorb it. Heat the pan on the stovetop, adding the mustard. Mix in with a whisk, then taste and adjust the flavors as necessary. Remove the star anise and cardamom pods and pour the sauce into a pitcher. Serve the rested pork with the sauce alongside.

HOW TO SEASON PORK SKIN
If you slightly bend the pork as you are rubbing in the salt and fennel seeds, it will open up the diamond incisions in the rind, making it easier for the flavors to penetrate.

CORIANDER, GINGER, AND CHILE BUTTER CHICKEN
SERVES 4

Butter chicken, or murgh makhani, is the dish I always order in Indian restaurants, as it's a favorite on UK menus. I had an amazing version at Moti Mahal restaurant in Delhi, where it originated, and this is my take on it. Start marinating the meat the night before to allow the flavors to develop.

1 pound boneless, skinless chicken thighs,
   cut into 1½-inch pieces
Olive oil or ghee
1 small onion, peeled and finely diced
Sea salt
2 garlic cloves, peeled and finely chopped
1-inch piece of fresh ginger, peeled and finely
   chopped
1 tsp ground coriander
1 tsp garam masala
½ tsp ground turmeric
Pinch of chili powder, or to taste (optional)
2 Tbsp tomato purée
2 Tbsp butter
Small bunch of fresh cilantro, leaves
   roughly chopped, to garnish

FOR THE MARINADE
2 garlic cloves, peeled and finely chopped
1½-inch piece of fresh ginger, peeled and grated
1 red chile, seeded and finely chopped
Juice of ¼ lemon
2 tsp coriander seeds
1 tsp cumin seeds
½ tsp ground turmeric
½ cup plain yogurt
Sea salt and freshly ground black pepper

1. Put the garlic, ginger, chile, and lemon juice from the marinade ingredients in a bowl. Toss the chicken in the mixture, then cover and set aside.

2. Continue preparing the marinade. Toast the coriander and cumin seeds in a dry pan for about 1 minute until aromatic and the coriander seeds are popping. Grind to a powder, then mix with the turmeric, yogurt, and a good pinch of salt and pepper.

3. Pour the yogurt mixture over the chicken. Mix well, cover, and leave to marinate for at least 2 hours (or, ideally, overnight if you have time).

4. When ready to cook the chicken, heat a large, heavy-bottomed pan over medium heat and add a little olive oil or ghee. When the pan is hot, sauté the onion with a pinch of salt for 5 minutes. Add the garlic and cook until lightly golden before adding the ginger and cooking for an additional minute.

5. Add the ground coriander, garam masala, turmeric, and chili powder (if using), and stir into the onions over medium heat until aromatic. Add the tomato purée and stir for 30 seconds. Add the butter and allow to melt before stirring it through.

6. Remove the chicken from the marinade and wipe off any excess. Add the chicken pieces to the pan and cook for 10 minutes, turning now and again, until cooked through. Lower the heat, add the remaining marinade to the pan, and cook gently for 5 minutes until piping hot (be careful not to let the sauce boil as this will cause it to split). Taste and adjust the seasoning as necessary. Serve garnished with chopped cilantro leaves.

MOROCCAN LAMB WITH SWEET POTATOES AND RAISINS

SERVES 4–6

Morocco is famed for its slow-cooked tagines, or stews, made in a distinctively shaped earthenware pot. This is my take on them, made in a regular casserole dish, but including all the sweet spices you'd expect. Make sure you get plenty of color onto the lamb as this is what gives the stock its wonderful depth of flavor. The dish will be even better if made a day in advance and reheated.

Olive oil
1½ pounds boneless leg or shoulder of lamb, cut into 1½-inch chunks
2 red onions, peeled and cut into eighths
Sea salt and freshly ground black pepper
2 garlic cloves, peeled and chopped
½ tsp ground ginger
Pinch of saffron strands
½ tsp ground coriander
½ tsp cumin seeds
½ tsp paprika
½ tsp fennel seeds
1 cinnamon stick
1 bay leaf
1 Tbsp tomato purée
¾ pound sweet potatoes, peeled and cut into 1-inch chunks
2 Tbsp raisins
2 cups chicken or lamb stock
Chopped parsley, to garnish

1. Heat a large, heavy-bottomed casserole dish over high heat. Add a little oil and brown the lamb pieces in batches for about 5 minutes until colored all over. Remove and set aside.

2. Add a little fresh oil to the pan, then add the onions and a good pinch of salt and pepper. Cook for 4–5 minutes until lightly colored, then add the garlic, ground ginger, saffron, ground coriander, cumin seeds, paprika, fennel seeds, cinnamon stick, and bay leaf. Stir for 2 minutes until aromatic.

3. Add the tomato purée and stir for 30 seconds, then add the sweet potato, coating well with the mixture in the pan. Return the lamb, plus any resting juices, to the pan along with the raisins and stock. Bring the stock to a boil, scraping up any bits stuck to the bottom of the casserole dish.

4. Lower the heat and simmer very gently, uncovered, for 1–2 hours, stirring occasionally, until the lamb is very tender. If the liquid is reducing too much, cover the casserole dish or add a cupful of water. This dish will be delicious if left overnight once cooked and gently reheated so that the flavors have even longer to develop.

5. Serve garnished with chopped parsley.

SLOW-COOKED BEEF WITH ORANGE GREMOLATA

SERVES 4–6

Veal shin is the classic cut used in the Italian dish osso bucco, but cheaper beef shin is just as good. The bone marrow gives the stock its melting richness, so do try to get shin from the upper end with a larger bone. For best results, make the day before and gently reheat from room temperature.

Olive oil
2 pieces of beef shin, about 1 pound each
1 carrot, peeled and diced
2 celery stalks, trimmed and diced
1-inch piece of fresh ginger, peeled and chopped
2 garlic cloves, peeled and sliced
7 ounces small shallots or pearl onions, left whole but peeled and trimmed
1 Tbsp tomato purée
Juice of 1 orange
¾ cup dry white wine
3 cups chicken stock
Sea salt and freshly ground black pepper

FOR THE MASHED SWEET POTATOES
1½ pounds sweet potatoes, peeled and chopped
Sea salt and freshly ground black pepper
Olive oil

FOR THE ORANGE GREMOLATA
1 orange, zest only
3 Tbsp chopped parsley
1 garlic clove, peeled and very finely chopped
2 Tbsp olive oil (optional)
Sea salt and freshly ground black pepper

1. Heat a heavy-bottomed casserole dish over high heat. Add a glug of oil and brown the beef shin in batches for about 5 minutes until well colored on all sides. Remove and set aside.

2. Add a dash of oil to the casserole dish if necessary and sauté the carrot, celery, ginger, garlic, and shallots for 5 minutes until lightly colored. Add the tomato purée and cook for 1–2 minutes. Put the beef back into the pan, then pour in the orange juice and wine, stirring and scraping up all the bits at the bottom. Bring to a boil, then lower the heat and simmer for 2 minutes until the alcohol has burned off.

3. Add the stock, season, and bring to a boil. Lower the heat, cover, and simmer gently for 1 hour, then remove the lid and continue to cook for an additional 20–30 minutes until the beef is completely tender but not falling apart.

4. Meanwhile, make the mashed sweet potatoes. Boil the sweet potatoes in salted water for 15 minutes until tender. Drain well and allow them to steam-dry for 5 minutes. Mash the sweet potatoes with a generous pinch of salt and pepper and a drizzle of olive oil until smooth. Taste and adjust the seasoning as necessary.

5. To make the gremolata, mix together the orange zest, parsley, and garlic, adding the olive oil, if using, until a thick spooning consistency is reached. Taste and season with salt and pepper.

6. Serve the beef shins immediately, topped with the gremolata and with the mashed sweet potatoes alongside.

SLOW-COOKED
BEEF SHORT RIBS
SERVES 2

Short ribs are going through a real renaissance, just like lamb shanks and pork cheeks have before them. They are a cheap cut full of fat and sinew that disappears as you slowly cook them in red wine and stock. Roasting the tomato purée—or "cooking it out," as we say in kitchens—rounds off the tart notes you sometimes get in tomatoes.

Olive oil
6 thick-cut meaty beef short ribs
Sea salt and freshly ground black pepper
1 large head of garlic, cut in half horizontally
1 heaping Tbsp tomato purée
One 750-ml bottle red wine
1 quart beef stock

5 ounces pancetta
8 ounces small cremini mushrooms, trimmed and halved
Chopped flat-leaf parsley, to garnish

1. Preheat the oven to 325°F.

2. Heat a deep-sided roasting pan on the stovetop and add a glug of olive oil. Season the short ribs with salt and pepper thoroughly, then cook for 10–15 minutes to brown very well on all sides.

3. Add the halved garlic head, cut side down, pushing it to the bottom of the pan. Add the tomato purée and heat for a minute or two to cook it out. Pour in the wine to deglaze the pan, scraping up the bits at the bottom. Bring to a boil and cook for 10–15 minutes until the liquid is reduced by half, then add stock to nearly cover the ribs (you'll need less stock if your roasting pan isn't very large). Bring to a boil again, basting the ribs with the juices.

4. Cover the roasting pan with foil and cook in the preheated oven for 3–4 hours, basting now and then until the meat is tender and falling away from the bone.

5. About 10 minutes before the short ribs are ready to come out, cook the pancetta for 2–3 minutes until crisp and golden. Add the mushrooms and cook for 4–5 minutes until tender. Drain off any excess fat.

6. When the short ribs are ready, remove from the oven and transfer to a serving dish. Squeeze the garlic cloves out of their skins and pass through a sieve. Spoon off any excess fat from the beef cooking liquid, then strain it through the sieve and mix with the garlic. (If the sauce is too thin, reduce the cooking liquid by heating for 10–15 minutes more after straining.)

7. Serve the short ribs topped with the hot pancetta and mushrooms and the sauce poured around. Garnish with chopped flat-leaf parsley.

BLONDIES

**MAKES 9 LARGE SQUARES OR 16 SMALLER
SQUARES**

As the name suggests, blondies are a white
chocolate version of brownies. I find them a bit
more subtle in flavor and they make a great end to
a meal, especially with chunks of white chocolate
and a few chewy cranberries thrown in for texture.

1 cup (2 sticks) butter, plus extra for greasing
1¾ cups dark brown sugar
Pinch of sea salt
1 tsp vanilla extract
2 eggs, lightly beaten
2¼ cups all-purpose flour
½ tsp baking soda
1 tsp baking powder
8 ounces white chocolate, chopped into small
    chunks
¼ cup dried cranberries

1. Preheat the oven to 350°F. Lightly butter a 9-inch
square cake pan and line with wax paper, allowing
the wax paper to come up the sides with a 1-inch
overhang.

2. Melt the butter in a saucepan and whisk in the
brown sugar and salt. (A good whisk now will make
the mixture slightly lighter and fluffier.) Add the
vanilla extract and whisk again. Remove from the
heat and cool.

3. Add the eggs to the butter mixture and stir well.
Sift the flour, baking soda, and baking powder into a
large bowl, then whisk in the egg and butter mixture
a little at a time. (It's important to do this in stages so
that you don't get any lumps.)

4. Fold in the chocolate chunks and the cranberries.

5. Spoon into the prepared cake pan and spread out
evenly. Bake for 35–40 minutes until the outer edges
are firm and the middle still a little soft.

6. Leave to cool on a wire rack for at least 10 minutes,
then cut into squares before serving. Once cooled,
the blondies will keep in an airtight container for up
to a week.

HOW TO BAKE WITHOUT STICKING
Lining the pan with wax paper acts as an insurance
policy to keep the blondies from sticking and
means you can have a higher ratio of chocolate in
the mix. Remember to smooth out the top of the
blondies when you fill the pan so that they bake
evenly.

CARAMELIZED FIGS WITH RICOTTA

SERVES 4

Slow cooking benefits not only meat: it allows fruit to develop its natural sugars too. The figs here are basted in a balsamic vinegar caramel and then roasted gently in the oven. True, we're talking about 15 minutes here, not several hours, but it is still enough to transform the fruit. Serve with ricotta to keep the dish light.

4 thick-stemmed rosemary sprigs
12 fresh figs
¼ cup confectioners' sugar
3 Tbsp balsamic vinegar
6 Tbsp granulated sugar
1 Tbsp butter, cubed

TO SERVE
½–¾ cup ricotta cheese
¼ cup toasted chopped almonds
Zest of 1 lemon

1. Preheat the oven to 350°F.

2. Remove the leaves from all but one end of each rosemary sprig and trim a point at the other. Use the pointed end to pierce through the figs, inserting horizontally through their tops, about ½ inch below the stalk. Thread 3 figs onto each sprig.

3. Place the threaded figs on a plate and dust generously with confectioners' sugar. Drizzle with 1 tablespoon of the balsamic vinegar.

4. Heat an ovenproof frying pan on the stovetop and add the granulated sugar in an even layer. Cook for 3–4 minutes until the sugar has completely melted and is starting to caramelize. As soon as it begins to take on a dark golden color, remove it from the heat and whisk in the butter. Add the remaining balsamic vinegar and 2 tablespoons of water and whisk to combine.

5. Add the figs to the pan and baste with the caramel until well coated. Place the figs in the preheated oven and cook for 10–15 minutes, basting now and again as they cook.

6. Place the figs on a serving plate, spooning over the caramel from the pan. Serve immediately with a spoonful of ricotta, toasted almonds, and a sprinkling of lemon zest.

COOKING FOR ONE OR TWO

MUCH AS I LOVE BIG-OCCASION COOKING— THE SOCIABILITY, THE CHANCE TO SHOW OFF A BIT —THE REALITY OF DAY-TO-DAY LIFE ISN'T LIKE THAT.

Much more often it's about coming back late from work and needing to get dinner on the table quickly, and that calls for a whole different set of skills. It's easy to be motivated when you've got the promise of an appreciative audience who will make all the right noises, but when you are cooking just for yourself or perhaps a partner, you can quickly lose heart and see the whole process as a chore. That's when the temptation to fall back on takeout is the strongest.

Don't be ashamed if that sounds like you—I'll let you in on every chef's dirty little secret. When they get home after evening service, what is the thing they are most likely to whip up before going to bed? A homemade burger? A cheese soufflé? I wish. No. Baked beans on toast—at least here in the UK. Half of them don't even bother warming them up, they just spoon them out of the can. I know, I know: it's late, they've spent all day in the kitchen, and they just want to collapse into bed. But it does show that it isn't skill or know-how that gets in the way of proper cooking, it's convenience.

So the solution to cooking for small numbers is to make it as easy as possible—so simple, in fact, that picking up the phone and waiting for the pizza boy to deliver will seem like too much of a hassle in comparison. That's my aim here. We think of fast food as being what comes in cardboard boxes from takeout shops, but in this chapter you'll find a bolognese sauce that will be ready before the pasta's even had time to boil (page 216), fishcakes you can assemble from a few cans and jars (page 218), and a chili hot dog that's in another league from anything you've had before (page 219). When everyday food is this fast and tastes this good, it soon becomes a pleasure. If you want

BASICS

cooking to be hassle-free, you've got to start with the basics, and make the shopping as uncomplicated as possible. Dishes should focus around two or three key flavors on the plate, maximum, as in Mushroom and Leek Pasta (page 215). Any more and you're not only making extra work for yourself, but you'll be confusing your palate.

In my years of filming *Kitchen Nightmares*, in which I go around to restaurants trying to sort out failing businesses, this has been by far the most common mistake. Young chefs, in particular, feel they have to put their all into every plate, and tend to overcomplicate their cooking to show what accomplished cooks they are. In fact the opposite is true. The best cooks know not to hide behind lots of competing flavors and are happy to let their main ingredients shine. Mushroom and leek pasta, for example, should taste of mushrooms and leeks. You might like to add some tarragon, perhaps, which marries the two ingredients together, or some bacon, but there really is no need to start throwing in lots of other strong flavors. It doesn't need them. Respect your main ingredients and they won't let you down.

A happy side effect of this is that the shopping is much easier too—even more so if you keep a well-stocked pantry. Think of this as the springboard for your cooking, so you need only pick up a couple of main ingredients—some sausages, say, or some eggs—to then take your cooking in whichever direction you choose when you get home.

I've listed opposite the kind of basics you might like to keep. The list is by no means exhaustive, but the main thing is to build it up as you go. I wouldn't recommend that you go out and buy everything in one massive shop. You'll soon see the kind of things that crop up in the recipes you like, and before you know it you'll have built up an arsenal of ingredients that arm you for happy evenings of cooking.

BEANS

I use a lot of kidney beans, cannellini beans, chickpeas, and lentils. It is always better to soak and cook your beans from dried as the flavor and texture will be better (you can add flavorings, such as thyme, bay, and smoked bacon, to the water when you boil them, but never salt as this will make their skins tough). That said, canned beans are very useful standbys, especially when you are cooking on the spur of the moment.

CANNED GOODS

Italian tomatoes (preferably whole, as the quality tends to be better); cannellini beans; anchovies; sardines; and mackerel.

CHOCOLATE

By using good-quality dark chocolate, with a minimum of 70 percent cocoa solids, you have much more control as you can always let it down with more sugar and/or milk if you find it too bitter. Valrhona is my favorite brand.

OILS

As a minimum, you need a good extra virgin olive oil for drizzling over finished dishes and making vinaigrettes, light olive oil for frying, and a neutral-flavored oil for when you want a less discernible flavor. Peanut oil is ideal, but canola oil is increasingly popular and has a very high smoking point, meaning you can cook at higher temperatures without it burning. Hazelnut, sesame, and truffle oils are useful for drizzling.

POMEGRANATE MOLASSES

Pomegranate juice that has been boiled down to a dark brown, sweetly tart liquid. Essential to much Middle Eastern cooking and available from Persian or Asian grocery shops, or online.

RICE

Long-grain basmati, which cooks and tastes better than other varieties; short-grain for puddings; bomba and calasparra rice for paellas; and risotto rice, which contains more starch and maintains the bite you need. I prefer carnaroli, but arborio is also good.

SAUCES

Naturally fermented soy sauce and fish sauce are essential in Asian cooking for delivering a salty kick. Other pantry essentials include Tabasco, tamarind concentrate, mustard, Worcestershire sauce, and good old tomato ketchup.

SPICES

I cover these in more detail on pages 111–114, but remember, they lose their flavor quickly, so buy little and often. Asian shops tend to be cheaper than supermarkets, and because of the higher turnover their spices are likely to be fresher.

VANILLA PODS

Fresh vanilla pods impart much more sweet, perfumed flavor than vanilla extract. Look for plump, oily pods from Madagascar. Once you have used the seeds, place the empty pod into a bag of sugar, which will take on the vanilla aroma and be ideal for baking.

VINEGARS

Essential not just for vinaigrettes and dressings but also to deglaze pans. Sherry, balsamic, white wine, cider, and red wine vinegars all have distinctive flavors. Rice vinegar is slightly milder and sweeter, and much used in Chinese and Vietnamese cooking.

Other staples I never like to be without are: flours (all-purpose, bread flour, and self-rising); pasta; maple syrup; leaf gelatin (easier to use than granules); instant (dried) yeast; capers; and nuts (like spices, they go stale very quickly, so buy in small quantities).

BRUSCHETTE WITH GARLIC, TOMATOES, CAPER BERRIES, AND PECORINO

SERVES 2

Bruschette make a great starter for a dinner
party, or equally a nice light supper dish if you
are feeling lazy. You can use any bread with
an open crumb, such as baguettes, sourdough,
or country bread—one that, once toasted,
has a dried surface that will really soak up the
garlic and tomato flavors.

8 slices good-quality baguette
Olive oil
½ garlic clove, peeled
8 cherry tomatoes, halved
Sea salt and freshly ground black pepper
8 caper berries, sliced diagonally
2 ounces pecorino cheese, cut into thin flakes
Extra virgin olive oil

1. Heat a grill pan until hot. Brush the baguette slices
with olive oil and toast for 1–2 minutes on
each side until golden brown and marked.

2. Remove the bread and, while warm, rub it lightly
with the cut side of the garlic clove. Rub two of the
cherry tomato halves, cut side down, into each slice
of baguette, pushing the flesh against the bread to
squash it into the surface.

3. Season the bruschette with salt and pepper.
Top with the sliced caper berries and the remaining
tomatoes, then scatter the pecorino over the top.
Serve with a drizzle of extra virgin olive oil.

HOW TO MAKE PECORINO SHAVINGS
The humble vegetable peeler is not just for peeling
vegetables, it's also ideal for making thin shavings
or ribbons of cheese, carrots, cucumbers, and
chocolate.

CANNELLINI BEAN CROSTINI WITH ANCHOVIES AND OLIVES

SERVES 2

Cannellini beans are rather bland on their own, so they need plenty of help. Here you are adding saltiness from the anchovies, bitterness from the olives, sweetness from the oil, and sourness from the vinegar. The four main tastes all covered on a single piece of bread. Genius.

6–8 slices ciabatta bread
Olive oil
One 14-ounce can cannellini beans, drained
10 pitted black olives, chopped
½ Tbsp red wine or sherry vinegar
2 Tbsp chopped parsley
Sea salt and freshly ground black pepper
4 preserved anchovy fillets, roughly chopped

1. Heat a grill pan until hot. Brush the bread with olive oil and toast for 2–3 minutes on each side until golden brown and marked.

2. Meanwhile, heat a small saucepan over medium heat, add the cannellini beans and a drizzle of olive oil, and heat through. Crush roughly with a fork or potato masher and stir in the olives, vinegar, parsley, and salt and pepper to taste.

3. Pile the crushed cannellini beans on top of the toasted bread and scatter the anchovy pieces over the top. Season with pepper and serve.

FARFALLE WITH RICOTTA, PANCETTA, AND PEAS

SERVES 2

Bacon, peas, and cream make a classic pasta sauce. I've lightened the whole dish here by using crème fraîche instead of heavy cream, and naturally low-fat ricotta cheese instead of Parmesan.

8 ounces dried farfalle pasta
5 ounces smoked pancetta
1 garlic clove, peeled and finely chopped
⅔ cup frozen peas
3 Tbsp crème fraîche
½ cup ricotta cheese
Sea salt and freshly ground black pepper
Olive oil

1. Cook the pasta in boiling salted water until al dente, according to the package instructions.

2. Meanwhile, put the pancetta in a dry frying pan large enough to hold the pasta when cooked. Cook for 5 minutes until cooked through and lightly colored on the outside, then add the garlic and cook for 1 minute until soft but not colored. Turn off the heat.

3. Three minutes before the pasta is ready, add the peas to it to cook through. Drain well, reserving a couple of tablespoons of the cooking water.

4. Tip the pasta and peas into the pan with the pancetta and stir well over low heat. Add the crème fraîche and stir until melted, adding a tablespoon or two of the pasta cooking water to loosen if necessary. Dot in the ricotta, gently mixing. Taste and adjust the seasoning as necessary.

5. Serve the farfalle hot, drizzled with a little olive oil.

HOW TO MAKE SILKY PASTA SAUCES
Whenever you make a creamy pasta dish, always stir in a little of the pasta water to make the sauce silky smooth.

FLATBREADS WITH FENNEL AND FETA

SERVES 2

You'll find countless variations of pizza around
the world, where a dough base is used as a plate
to carry other ingredients. In this version the
saltiness of the feta works beautifully with the sharp
sweetness of the pomegranate molasses and the
anise crunch of fennel.

2 Middle Eastern flatbreads
Olive oil
Sea salt and freshly ground black pepper
1 tsp fennel seeds
1 small fennel bulb, trimmed
4 ounces feta cheese, crumbled
1 Tbsp pomegranate molasses (see page 205)

1. Drizzle the flatbread with a little olive oil on each side and season with salt and pepper. Heat a frying pan over medium heat and toast the flatbreads individually for 2 minutes on each side until golden and turning crisp.

2. Remove the flatbreads from the pan and keep warm. If necessary, wipe away any remaining oil in the pan, then toast the fennel seeds for about 1 minute until aromatic. Remove and set aside.

3. Shave the fennel bulb into thin slices using a mandoline or vegetable peeler.

4. Sprinkle the shaved fennel over the flatbreads, then scatter with the feta and fennel seeds. Drizzle some pomegranate molasses over each flatbread and serve.

CORN FRITTERS WITH YOGURT DIP

MAKES 6–8 FRITTERS

We've all got a can or two of corn lurking in a cabinet somewhere, and these thick savory pancakes show how easily you can transform them into an interesting light lunch or supper. The secret here is not to make the batter too wet. You are aiming for a balance of one-third batter to two-thirds filling.

¾ cup all-purpose flour
½ tsp baking powder
Sea salt and freshly ground black pepper
1 egg, beaten
¼ cup whole milk
Olive oil
2 scallions, trimmed and thinly sliced
1 red chile, seeded and finely chopped
  (see tip below)
2 Tbsp chopped cilantro
One 8-ounce can corn kernels, drained and dried
  on paper towels

FOR THE YOGURT DIP

1 cup plain yogurt
½–1 red chile, seeded and finely chopped,
  to taste
Juice of ½ lime
3 Tbsp chopped cilantro
Salt and freshly ground black pepper

1. First, mix together all the ingredients for the dip. Taste and season with salt and pepper as necessary, then set aside.

2. Sift the flour and baking powder into a mixing bowl. Season with salt and pepper. Mix together, make a well in the middle, and add the egg and milk. Whisk, gradually bringing the flour into the wet mixture until it forms a smooth batter. Add 1 tablespoon of olive oil and whisk again until smooth, adding a little more milk if necessary.

3. Stir the scallions, chile, cilantro, and corn into the batter and mix well.

4. Heat a large frying pan and add a glug of oil. Put about ¼ cup of the mixture per fritter into the hot pan, pushing it down lightly. Fry in batches for 1–2 minutes on each side until golden. Keep warm.

5. Serve the warm fritters with the yogurt dip alongside.

HOW TO CHOP CHILES FINELY
Press a chile against a work surface and cut a line along its length, stopping just short of the stalk. Rotate the chile by an eighth of a turn and cut again. Repeat this until you have 8 cuts and the chile looks like a tassel when you hold it by the stalk. Now hold the chile down firmly with three fingers, the middle one slightly in front of the others, and, using the knuckle of your middle finger to guide the blade, slice across the chile, gradually working your way toward the stalk.

MUSHROOM
AND LEEK PASTA
SERVES 2

There are very few dishes you can't simplify and strip back to their essence. This is a fast and simple open lasagne that doesn't need any time in the oven. Put the pot on for the pasta before you've even taken your coat off, and you'll have dinner on the table in 10 minutes.

Olive oil
8 cremini mushrooms, trimmed and sliced
Sea salt and freshly ground black pepper
1 garlic clove, peeled and chopped
1 leek, trimmed, quartered, and sliced
1 cup chicken stock
4–6 lasagne sheets, dried or fresh
½ cup heavy cream
2 Tbsp roughly chopped tarragon leaves

FOR THE GARLIC BRUSCHETTE
2 slices ciabatta bread
Olive oil
1 garlic clove, peeled and halved

1. Heat a large frying pan and add a dash of oil. Season the mushrooms with salt and pepper and start to sauté them, adding the garlic after 2 minutes and the leek a minute later. Cook for 6–8 minutes until the leek is soft and the mushrooms are colored on the outside. Taste and adjust the seasoning.

2. Add the stock and boil for 5 minutes until reduced by half.

3. Meanwhile, cook the lasagne sheets in a large saucepan of boiling salted water for 4 minutes or until just al dente.

4. While the lasagne is cooking, add the cream to the frying pan and simmer for 2–3 minutes to reduce a little.

5. When the lasagne sheets are cooked, drain and add to the pan with the sauce, stirring until well coated. Turn off the heat, add the tarragon leaves, and allow to sit while the bread toasts.

6. To prepare the bruschette, preheat a grill pan or the broiler. Rub the slices of ciabatta with olive oil and the cut side of the garlic clove and toast for 1–2 minutes on each side until golden brown.

7. To serve, spoon the lasagne and mushroom mixture onto serving plates, layering them up attractively. Serve the toasted bruschette slices on the side.

HOW TO COOK LASAGNE WITHOUT STICKING
Simply bring the water to a rolling boil and then gently tilt the pan from side to side as you add the lasagne to stop the sheets from sticking. Allow it to simmer gently until al dente. To test if it is ready, nip it between your fingers. If you can feel them meeting in the middle, it is perfectly al dente.

TAGLIATELLE WITH QUICK SAUSAGE-MEAT BOLOGNESE

SERVES 2

Sausage always makes a great quick-supper standby. Rather than cooking them whole, though, I'll often split them open to get at all the meat inside. Because it's already beautifully seasoned, it gives you a head start and means you achieve greater depth of flavor in double-quick time.

Olive oil
1 small onion, peeled and finely diced
1 garlic clove, peeled and chopped
3–4 best-quality Italian sausages
5 ounces dried tagliatelle
8 ounces cherry tomatoes, halved
Sea salt and freshly ground black pepper
Freshly grated Parmesan cheese, to serve

1. Heat a frying pan large enough to contain the pasta once cooked. Add a little oil and sweat the onions and garlic together for 3–4 minutes until the onions have softened. Remove the meat from the sausage skins, add to the pan, and brown for 4–5 minutes. Break up the sausage meat as you fry so that it resembles small pieces of ground pork.

2. Meanwhile, cook the tagliatelle in boiling salted water until al dente, according to the package instructions.

3. When the sausage meat is lightly colored, add the halved tomatoes and a little salt and pepper to the pan and continue to cook over medium heat for 5 minutes until the tomatoes begin to break down. Add a tablespoon or two of the pasta water to the pan as it cooks to create a sauce.

4. Drain the pasta, reserving an additional couple of tablespoons of the cooking water. Add the drained pasta directly to the pan with the sauce. Toss well, and loosen with a little more of the cooking water if necessary. Taste and adjust the seasoning. Serve hot with freshly grated Parmesan cheese.

SPICY TUNA FISHCAKES

MAKES 8 SMALL CAKES

Another miraculous transformation of the kind of ingredient we all have knocking about in a kitchen cabinet. Texture is always important in fishcakes, and the water chestnuts add a lovely light, pickled crunch. Grating the ginger releases all of its fresh, fiery juices, so make sure you catch them all in the bowl.

Three 5-ounce cans good-quality tuna
6 canned water chestnuts, drained and thinly sliced
3 scallions, trimmed and sliced
1-inch piece of fresh ginger, peeled and grated
3 Tbsp chopped cilantro
1 red chile, seeded and finely chopped
3 kaffir lime leaves, finely chopped (rehydrated
    for 5 minutes in boiling water if dried)
Sea salt and freshly ground black pepper
2 tsp Thai fish sauce
2 eggs, beaten
Vegetable oil

FOR THE DIPPING SAUCE
Good pinch of sugar
2 Tbsp Thai fish sauce
1 Tbsp rice vinegar
Juice of ½ lime
2 Tbsp chopped cilantro

1. First make the dipping sauce. Mix together all the sauce ingredients, stirring until the sugar has dissolved. Taste and adjust the flavors as necessary. Set aside.

2. Drain the tuna and place in a bowl; use a fork to separate the chunks. Add the water chestnuts, scallions, ginger, cilantro, chile, and lime leaves and season with salt and pepper. Add the fish sauce and beaten eggs. Mix well.

3. Squeezing the mixture to tightly compress it and get rid of any excess liquid, shape it into balls the size of golf balls. Flatten them lightly into patties.

4. Heat a frying pan over medium heat, add a little oil, and pan-fry the fishcakes on each side for 1–2 minutes until golden on all sides and heated through. Serve with the dipping sauce.

HOW TO HANDLE CHILES
When you've been chopping chiles, rub your hands with olive oil before washing them. The oil helps dissolve the capsaicin, the source of the chiles' heat, which is more soluble in oil than in water, and it will then rinse away easily.

CHILI DOGS

SERVES 2

I'm a real sucker for proper American hot dogs — a juicy frankfurter covered with caramelized onions and that weirdly addictive sweet mustard. Even better when it is topped with an easy chili con carne. The quantity of chili here will produce enough for leftovers for another night.

2 large hot dogs
2 hot dog buns
2 ounces Cheddar cheese, crumbled or grated
1 scallion, trimmed and finely chopped

FOR THE QUICK CHILI CON CARNE
Olive oil
1 small onion, peeled and finely diced
2 garlic cloves, peeled and finely chopped
½ tsp cumin seeds
½–1 tsp chili powder, to taste
10 ounces ground beef
Sea salt and freshly ground black pepper

1 tsp Worcestershire sauce
2 tsp tomato purée
One 14-ounce can chopped tomatoes
Pinch of granulated sugar
½ tsp dried oregano

FOR THE CARAMELIZED ONIONS
Olive oil
2 red onions, peeled and thinly sliced
Sea salt
1 Tbsp brown sugar
1 Tbsp balsamic vinegar

1. First make the quick chili con carne. Heat a saucepan over medium heat. Add a dash of oil and, once hot, sweat the onion for 4–5 minutes, then add the garlic and cook for another minute until soft. Add the cumin seeds and stir over medium heat for 1–2 minutes until aromatic. Add the chili powder and mix well.

2. Season the beef with salt and pepper. Turn up the heat and add another dash of oil to the pan. Cook the beef over high heat for 6–8 minutes, stirring well to break it up. When it is lightly browned, add the Worcestershire sauce, turn down the heat, and add the tomato purée, cooking for 1–2 minutes.

3. Add the tomatoes, granulated sugar, and oregano along with a pinch of pepper. Bring to a simmer, cover, and simmer gently for 20 minutes, stirring frequently.

4. Meanwhile, prepare the caramelized onions. Heat a small frying pan over medium-low heat and add a dash of oil. Add the onions with a good pinch of salt and gently sweat for 10–15 minutes until completely softened and turning a rich golden color. (Don't increase the heat to speed up this process as you'll end up with burnt onions.) Once the onions are golden and very soft, add the brown sugar and balsamic vinegar. Increase the heat to medium and allow to caramelize gently. Cook for about 5 minutes until the liquid is reduced and the onions are nice and sticky. Taste and adjust the seasoning as necessary.

5. When ready to serve, boil or grill the hot dogs for 6 minutes or until heated through. Remove and drain. Divide the caramelized onions between the opened hot dog buns. Top with the cooked hot dogs and a generous spoonful or two of chili con carne. Crumble over the cheese and finish with a sprinkling of chopped scallion.

BEEF TACOS WITH WASABI MAYO

MAKES 6–8 TACOS

This mix of Mexican and Japanese flavors—seared steak marinated in a rich, sweet sauce and wrapped in a taco—makes a really quick meaty feast. Normally, meat is marinated before cooking, but here you cook the steak and then let it cool in the marinade to absorb all that flavor. The steaks can be left to marinate for up to four days—the longer the better.

2 beef sirloin steaks
Salt and freshly ground black pepper
Olive oil
6–8 small (6-inch) corn tortillas, to serve

FOR THE MARINADE
2 Tbsp light miso paste
2 Tbsp mirin
1 Tbsp sugar
2 Tbsp olive oil
Sea salt and freshly ground black pepper

FOR THE QUICK PICKLED CABBAGE
½ head of Chinese cabbage, finely shredded
Sea salt and freshly ground black pepper
1–1½ Tbsp rice vinegar or lemon juice
½ tsp toasted sesame oil
1 tsp dried chile flakes

FOR THE WASABI MAYO
½ tsp wasabi, to taste
2 heaping Tbsp mayonnaise

1. First prepare the marinade. Mix the miso paste, mirin, sugar, and olive oil, stirring well to dissolve the sugar. Season with salt and pepper and add a tablespoon of water if the mixture needs loosening a little.

2. Leave the fat on the steaks to keep them from drying out as you cook them. Season them well with salt and pepper and sear in a hot oiled frying pan for 2–3 minutes on each side for rare/medium-rare, or until cooked to your liking. (Shake the pan gently as you put the steaks in the pan to keep them from sticking, otherwise they might burn.) Render the fat by tipping the steaks onto their sides and cooking until the fat is golden and crisp. Keep basting the steaks as you cook.

3. When the steaks are cooked, remove from the pan and cut off the remaining layer of fat. Place the steaks in the marinade, coating all sides. Leave to rest, spooning the marinade over now and again.

4. Meanwhile, prepare the quick pickled cabbage. Put the cabbage in a bowl and season with salt and pepper. Add the rice vinegar, sesame oil, and chile flakes. Toss the mixture to coat, then leave to soften slightly for a couple of minutes.

5. Meanwhile, mix together the wasabi and mayonnaise, taste, and add a little more wasabi if you like a stronger flavor.

6. Heat the tortillas for 30–60 seconds over a naked gas flame until charred and lightly toasted (use a pan if you don't have gas). Roll them around a rolling pin while they're still hot, and hold until cooled to set in half-moon taco shapes.

7. Drain the beef of any excess marinade, then slice and place in the tacos. Top with the cabbage (drained of excess liquid) and a little wasabi mayo.

GRILLED PINEAPPLE
WITH SPICED CARAMEL

SERVES 2

Desserts for one or two have to be really easy or
else you won't bother. This grilled pineapple strikes
just the right balance. It can be ready in minutes
and adds another dimension to a familiar fruit. To
test if your pineapple is ripe, try pulling
a leaf from the top. It should come out easily.
If it doesn't, leave the pineapple in the fruit bowl
for a day or two and try again.

1 ripe pineapple
¼ cup sugar, plus a little extra for sprinkling
Seeds from 1 vanilla pod
Pinch of Chinese five-spice powder
1½ Tbsp butter, cut in half
⅔ cup heavy cream

1. First prepare the pineapple. Using a serrated knife,
cut off the top and base, then cut the pineapple into
8 long wedges. Cut along the inside edge of the
wedges to remove the core. Slice between the flesh
and the skin as you would a piece of melon, but leave
the last ¾ inch of skin attached.

2. Heat a grill pan. Place the pineapple wedges
in the hot pan, pushing the fruit against the grill bars
to help it color. Cook for 2 minutes on each side until
marked. Sprinkle over a little sugar 1 minute before
the end of cooking to glaze the fruit.

3. To make the caramel, tip the sugar, the vanilla seeds,
and five-spice powder into a heavy-bottomed frying
pan and cook over medium heat for 3–4 minutes
until the sugar has dissolved and is turning a dark
golden brown. Remove from the heat and add the
butter and 2 tablespoons of the cream. Shake the pan
to melt the butter, whisk to combine, then add the
remaining cream.

4. To serve, drizzle the caramel sauce over the
pineapple wedges and serve immediately.

HOW TO GRILL ON A PAN
Whenever you use a grill pan, always press down
hard what you are cooking and hold it there for a
few seconds. This will help achieve those
characteristic scorch lines, which not only look
attractive but mean more flavor.

BLUEBERRY AND RICOTTA PANCAKES WITH YOGURT AND HONEY

MAKES 8

Who says pancakes are only for breakfast? These are certainly good enough to eat at any time of the day. If you beat the ricotta with a fork first, it will loosen up and be easier to fold into the batter. And remember, when whisking egg whites, make sure your bowl and whisk are spotlessly clean. Any grease will keep the whites from fluffing up.

1 cup all-purpose flour
1 tsp baking powder
Pinch of salt
1 Tbsp sugar
2 eggs, separated
½ cup whole milk
½ cup ricotta cheese
⅔ cup fresh blueberries, plus extra to serve
Oil and butter
Greek yogurt and runny honey, to serve

1. Sift the flour, baking powder, salt, and sugar into a large bowl and mix together. Make a well in the middle and add the egg yolks. Gradually add the milk and whisk slowly, bringing the flour in from the edges until it is all combined. Fold in the ricotta, then the blueberries.

2. In a separate bowl, whisk the egg whites until they almost reach soft peaks. Fold a spoonful of the egg whites into the pancake mix to loosen it slightly, then fold in the rest.

3. Heat a wide, nonstick frying pan over medium heat. Add a dash of oil and a small chunk of butter. Once the butter has melted, cook the pancakes in batches, using ¼ cup of batter per pancake. Shape them into round discs in the pan. Cook for about 5 minutes on each side until golden and fluffy and hot all the way through. Keep warm in a low oven while you repeat with the remaining batter.

4. To serve, divide among serving plates and top with a dollop of Greek yogurt, a sprinkling of fresh blueberries, and a drizzle of honey.

COOKING
FOR
FRIENDS

SOMETIMES COOKS CAN BE THEIR OWN WORST ENEMIES.

I occasionally go round to friends for dinner and when I see what they are putting themselves through, it almost makes me cry. They'll be manfully struggling to carve a roast, with four different vegetables all coming to a boil, a gravy still to be made, *and* they want to plate it all up themselves *and* bring it to the table. Meanwhile, we guests sit there, watching as the stress levels go through the roof, wishing they'd let us help.

And I just want to say, "Are you mad?" No one can get food out under those conditions. I've worked in professional kitchens for more than 25 years, and I'd never dream of trying to do all that on my own.

In a restaurant you've got chefs on all the different sections, each cooking their own elements: the meat, the vegetables, the sauces. You've got a head chef whose job it is to check that each plate is perfect. You've got waiters ferrying the dishes to the table, and you've even got a kitchen porter to do the washing up. That's—what?—a minimum of six people. And there you are trying to do the whole thing on your own. No wonder you're stressed.

The first thing to remember when you are cooking for a crowd is that it hasn't got to be perfect. You're not running a restaurant here. Your guests have hopefully come because they want to spend time in your company, not because they want a Michelin-starred meal on the cheap. So relax and make sure the meal will work for you in order that you can enjoy yourself at the same time.

That means choosing the right menu. It doesn't matter if it's one course or five, it's got to be something you can produce without breaking a sweat. Cooking can be stressful, there's no denying it, but if you plan ahead, you'll be able to minimize the stress. Think about what you are setting yourself up to do. Are you going to have to do lots of last-minute prepping, or can everything be made ready in advance? Will you be trying to cook eight steaks with only one frying pan, or can it all be left alone in the oven? Will the fish need filleting before you can plate it up? This is the kind of forward thinking that makes most disasters avoidable and will, hopefully, save you a world of hurt.

Let's start by talking about timing. I find a lot of people misunderstand this. They think of those countdowns you often see in magazines around Christmastime—you know the sort: 10:30 Put in the turkey; 12:15 Put on the potatoes; 12:50 Boil the vegetables. These are always geared toward everything coming together at the same moment so that on the stroke of 1 p.m. your bird is ready, your potatoes are roasted, your sprouts and carrots are perfectly cooked. Success, you think. Except that you then have the most almighty panic as you try to drain the vegetables, carve the turkey, and put the potatoes in the serving dish all at the same time.

When chefs talk about timing, it is almost the opposite. We are trying to make sure that everything doesn't come together at the same time. Far better that the bird has come out of the oven half an hour earlier (it will always benefit from having time to relax), that the vegetables are keeping warm in a low oven, that only the gravy is still to be finished off.

Anything you can make ahead is a good thing. That doesn't just mean the kind of slow braises and casseroles I covered in Cooking in Advance (although, of course, they are ideal for feeding a crowd). Just as important are dishes that can be prepared a few hours ahead and then finished off at the last minute. The Sticky Pork Ribs on page 240, for example, is ideal for crowds, as it can be taken to the final stage and then finished off on the stovetop, leaving you in total control.

A cold starter or side dish is always a fantastic stress-busting option, one you can get ready hours before your guests arrive. The only problem with salads is that once you add the vinaigrette, the greens will start to wilt, and within minutes they will turn limp and slimy. One trick is to put the vinaigrette in the base of the bowl, then cross the salad servers over it to form a kind of stand you can rest the salad greens on, so they aren't in contact with the dressing. Then, when the time comes to serve, a quick toss and you are good to go. Alternatively, there are all manner of robust salads that often benefit from being dressed ahead of time. The Green Papaya Salad on page 232 is a good example. You can make that a few hours in advance and it will actually improve with the extra time.

If you are super-organized, don't forget that vegetables can be blanched in boiling water for a couple of minutes and then refreshed in iced water, ready for reheating at the last minute, either in the microwave or by plunging them into boiling water.

A quick word about boiling vegetables for crowds. As a general rule, you shouldn't use more liquid in a saucepan than you need to cover the thing you want to cook; otherwise, you encourage more flavors to leach out. However, when boiling vegetables, particularly frozen ones, you should always bring a generous amount of water to a boil. That way the water will return to heat much more quickly once you've added the vegetables, and they'll stay firmer and greener as a result.

Sometimes a dish will require lots of last-minute work, so don't be afraid to ask for help. Kitchens work on delegation, and one of the first tasks a head chef has to learn is to organize his brigade. I always assign tasks to my guests, from pouring drinks to laying the table. Get them involved. Even better, make the food preparation part of the entertainment. Get your guests to make their own Vietnamese shrimp rolls; ask them to mix the salad.

You also need to think about how you will present your food. Will you plate it all up in the kitchen, or will you let guests help themselves? For me, it depends entirely on what I am serving. If I've got a big centerpiece dish, like a magnificent rib of beef, I'll let guests share in the excitement and carve it at the table. Eight fillets of fish, on the other hand, aren't going to look too impressive sitting in their hot frying pans, so I'll tend to plate those up, but ask someone to come and help. That way they can be served on hot plates straight out of the warming oven (particularly important with fish as it will go cold quickly). I'll tend to let the guests help themselves to vegetables.

If it's a more casual gathering (and to be honest, we are all heading this way more and more with our home cooking), I'll simply put big bowls of salad or stew or whatever out on the table and let everyone dig in. If you invest in some nice serving bowls or cast-iron casserole dishes this can still look elegant—just remember to warn guests when pans are hot if you want to avoid any lawsuits.

Finally, the dessert. This is one area where I think you can afford to show off a bit. It's the last thing your guests will taste, the memory they'll take home with them, so why not finish on a bang? It hasn't got to be super-complicated, but it should look the part, so stick to something you can take your time over and that won't need lots of last-minute work. Then put it in the center of the table and let your guests dig in.

GREEN PAPAYA SALAD

SERVES 6–8

This is a great salad to serve at a party. It is delicious and robust enough to last the whole evening without wilting. The secret is in the sour, tangy paste, which is a staple of Thai cooking and adds the salty depth of flavor you'll find in so many of their dishes. I'm using super-hot bird's eye chiles here, so do be careful. The sugar will soften the blow of the heat, but won't hide it. If serving fewer numbers, the ingredients below can easily be halved.

4–6 Tbsp dried shrimp, to taste
Sea salt
2 garlic cloves, peeled and roughly chopped
2 red bird's eye chiles, chopped
¼ cup sugar
2 Tbsp tamarind paste
¼ cup fish sauce
Juice of 2 limes
2 large green papayas, peeled and grated, central core and seeds discarded (see tip below)
2 shallots, peeled and grated
2 carrots, peeled and grated
6 Tbsp roughly chopped cilantro
6 Tbsp roughly chopped Thai basil
6 Tbsp roughly chopped skinless peanuts

1. Using a large mortar and pestle, grind the dried shrimp with a pinch of salt until it's broken into small pieces. Add the garlic, chiles, sugar, tamarind paste, and fish sauce and grind until the mixture has a paste-like consistency. Stir in the lime juice to loosen.

2. Mix the papaya, shallots, carrots, cilantro, and basil together in a bowl.

3. Toast the chopped peanuts, rolling them around in a dry pan with a pinch of salt for 2–3 minutes until golden. This will make the nuts sweeter and more intensely flavored. (Don't chop them too small or they will burn.)

4. Add 6 tablespoons of the shrimp paste to the salad and toss well. Taste and add a little more of the paste if needed. Garnish the salad with the peanuts and serve.

HOW TO PREPARE GREEN PAPAYA
Green papaya doesn't look like much from the outside, but it has a unique flavor. The texture is very strong and durable, like a palm heart, so it takes the dressing but doesn't wilt. To peel it, stand it up and cut down around the sides, as if paring an orange.

ROASTED RED PEPPER, LENTIL, AND HERB SALAD

SERVES 6–8

I love to add lentils to my salads as a way of bulking them up for a hungry crowd. That way they work as both vegetable and carbohydrate, freeing you up to concentrate on the main element —perhaps a lemony roast chicken, or butterflied leg of lamb grilled on the barbecue. Don't dice the avocado until the last minute or it will discolor.

1 pound Puy lentils
2 quarts hot vegetable stock
2 bay leaves
4 zucchinis, trimmed
4 red peppers
Olive oil
Sea salt and freshly ground black pepper
12 ounces sun-dried tomatoes in olive oil
2 ripe avocados
Juice of 1 lemon
½ cup chopped chives
Bunch of basil, leaves roughly torn

1. Preheat the oven to 400°F.

2. Boil the lentils in the stock with the bay leaves for about 15 minutes until just cooked. Drain and leave to cool in a large bowl.

3. Meanwhile, chop the zucchini and peppers into bite-sized pieces. Toss with olive oil and season with salt and pepper. Place in a single layer on a roasting pan and place in the oven for 12–15 minutes until tender and slightly coloring at the edges. Leave to cool.

4. Drain the tomatoes, reserving the oil, and chop into small chunks. Add 1–2 tablespoons of the reserved oil to the lentils. Add the tomatoes, zucchini, and red peppers and season well.

5. To serve, dice the avocado and stir into the cooled lentils along with the lemon juice, chives, and basil.

HOW TO SEASON LENTILS
Lentils and beans are great bargain ingredients, but they have a protective membrane that can toughen if salted too early. For this reason, always wait until they are cooked before you add the salt.

CHOPPED SALAD

SERVES 6–8

Another robust salad that's pretty much a meal in itself. You may not think you like chicory because it is quite a bitter leaf, but trust me, it works really well here as a foil to the sweetness of the cheese and tomatoes. Don't add the vinaigrette until you are ready to serve or the lettuce will get limp.

2 shallots, peeled and very thinly sliced
8 ounces baby plum tomatoes or cherry
    tomatoes, halved
Sea salt and freshly ground black pepper
Olive oil
4 heads romaine lettuce, shredded
4 small heads red chicory, shredded
2 red peppers, seeded and diced
Two 14-ounce cans chickpeas, drained and rinsed
10 ounces Edam cheese, sliced into matchsticks
9 ounces salami, sliced into strips
Juice of about ½ lemon
2 Tbsp dried oregano, to garnish

FOR THE SALAD DRESSING
2 Tbsp sherry vinegar
1 Tbsp Worcestershire sauce
2 tsp sugar
2 garlic cloves, peeled and finely chopped
¾ cup olive oil
Sea salt and freshly ground black pepper

1. Place the shallots and tomatoes in a large serving bowl. Season with salt and pepper, then drizzle with a little olive oil. Toss to mix evenly and let stand.

2. To make the dressing, mix together the sherry vinegar, Worcestershire sauce, and sugar and stir until the sugar has dissolved. Add the garlic and mix well. Slowly pour in the olive oil, whisking continuously until thick and glossy. Taste and season with salt and pepper, adjusting the oil or vinegar level as necessary.

3. Mix the lettuce, chicory, peppers, chickpeas, cheese, and salami into the bowl with the tomatoes. Toss to mix, then season with a little more salt and pepper.

4. When ready to serve, squeeze over the juice of half a lemon and add three-quarters of the salad dressing. Mix thoroughly and taste, adding a little more lemon juice and/or salad dressing as necessary. Sprinkle over the dried oregano, toss once more, and serve.

HOW TO KEEP YOUR CUTTING BOARD FROM SLIPPING
An unstable cutting board is a dangerous one; to keep it securely in place, wet a dishcloth or kitchen towel and place it underneath the board to keep it from slipping around.

GREEN BEAN SALAD
WITH MUSTARD DRESSING

SERVES 6–8

Green beans seem to have replaced frozen peas
as the ubiquitous all-year-round vegetable. This is
a very simple way of jazzing them up during the
summer months. Roasting the garlic brings out its
natural sweetness so it has none of the astringency
you find in the raw bulb.

2 pounds green beans, topped and tailed
7 ounces flaked almonds
Sea salt and freshly ground black pepper

FOR THE DRESSING
2 small heads of garlic
2–3 Tbsp white wine vinegar
2 tsp Dijon mustard
2 tsp runny honey
⅔ cup olive oil
Sea salt and freshly ground black pepper

1. Preheat the oven to 350°F.

2. Wrap the garlic for the dressing in foil and roast in
the oven for 20–25 minutes until soft. Remove and
leave to cool.

3. Meanwhile, blanch the green beans by plunging
them into plenty of boiling salted water for 1½
minutes until their rawness has been removed but
they are still crunchy. Refresh immediately under cold
running water, then drain and set aside.

4. Lightly toast the almonds in a medium-hot dry
frying pan for 2–3 minutes until golden. Leave to cool.

5. Mix together the cooled beans and almonds with
a little salt and pepper.

6. Remove the flesh from the garlic heads and mash
with 1 tablespoon of the white wine vinegar until
a smooth paste is formed. Add the mustard and honey
and mix well. Pour in the olive oil in a slow drizzle,
stirring constantly to thicken. Taste and season with
salt and pepper as necessary, and add a little more
vinegar if needed.

7. Dress the green beans, toss to coat well, and serve.

HOW TO MIX DRESSINGS EASILY
Instead of whisking the ingredients in a bowl,
put them in a jar with a tight-fitting lid and shake
vigorously. This emulsifies the mixture more easily
than whisking, and any leftover dressing can be
stored in the jar for future use.

FRESH SHRIMP ROLLS
MAKES 24–28 ROLLS

I grew up loving spring rolls, but traveling around Asia gave me a new respect for this really simple dish. The shrimp give a really nice sweetness to the wraps, but you need to think about texture too. That's why I've included baby Boston lettuce and carrots—to provide some crunch. You can make these rolls in advance and take them out of the fridge minutes before your guests arrive.

8 ounces dried vermicelli or fine rice noodles
1 pound cooked large shrimp, peeled, deveined, and roughly chopped (see page 167)
2 baby Boston lettuces, shredded
4 scallions, trimmed and chopped
2 large carrots, peeled and grated
¼ cup chopped cilantro
¼ cup chopped Thai basil
¼ cup chopped mint
Juice of 2 limes
24–28 round rice paper sheets (6-inch diameter)

FOR THE DIPPING SAUCE
¼ cup sugar
¼ cup rice vinegar
¾ cup fish sauce
2 red chiles, seeded and finely chopped
2 garlic cloves, peeled and finely chopped
2 scallions, trimmed and thinly sliced
¼ cup chopped cilantro
¼ cup chopped mint

1. To rehydrate the vermicelli noodles, soak in boiling water for 3–4 minutes; drain and refresh under running cold water. When cool, shake off any excess water and set aside.

2. To make the dipping sauce, mix together the sugar, rice vinegar, fish sauce, chiles, and garlic. Mix well, stirring until the sugar has dissolved. Add the remaining ingredients. Mix, taste, and adjust the seasonings as necessary, then set aside.

3. To make the rolls, roughly chop the noodles in a bowl. Mix in the shrimp, lettuce, scallions, carrot, cilantro, basil, and mint. Add the lime juice along with 2 tablespoons of the dipping sauce and mix together. Taste and adjust the seasoning, adding a little more sauce if needed.

4. Dip a rice paper into a bowl of hot water for about 20 seconds until softened and pliable. Splash a board with a little water before placing a rice paper on it (this will keep it from sticking), then put a spoonful of the mixture into the center of the rice paper and fold the sides over the filling. Roll up tightly into a spring roll shape and repeat with the remaining mixture and rice papers.

5. Serve the rolls with the dipping sauce on the side.

HOW TO MAXIMIZE CITRUS JUICE
To get the maximum amount of juice from a lemon or lime, roll it hard under your palm for a minute before juicing.

STICKY PORK RIBS

SERVES 6–8

Sticky, chewy, sweet, and sour, these ribs are
impossible to resist. The glaze is packed full
of vibrant, citrusy flavors, with the sweetness
of the honey counteracting the spices. The secret
is to get the ribs really well caramelized before
you add any of the other ingredients. As they
braise in the oven, all that color will turn into
the most amazing flavor.

4½ pounds pork ribs, separated
Sea salt and freshly ground black pepper
Olive oil
6–8 garlic cloves, peeled and sliced
4-inch piece of fresh ginger, peeled and sliced
2–4 tsp dried chile flakes, to taste
2 tsp Sichuan peppercorns
8 whole star anise
½ cup runny honey
1¼ cups soy sauce
4–5 Tbsp rice vinegar
2½ cups Shaoxing rice wine or medium-dry sherry
10 scallions, trimmed and sliced
3½ cups chicken stock

1. Preheat the oven to 350°F.

2. Season the ribs with salt and pepper, pushing
the seasoning into the meat. Heat a roasting pan on
the stovetop with a little olive oil and brown the ribs
for 5–10 minutes until they are colored on all sides.

3. Add the garlic, ginger, chile flakes, Sichuan
peppercorns, star anise, and honey and continue to
cook over the heat for 2 minutes until the honey
begins to caramelize. Add the soy sauce, rice vinegar,
and Shaoxing wine and bring to a boil, simmering
for 1 minute. Taste and adjust the flavors, adding
a little extra vinegar if necessary. Add the scallions and
stock and bring to a boil. Place in the preheated oven
and cook for 1 hour until tender, turning the ribs
halfway through the cooking time.

4. Remove the pan from the oven and place back
on the stovetop. Heat the marinade and reduce for
8–10 minutes until the sauce is thick and syrupy. Turn
the ribs in the sauce to coat them well, then serve.

HOW TO GIVE RIBS EXTRA FLAVOR
Once the ribs have cooked in the oven, you can
leave them sitting in their sticky marinade for a day
or two, which really helps to develop the flavor.
Then, when you come to finish them off, give them
about 20 minutes on the stovetop, making sure
they are well heated through.

STUFFED LAMB WITH SPINACH AND PINE NUTS

SERVES 6–8

People often think lamb should go with mint, but it's nice to go off piste, as here, with feta, pine nuts, and spinach. A lovely yogurt and cucumber dressing completes this dish. Make sure you sear the saddle on the stovetop before putting it into the oven to kick-start the roasting process and get a well-colored crisp outside in contrast to a perfectly pink inside.

1 small onion, peeled and chopped
2 garlic cloves, peeled and sliced
Olive oil
Sea salt and freshly ground black pepper
3 Tbsp pine nuts
8 ounces baby spinach, washed
5 ounces feta cheese, crumbled
1 boned saddle of lamb, about 4 pounds
  (ask your butcher to bone it for you)
1–2 tsp sumac (see page 113), to taste

FOR THE DRESSING
½ large cucumber, peeled, seeded, and sliced
  into rings
⅔ cup plain yogurt
Small bunch of mint, shredded
1 Tbsp pomegranate molasses (see page 205),
  to taste
Zest of 1 lemon, squeeze of juice
Salt and freshly ground black pepper

1. Sauté the onion and garlic in a medium–hot pan with a dash of olive oil for 5 minutes until softened. Season with salt and pepper, then add the pine nuts and cook for about 1 minute until golden. Add the spinach and wilt briefly in the pan, tossing to mix well. Remove from the heat and stir in the feta.

2. Lay the saddle of lamb open on a board, flesh side up. Season with salt and pepper and sprinkle over the sumac. Spoon the spinach mixture along the middle of the meat, using the fillets that run down the inside length of the meat to support the sides of the stuffing.

3. Roll the meat around the filling and tie at intervals with string. Season the outside of the lamb with salt and pepper all over, then chill for at least 30 minutes or overnight to help it firm up and make it easier to brown.

4. Preheat the oven to 375°F.

5. Put a roasting pan on the stovetop and heat until hot. Add a glug of oil and cook the lamb for 10 minutes until browned all over. Transfer to the preheated oven and cook for 45–55 minutes, depending on the weight of the lamb and how pink you like it. When cooked, set aside to rest.

6. Meanwhile, mix all the dressing ingredients together and add a little salt and pepper.

7. Serve the rested lamb hot or at room temperature, thickly sliced, with the dressing on the side.

HOW TO STUFF MEAT
The secret of any stuffing is to partially cook it first. Raw onions and raw garlic will take forever to cook inside the meat. If you are not going to be roasting the meat immediately, you must let the stuffing cool before using it. When filling the saddle, put extra stuffing at the edges as some will inevitably squeeze out as you roll, and don't tie it too tightly.

PAELLA
SERVES 8–10

The original one-pot Spanish dish. Unlike risotto, paella does not have to be stirred as it cooks, so it is better suited to entertaining. As always when cooking rice, you need twice the amount of liquid to rice. The other thing to watch is that you add the seafood according to how long it needs to cook: squid goes in last as it becomes rubbery if cooked for too long.

Olive oil
1 large onion, peeled and chopped
1 large red pepper, seeded and diced
3–4 garlic cloves, peeled and thinly sliced
8 ounces chorizo sausage, skinned and sliced
1 tsp smoked paprika
1 pound skinless and boneless chicken thighs
Sea salt and freshly ground black pepper
2½ cups paella rice, such as calasparra or bomba
1 cup dry white wine
1 quart hot chicken stock

Generous pinch of saffron strands
One 14-ounce can chopped tomatoes
24 mussels, cleaned
10 ounces raw jumbo shrimp, whole or heads removed
10 ounces squid, cleaned and sliced into thin rings
2½ cups peas, thawed if frozen
Handful of chopped flat-leaf parsley, to garnish
2 lemons, cut into wedges, to serve

1. Heat a little olive oil in a large paella pan or frying pan. Add the onion and red pepper and sauté for 2–3 minutes to soften. Add the garlic and sauté for an additional 2 minutes before adding the chorizo and paprika.

2. Meanwhile, cut the chicken into bite-sized pieces and season with salt and pepper. Add to the pan and cook for a few minutes over high heat, stirring frequently, to lightly seal the meat.

3. Add the rice and stir for 2–3 minutes, then add the wine and cook for about 5 minutes to evaporate before adding the stock. Bring up to a simmer, then add the saffron and tomatoes. Season with salt and pepper and stir well.

4. Simmer for 10 minutes, then gently push the mussels and shrimp into the top of the rice. Cook over medium heat for 5 minutes until the shrimp are opaque and the mussels have opened (discard any that haven't). Stir in the squid and the peas and cook for an additional 2–3 minutes. (The rice should now be cooked and all the liquid absorbed.)

5. Taste and adjust the seasoning as necessary.

6. Remove the pan from the heat, cover tightly with foil, and allow to rest for 10 minutes. Garnish with the parsley and lemon wedges and serve.

ROAST BEEF SIRLOIN

SERVES 6–8

If you buy a good piece of beef, you need do nothing more than rub it with a little olive oil and season it generously before putting it into a very hot oven. The fat will baste the meat as it cooks, resulting in a beautifully flavorful roast.

Don't forget to leave the meat to relax for at least 15 minutes so that it has time to reabsorb its juices. If you want to have a traditional meal, serve with roasted potatoes and steamed broccoli. Alternatively, serve at room temperature with a salad (see pages 232–237).

4-pound beef sirloin, trimmed
2 Tbsp olive oil
Sea salt and freshly ground black pepper
A few rosemary sprigs, leaves chopped

FOR THE GRAVY
2 shallots, peeled and thinly sliced
1 garlic clove, peeled and crushed
Sea salt and freshly ground black pepper
2 Tbsp all-purpose flour
1–2 Tbsp balsamic vinegar
⅔ cup red wine
2 cups beef stock
A few tarragon sprigs, leaves chopped

1. Preheat the oven to 450°F. Put the beef in a large roasting pan and drizzle with the olive oil. Sprinkle over some salt, pepper, and the chopped rosemary and rub the seasoning all over the beef. Turn the beef so that the fat is on top. Roast in the hot oven for 20 minutes, then reduce the heat to 400°F. Roast for 5–10 minutes per pound for medium-rare meat, or 10–15 minutes per pound for medium. Turn the beef halfway through cooking for an even roast.

2. Transfer the beef to a warm platter, cover loosely with foil, and leave to rest for 15–20 minutes. To make the gravy, pour off any excess fat from the roasting pan, leaving behind a couple of tablespoons, then place the pan over medium heat. Add the shallots, garlic, and a little salt and pepper. Cook for about 4–6 minutes, stirring frequently, until the shallots begin to soften. Add the flour and stir for a few more minutes.

3. Pour in the vinegar and red wine and bring to a boil. Add the stock and return to a boil for about 10 minutes until the sauce has reduced and thickened, then stir in the tarragon.

4. Carve the beef thinly and serve the gravy in a warm gravy boat.

POACHED WINTER FRUITS WITH ZABAGLIONE

SERVES 6

This dessert shows that you don't have to spend hours in the kitchen to create a stunning and delicious end to a meal. Although a little muscle power is needed for the zabaglione, it's simple to make just before it's eaten. Cooking times for the fruit will vary depending on how ripe it is to begin with—you want it tender but not falling apart.

One 750-ml bottle red wine, such as Chianti
2 cups ruby port
¼ cup sugar
2 cinnamon sticks
2 firm ripe pears
2 dessert apples
3 ripe fresh figs
3 ripe plums
Amaretti cookies, to serve

FOR THE ZABAGLIONE
5 egg yolks
½ cup sugar
½ cup sweet dessert wine, such as Marsala
1½ Tbsp whisky
1½ Tbsp brandy

1. Pour the wine and port into a pan, stir in the sugar, and add the cinnamon sticks. Place over low heat and warm for about 5 minutes until the sugar has completely dissolved. Bring to a rolling boil and allow to bubble for 5–10 minutes until reduced by half.

2. Meanwhile, prepare the fruit. Peel, quarter, and core the pears and apples. Halve the figs and plums, and remove the pits from the latter.

3. Add the fruits to the reduced wine mixture and simmer over low heat for about 10 minutes until deep red in color and soft but holding their shape. Transfer the fruit to a large bowl, return the poaching liquid to a boil, and continue to cook for 5–10 minutes until it has reduced by another two-thirds, or until you are left with a syrupy glaze. Pour this over the fruit and leave to steep.

4. Meanwhile, make the zabaglione. Pour a shallow depth of water into a saucepan and bring to the simmering point. Put the egg yolks and sugar in a heatproof mixing bowl that will fit snugly on top of the pan without its base touching the water. With the bowl on a work surface, whisk the yolks and sugar together with a hand-held electric mixer for 2–3 minutes until pale and thick. Add the dessert wine and spirits and whisk again.

5. Place the bowl over the pan of simmering water and continue to whisk for 8–10 minutes until the mixture is thick and creamy and has almost tripled in volume (you'll know it's ready when you lift the beaters and the mixture leaves a trail on the surface).

6. Divide the fruit and poaching liquor among serving bowls and spoon over the hot zabaglione. Pass a kitchen torch over the surface or place under a hot broiler for a few minutes until the zabaglione turns lightly golden. Serve immediately with amaretti cookies.

RASPBERRY MILLEFEUILLE

SERVES 4–6

Desserts should always have that wow factor, and this dish is incredibly simple to prepare, yet looks and tastes absolutely stunning. By lightly dusting the top of the pastry with confectioners' sugar, it caramelizes the top and allows all the layers to separate into the "thousand leaves" that give the dessert its name.

One 11-ounce package frozen all-butter puff
    pastry, thawed
3 Tbsp confectioners' sugar, plus extra to dust
Seeds from 2 vanilla pods
2½ cups heavy cream
Zest of 1 orange
½ Tbsp orange-flavored liqueur,
    such as Grand Marnier
1½ cups fresh raspberries

1. Preheat the oven to 425°F.

2. Unroll the pastry and place on a nonstick baking sheet. Dust generously with confectioners' sugar and bake in the preheated oven for 8 minutes, then reduce the temperature to 400°F and cook for an additional 7–12 minutes until the pastry is golden and glazed. Remove and leave to cool slightly on a wire rack.

3. Meanwhile, mix the vanilla seeds into the cream. Add the 3 tablespoons of sugar and whip the mixture until it forms soft peaks. (Don't overbeat or it will separate.) Add the orange zest and liqueur and fold in using a spatula.

4. Spoon the cream into a piping bag fitted with a plain nozzle, twisting slowly to move the cream to the pointed end. Chill until ready to use.

5. When the pastry has cooled, slice it very gently into 3 equal-sized lengths with a bread knife.

6. Assemble the millefeuille just before serving. Take the piping bag from the fridge, add a dot of cream to the serving plate to act as "glue," and put a piece of pastry on top. Pipe a layer of cream over the pastry and add a border of raspberries around the outer edges. Pipe another layer of cream inside the raspberry border, then top with another layer of pastry and repeat the cream and raspberry stages. Finish with a top layer of pastry. Serve immediately, dusted with more confectioners' sugar.

HOW TO VARY THE MILLEFEUILLE FILLING
You can vary the filling of the millefeuille as much as you like. Use crème fraîche, mascarpone, strawberries, lime … whatever you like.

APRICOT AND FRANGIPANE TART

SERVES 8–10

This almond-flavored tart can be paired with any fruits in season: cherries, pears, peaches, or, as here, apricots. Serve warm or cold with a dollop of crème fraîche for a simple, make-ahead dessert.

Butter, for greasing
1 recipe pie pastry (see page 269)
All-purpose flour, for dusting
4 large, or 6 small, apricots, halved and pitted
¼ cup apricot jam

FOR THE FRANGIPANE
½ cup (1 stick) unsalted butter, softened to
   room temperature
½ cup sugar
¼ cup all-purpose flour
1½ cups almond meal or almond flour
1 large free-range egg, beaten

1. Lightly butter a 10-inch removable-bottomed tart pan.

2. Roll out the pastry on a lightly floured surface to ⅛-inch thickness. Use the pastry to line the pan, gently pressing it into the sides and leaving about ½ inch overhanging the top edge.

3. Use a fork to prick the base, then line with parchment paper and fill with ceramic baking beans or uncooked rice. Chill for 20 minutes.

4. Meanwhile, preheat the oven to 375°F.

5. When the tart case has chilled, place it on a baking sheet and blind-bake it in the preheated oven for 15 minutes. Remove the paper and beans, then return the pastry to the oven for 5 minutes to cook the base.

6. When cooked, use a sharp knife to trim the excess pastry level with the top of the pan and set aside to cool.

7. Reduce the oven setting to 300°F.

8. To make the frangipane, cream the butter, sugar, flour, and almond meal together, then slowly add the egg, mixing until fully incorporated. Allow the frangipane to rest for 5 minutes before smoothing it inside the pastry case.

9. Cut each apricot half into 3 or 4 wedges and arrange them on top of the frangipane, skin side up. Push the apricots gently into the mixture, then return the tart to the baking sheet and bake in the preheated oven for 30–35 minutes until the frangipane is puffed and golden and the apricots are soft and golden brown.

10. Heat the apricot jam gently in a small pan for about 2 minutes until warmed. Remove the tart from the oven and brush with the melted jam while still warm.

11. Leave the tart to cool slightly before removing from the pan and serving in slices.

PIMM'S FRUIT GELATIN DESSERT

MAKES 6–8

This is such a beautiful dessert to have in the garden on a summer's afternoon, especially if served in some pretty glasses or teacups. Its key ingredient is Pimm's No. 1, a bittersweet, very British, gin-based liqueur. Depending on the size of your containers, you may find the fruit floats to the surface. If so, fill them in two stages, setting them in between, so that the fruit is trapped throughout the gelatin.

8 sheets of leaf gelatin
2 cups lemonade
1 ½ cups small strawberries, hulled
2 small oranges
1 Granny Smith apple, peeled, cored
    and quartered
Juice of 1 lemon
¾ cup Pimm's No. 1
2 Tbsp sugar
½ cup mascarpone cheese
⅔ cup heavy cream
A few mint sprigs
Shortbread cookies, to serve (optional)

1. Soften the gelatin in cold water for about 5 minutes. Meanwhile, heat half the lemonade until almost boiling, then remove from the heat. Squeeze the water from the gelatin, then stir it into the hot lemonade until completely dissolved.

2. Quarter the strawberries and peel and segment 1 of the oranges. Chop the apple into equal-sized pieces and toss in half of the lemon juice.

3. Once the lemonade and gelatin mixture has cooled, stir in the Pimm's, the remaining lemonade, and the lemon juice. Pass through a sieve. Divide the prepared fruit among 6–8 molds, tumblers, or teacups (the number depends on their capacity), then pour the gelatin mixture over and chill for 2–3 hours until completely set.

4. To make the cream, finely zest and juice the second orange. Mix with the sugar and boil in a small pan for about 5 minutes until reduced to about 2 tablespoons. Beat into the mascarpone. Softly whip the cream and fold into the orange mascarpone. Chill until ready to use.

5. Remove the gelatin molds from the fridge 20–30 minutes before serving, placing them on small plates or saucers and turning them out if you wish. Spoon some of the orange cream on top of each serving and garnish with mint leaves. Serve with a cookie on the side if you like.

BAKING

IF YOU ARE LUCKY ENOUGH TO HAVE PARENTS OR GRANDPARENTS WHO COOKED A LOT WHEN YOU WERE A CHILD, I'M SURE FRESH BAKING IS ONE OF THE MOST EVOCATIVE SMELLS YOU CAN COME ACROSS.

It always transports me back to the times when my mother ran a tearoom in Stratford-upon-Avon, and we'd come home from school to all these wonderful scents. There's something so homey and comforting about the smell of cakes cooling on wire racks, or freshly baked bread coming out of the oven.

It's curious how the cycles of food fashion go. Baking used to be one of the first things that cooks would master, but often nowadays even those who cook regularly don't necessarily bake very much. Maybe they see it as being too time-consuming or too much of a hassle, and it's true that food manufacturers have gone out of their way to make sure you need never be short of a sweet treat. But baking is about so much more than cookies and cake. It opens up a whole world of savory dishes, too, and once you master the art of the perfect pastry or lightest sponge, your cooking will be all the stronger for it.

A lot of people give up before they've even started and claim they can't bake, period. "My hands are too warm," they'll say, or "My kitchen's too cold." It's all nonsense, of course. The truth is that baking, more than any other discipline in the kitchen, is a science and you've got to follow the formula. Just like in those chemistry lessons you hated at school, accuracy is all-important. You need the right ingredients and you need to combine them in the right way. Self-rising flour is not the same as all-purpose flour; all-purpose flour is not the same as bread flour. If you don't put enough baking powder in a cake batter, it won't rise; put too much in and it will rise too much and then collapse. I'm an instinctive cook, and I judge most things by eye, but baking is the one time you'll see me reaching for the scale. A bit too much flour in corn pancakes is not going to make a whole world of difference, but too much flour in hazelnut shortbread and it will. So follow the recipe, pay attention, and measure precisely. This is no time to come over all creative. Stick to the rules and you'll get perfect results.

BREAD

I absolutely love making bread. There's something so satisfying—magical almost—about the process. You can really switch off and lose yourself in it. I learned my craft as a 22-year-old working in Paris. I'd start at midnight and by 7 a.m. had to have produced white, brown, sourdough, and cheese breads worthy of a three-star establishment. That's a lot of pressure, and the sense of danger, that everything would go wrong, never quite left me. But I did learn to have no fear and to enjoy it. That's the secret.

If you ever stop to read the list of ingredients in your average supermarket bread, with its emulsifiers and stabilizers, you'll be amazed at how little goes into a proper old-fashioned loaf: flour, salt, yeast, and water. And that's it. If ever you needed an incentive to make your own, you've got it right there.

Yeast is what gives most breads their lift and texture, and it takes time to "wake up" and feed on the sugars in the flour. So the quickest and easiest breads of all are those without yeast—soda bread and flatbreads being two of the most common. As its name suggests, soda bread, which is typical of Ireland, relies on baking soda to aerate it. It's a simple combination of ingredients that barely even need kneading, yet it produces this fantastically dense loaf. Flatbread is entirely unleavened and can be ready to eat within 30 minutes.

Of breads made with yeast, the Italian focaccia is a good one to start with. It's a very simple hands-on bread that produces really impressive results, with a lovely silky, rich texture. Because it's baked on a baking sheet, it's easy to shape—you simply massage it into the corners—and you can top it with almost anything that takes your fancy, from tomatoes, olives, and rosemary to bacon, onion, or chorizo. Yes, you can buy bread, but once you've tried this, you'll be addicted.

Making bread can also be a good workout, as kneading requires a bit of effort. This is where you stretch and aerate the dough by pushing it away from you with the heel of your hand, then pulling it back over itself and pinching it in. You repeat this process until the dough feels smooth and elastic and comes cleanly away from the work surface. This can take anywhere up to 15 minutes.

PASTRY

The cornerstone of any proud home cook. You can buy very good ready-made pastry these days, and I must admit I seldom bother making my own puff pastry at home (I'll only buy a good all-butter version, though), but pie pastry is another matter. Rich, buttery, and robust, it is one of the staples of the kitchen and is very versatile and easy to make. There is a certain knack to making pastry, but once you crack it, it will make such a difference in your cooking.

For savory pie pastry, I normally use the "rub-in" method, where you rub cold butter into flour using your fingertips until the mixture resembles fine breadcrumbs. It's important not to handle the mixture any more than necessary at this stage or the butter will become oily, resulting in tough pastry (that's where the hot hands myth comes in). Then you add enough water (or beaten egg if you want a richer result, although I don't think it often needs it) for the dough to come together. This is another crucial stage that you will learn to judge with practice. If the dough is too dry now, it will end up too crumbly to roll or crack as you cook it. If it is too wet, it may be easier to handle, but when you cook it, the water will evaporate and the dough will shrink in the oven. You can do all this mixing in a food processor, but it is good to do it by hand so that you learn to identify the texture you are looking for. Give the dough a very quick knead, folding it and pushing it away with the heel of your hand, until it is homogeneous.

Next, it is really important to allow the dough to relax for about 20 minutes in the fridge so that the butter and flour can synchronize together. The strands of gluten will absorb some of the moisture, making them more durable and less likely to crack when you roll out the dough. Once rested, it will be much firmer. No matter how tempting, you shouldn't rush this stage.

Next comes the rolling out. Sprinkle the work surface with flour, place your flattened disc of dough in front of you, and, using a floured rolling pin, roll once away from you. Give the dough a one-eighth turn and roll again. Turn, roll, turn, roll, turn, roll, and so on, re-flouring the pin if the dough starts to stick, until you have the size and shape you need. This rotating process will ensure that you have evenly rolled dough.

To line your pan, lift the pastry up by half-rolling it onto the pin, then drape it over the pan, allowing it to overhang the edges. Take a little ball of leftover dough and use it like a soft mallet to gently push the dough into the corners to give it a snug fit. Be sure not to trap any air under the pastry or it will bubble up when it is cooking.

Although ceramic pie dishes may look attractive, they are poor conductors of heat and often result in a soggy base, and that's the last thing you want. Always use metal containers, either a tart pan with a removable base, or an ovenproof frying pan, and place them on a preheated metal pan rather than directly on a rack. This will ensure that more heat is directed at the bottom of the pastry and result in a crisper base.

Recipes will often call for you to cook the pastry "blind," which means giving it an initial cooking without its filling. This is particularly the case when you are adding a liquid filling, which would otherwise make the pastry soggy. To do this, line the pastry case with foil or parchment paper and fill it with something inert that will weigh it down. You can buy special ceramic baking beans, but dried rice or lentils will work just as well (store them for use again, but don't eat them). After 10–15 minutes, take out the beans and paper and cook the pastry case uncovered for another 5–10 minutes to crisp up the base. (To seal the base even more, you can brush it with beaten egg and cook for another minute.) Trim the excess pastry with a knife. The pastry case is now ready for filling.

Sweet pie crust is very similar to savory pie crust, but is enriched with granulated or confectioners' sugar and egg. This one I tend to make in the processor, creaming the butter, sugar, and egg together first, then adding the flour and pulsing briefly to bring the dough together. This results in a slightly more pliable, user-friendly dough. It will be slightly less flaky, perhaps, but easier to handle and still very crisp, as you want any good pastry to be. You then treat it just as you would a savory pie crust.

These are just beginnings, of course. You can add any flavors you like. Try substituting a quarter of the flour with peanut flour or cocoa powder, or add some chopped thyme, lavender, lemon zest, or vanilla seeds. Take it in any direction you like.

CAKES AND COOKIES

There are various ways of making cakes, but the most common is the creaming method, where you beat together butter and sugar, add eggs one by one, and then fold in the sifted flour. Air is the key ingredient here, the thing that gives cakes their lightness, so everything you do is geared toward incorporating as much of it as possible.

Unlike in pastry, butter should be at room temperature; too cold and it won't cream properly, too warm and it will be oily and coat too much of the flour. Start by beating it until creamy, then add the sugar and whisk for at least 5 minutes, ideally with an electric mixer, until it is pale and fluffy. It's so important to start this aeration process properly at the beginning, and it's where so much cake-making fails. The eggs should also be at room temperature or else they are more likely to curdle when you add them to the butter and sugar mixture. (If that starts happening, add a tablespoon of flour at this stage to bind the mixture together again.)

Once the eggs are incorporated, sift in the self-rising flour and use a metal spoon or spatula to cut and fold the mixture together. Again, you are trying to keep as much air as possible in the batter, so don't be too heavy-handed. You are looking for what's called a dropping consistency, when the batter falls slowly from your spatula, so you might need to loosen the batter with a little milk. Again, with practice you'll learn to judge this.

Have a buttered cake pan ready and dust the inside with flour so that nothing will stick, then spoon in the batter. Level it out with your spatula and then bang the pan on the work surface a couple of times to help settle the mixture and get rid of any air pockets that would make the cake rise unevenly.

You can smell when a cake is ready, so trust your instincts more than the time given in a recipe. All ovens and flours vary, so it is impossible to give entirely accurate cooking times. When you think the cake is cooked, take it out and insert a knife blade or metal skewer into the middle. If it comes out clean, the cake is ready. If not, bake it for five minutes more.

Cookies often have the same mix of ingredients—butter, flour, sugar, and eggs—but you change the chemistry of them by incorporating less air to produce a shorter, crumblier texture. That means less beating, and using all-purpose flour instead of self-rising. The key thing to remember when making things like Lemon Thyme Shortbread (page 279) is to make even-sized biscuits so that they bake at the same rate. A good trick with a solid dough such as this is to roll it into a cylinder, wrap it in plastic wrap, and then chill it. This way, not only can you cut beautiful, even slices of dough, but also, because the dough is chilled, the cookies are more likely to keep their shape as they bake.

OLIVE, TOMATO, AND ROSEMARY FOCACCIA

SERVES 6–8

Focaccia is a great place to start when making bread. It is hands-on but very quick and tasty. Adding oil to the white dough makes the finished loaf silky soft, and the semolina gives it a more rustic edge. You can finish your dough with anything from tomatoes, rosemary, and roasted garlic to olives, or even salami. Some people like to push these ingredients into the dough, but I think that stops the aeration so I leave mine on top.

4 cups bread flour
1 heaping Tbsp coarse semolina
Two ¼-ounce packets active dry yeast
Sea salt and freshly ground black pepper
¼ cup olive oil, plus a little extra
½ cup pitted black olives, sliced
5 ounces sun-dried tomatoes in olive oil
2–3 rosemary sprigs, leaves only

1. Thoroughly mix the flour, semolina, and yeast with a couple of generous pinches of salt. Mix 1½ cups warm water with the olive oil. Make a well in the middle of the flour mixture and gradually add the liquid. (It's easiest to mix this together with a fork to start with and then, when it is just coming together, use your hands to make it into a ball.) Tip the dough out onto a lightly floured surface and knead for about 10 minutes until smooth, elastic, and springy to the touch.

2. Place the dough in a large floured mixing bowl and leave to rise in a warm place for 30–60 minutes until doubled in size.

3. Preheat the oven to 400°F.

4. Place the risen dough on an oiled baking sheet (about 8 x 12 inches) and sprinkle with a little salt. Grease your fingers with a little olive oil and prod out the dough to the edges of the sheet.

5. Press the olives and tomatoes into the dough so that they are slightly poking above the surface. Season with salt and pepper and scatter over the rosemary leaves.

6. Drizzle the bread with a little extra olive oil and place in the preheated oven for 30 minutes until golden and cooked through.

7. Turn out of the sheet, then transfer to a board, slice, and serve.

SODA BREAD
MAKES 1 LOAF

This traditional Irish loaf uses baking soda instead
of yeast as its leavener. The advantage is that you
don't have to wait for it to rise or proof, but the
resulting loaf will not keep as long and
is best eaten the same day. If you can't find
buttermilk, use regular milk instead and add
a level teaspoon of cream of tartar.

3 cups all-purpose flour, plus extra for dusting
1 ¼ cups whole wheat flour
1 ½ tsp baking soda
1 tsp table salt
1 tsp sugar
2 cups buttermilk

1. Preheat the oven to 400°F.

2. Sift the dry ingredients into a bowl and make
a well in the middle. Reserve 2 tablespoons of the
buttermilk and add the rest to the bowl, mixing
lightly with a fork as you add it. (Be careful not to
overwork the dough, but make sure all the dry
ingredients are mixed in. Add the remaining
buttermilk if necessary.)

3. Tip the dough onto a floured work surface and
knead gently for 30 seconds to combine. Do not
overwork. Line a baking sheet with parchment paper
and dust with flour. Form the bread into a round,
place on the sheet, and flatten slightly. Use a serrated
knife to cut a deep cross in the top of the loaf.

4. Place in the preheated oven and bake for 30–35
minutes until the soda bread is golden on the
outside and cooked through. A good way to check
is by tapping the bottom—it should sound hollow
when cooked.

5. Cool on a wire rack before enjoying warm or cold.

MOZZARELLA AND ROSEMARY PIZZA
MAKES 4

Making your own pizza dough couldn't be simpler, and is always so much nicer than buying a prepared base. Most domestic ovens don't get hot enough to achieve that really crisp crust flecked with scorch marks, so I tend to cook pizzas in a very hot frying pan and finish them under the broiler.

Two ¼-ounce packets active dry yeast
1 Tbsp sugar
4 cups bread flour or Italian "00" flour
1 Tbsp fine sea salt
¼ cup extra virgin olive oil

FOR THE MOZZARELLA AND ROSEMARY TOPPING
½ cup tomato sauce
2 balls of mozzarella cheese
Freshly ground black pepper
2 rosemary sprigs
Olive oil

ALTERNATIVE GORGONZOLA AND RADICCHIO TOPPING
½ cup tomato sauce
5 ounces Gorgonzola cheese
2 small heads of radicchio, shredded
2 rosemary sprigs
Freshly ground black pepper
Olive oil

ALTERNATIVE MEAT AND CHILE TOPPING
½ cup tomato sauce
1 red chile, seeded and thinly sliced
6 slices of salami
1 ball of mozzarella cheese
Freshly ground black pepper
Olive oil

CONTINUED ON PAGE 268

CONTINUED FROM PAGE 266

1. First make the pizza dough. Mix together the yeast and sugar with 1⅓ cups warm water and leave for a couple of minutes. Meanwhile, sift the flour into a mixing bowl, add the salt, and make a well in the middle. Pour the oil into the well, followed by the yeast mixture. Using a spoon, bring the flour into the middle from the sides, mixing slowly, bit by bit, until a dough begins to form. Once you reach this stage, work the rest together with your hands.

2. When combined, tip the dough onto a floured work surface and knead for 10 minutes until smooth. Clean out your mixing bowl, dust it with flour, and put the dough back into the bowl. Cover with a dish towel and leave to rise in a warm place for about 1 hour until doubled in size.

3. When the dough is risen punch out the air and tip onto a floured work surface. Knead the dough for 1–2 minutes to push out any excess air, then wrap in plastic wrap and chill if not using immediately.

4. When you're ready to make the pizzas, divide the dough into 4 equal balls and keep them covered. Put a large (10-inch) broilerproof frying pan on the heat (you can cook 2 bases at a time if you have 2 pans) and roll out one ball of dough on a floured work surface with a floured rolling pin until it's the same size as your pan. Pour a little olive oil into the pan and add the pizza base, pressing it down. Cook over medium heat for 5–8 minutes until the base crisps and the dough starts to cook through and bubble up.

5. Spread 2 tablespoons of the tomato sauce over the pizza base. Tear the mozzarella balls in half, then tear one half into 4 pieces and dot them over the base. Season with pepper and scatter over a few rosemary leaves. Remove from the pan and set aside. Repeat with the remaining pizzas. (If you want to try the alternative toppings, build them up in a similar way.)

6. Drizzle the pizzas with a little olive oil before placing under a preheated broiler. Cook for about 4 minutes until the topping is golden and bubbling and the dough along the edges is nice and crisp.

7. Serve warm, cut into slices, and drizzle with extra olive oil with a couple of extra rosemary sprigs sprinkled on top.

LEEK AND PANCETTA QUICHE

SERVES 2

Quiche is a really versatile dish that you can take in any direction you like—just be generous with the filling: you want about two-thirds flavoring ingredients to one-third custard. Quiches are often better the next day, once the custard has had a chance to set properly and the flavors to mingle.

7 ounces pancetta
Olive oil
2 leeks, trimmed and finely chopped
4 eggs
¼ cup heavy cream
Sea salt and freshly ground black pepper
4 ounces Gruyère cheese, finely grated
2 Tbsp chopped flat-leaf parsley

FOR THE PIE PASTRY
1½ cups all-purpose flour, plus extra for dusting
Pinch of salt
½ cup (1 stick) butter, cubed, at room temperature

1. First make the pastry. Sift the flour and salt into a mixing bowl. Using your fingertips, rub the butter into the flour, lifting the mixture up and dropping it back into the bowl—you want to keep the mixture light and airy. When it resembles fine breadcrumbs, mix in 2–3 tablespoons of cold water. Bring the pastry together, adding a little more water if needed, then knead lightly on a floured work surface to create a smooth, solid ball. Wrap in plastic wrap and chill for 20 minutes.

2. Preheat the oven to 375°F. Oil a 10-inch loose-bottomed tart pan.

3. Flour a work surface and roll out the pastry to the thickness of ⅛ inch. Use to line the prepared pan, pushing it into the corners and sides with a small ball of leftover pastry. Leave some excess pastry overhanging the edges, then prick the base with a fork. Chill for 10 minutes.

4. Line the chilled pastry case with parchment paper and fill with ceramic baking beans or uncooked rice. Place it on a baking sheet and blind-bake in the preheated oven for 10–15 minutes. Remove the paper and beans, then bake for an additional 5–8 minutes until golden. Trim off the excess pastry with a sharp knife, then set the pie shell aside.

5. Meanwhile, cook the pancetta in a large oiled frying pan over medium heat for 3–4 minutes until colored and almost crisp. Add the leek and sauté for 3–4 minutes until soft and completely cooked through. Drain to remove excess oil if necessary.

6. Mix the eggs and cream together in a bowl. Season with a pinch of salt and pepper. Add three-quarters of the Gruyère and stir in the leek mixture. Mix well then add the parsley. Taste and adjust the seasoning as necessary. Pour the mixture into the cooked pie shell, sprinkle the top with the remaining cheese, and cook in the preheated oven for 15–20 minutes until golden and set.

7. Remove the quiche and allow to cool slightly before serving.

HOW TO MAKE PIE PASTRY IN A FOOD PROCESSOR
Blend the flour, butter, and salt together first, then add the cold water and pulse until combined. Tip the dough onto a floured surface and knead once or twice to bring it together in a smooth ball.

BEEF EMPANADAS
MAKES 18 EMPANADAS

The empanada resembles a turnover and probably started out in Spain but soon spread throughout Latin America and Asia. The piquant chimichurri sauce is a great accompaniment.

Two 11-ounce packages frozen all-butter puff
   pastry, thawed
Olive oil
1 onion, peeled and finely diced
2 garlic cloves, peeled and finely chopped
Pinch of ground cumin
Pinch of ground cinnamon
½ tsp paprika
10 ounces ground beef
Sea salt and freshly ground black pepper
¼ cup pitted green olives, chopped
1 tsp dried oregano
½ tsp dried chile flakes
Pinch of sugar

2 hard-boiled eggs, finely chopped
1 large egg, beaten

FOR THE CHIMICHURRI SAUCE
Leaves of 1 bunch of flat-leaf parsley
3 garlic cloves, peeled
1 Tbsp chopped fresh oregano leaves,
   or 1 tsp dried oregano
1 tsp dried chile flakes, to taste
1 Tbsp red wine vinegar
1 Tbsp lemon juice
5 Tbsp olive oil
Salt and freshly ground black pepper

1. Roll out both blocks of pastry to a thickness of ⅛ inch and cut out 18 discs, using a 4-inch cutter or saucer. Cover the discs with plastic wrap and chill while you prepare the filling.

2. Heat a saucepan over medium heat and add a little olive oil. Sweat the onion and garlic gently for about 5 minutes until soft but not colored. Add the cumin, cinnamon, and paprika and stir until aromatic.

3. Add the beef, season with salt and pepper, and cook for about 5 minutes until lightly browned. Mix in the olives, oregano, chile flakes, sugar, and hard-boiled eggs. Taste and adjust the seasoning as necessary. Leave to cool.

4. Once the beef has cooled, spoon about 1 tablespoon onto each pastry disc, leaving a ¼-inch border around the edge. Brush beaten egg around half the border, then fold the pastry over and press the edges together to seal and create a half-moon shape. Crimp the edges, removing any air pockets as you go.

5. Chill the empanadas for 20 minutes to firm up. Meanwhile, preheat the oven to 350°F.

6. Place the empanadas on a baking sheet. Make a steam hole in the top of each one with a skewer, then brush with beaten egg. Bake in the preheated oven for 18–20 minutes until the pastry is golden brown.

7. Meanwhile, make the chimichurri. Place the parsley, garlic, and fresh oregano (if using) in a small food processor and roughly chop. Add the rest of the ingredients and process briefly to combine. Taste and season with salt and pepper. (If using dried oregano, add it at this stage.)

8. Once the empanadas are cooked, cool on a wire rack. Serve warm or at room temperature with the chimichurri on the side to spoon over or dip into.

EASY CHICKEN PASTILLA
SERVES 4

Chicken instead of beef, filo pastry instead of puff, but the concept is the same as for the empanada. In Morocco, where the pastilla originated, they are fond of mixing sweetness and spice in savory dishes—hence the combination of cinnamon, sugar, and almonds in these delicate parcels.

4 skinless, boneless chicken thighs
Olive oil
Sea salt and freshly ground black pepper
1 onion, peeled and thinly sliced
¾-inch piece of fresh ginger, peeled and finely chopped
1 tsp ground cinnamon, plus extra to dust
Pinch of sugar
¾ cup chicken stock

3 eggs, lightly beaten
3 ounces toasted flaked almonds
2 Tbsp butter, melted
10 sheets filo pastry
Confectioners' sugar and/or extra ground cinnamon for dusting (optional), to serve

1. Preheat the oven to 400°F.

2. First cook the chicken. Place the thighs in a roasting pan, drizzle with oil, and season with salt and pepper. Roast in the preheated oven for 35 minutes until golden brown and cooked through. Set aside to cool, but keep the oven on. When the thighs are cool enough to handle, chop them into bite-sized pieces.

3. Heat a wide pan over medium heat and add a dash of oil. Sweat the onion and ginger for 8 minutes until softened. Stir in the cinnamon and sugar. Add the chicken, season with salt and pepper, and cover with the stock. Bring to a simmer and cook for 5 minutes so that the stock is reduced by half. Stir the eggs into the chicken mixture as the stock reduces so that they are well combined. When the stock is reduced, add the almonds, then taste and adjust the seasoning as necessary. Leave to cool.

4. Brush a 9-inch cake pan or pie plate with some of the melted butter. Line the dish with 4 sheets of filo, brushing melted butter between each layer and letting the ends of the filo drape over the sides.

5. Place half the chicken mixture in the pastry cases, then cover with 4 more sheets of filo, brushing with butter and overlapping the edges as before. Flatten down and spoon in the remaining chicken mixture. Cover with the remaining sheets of filo, brushing with melted butter between the layers. Fold the overhanging filo onto the top of the pie, tucking any other edges into the sides. Give one final brush with melted butter before placing in the preheated oven. Cook for 10–15 minutes until golden and crisp on top.

6. Remove from the oven, place a plate over the dish, and, using an oven mitt, flip the dish upside down to turn out the pastilla. Slide it from the plate onto a nonstick baking sheet. The bottom should now be facing up. Continue to cook for an additional 5–10 minutes until golden.

7. Remove and cool before serving, dusted with a little confectioners' sugar and extra cinnamon if you like.

FLATBREADS WITH LEMON THYME RICOTTA

SERVES 2–4

Flatbreads are the simplest of all breads to make because, as the name suggests, you don't need any leavener at all. They are simply a mix of flour, water, and oil, and are cooked on the stovetop or a fire rather than in an oven. I've added sautéed leeks to the dough here for extra interest. Serve with any curry or Lebanese rice dish, or simply with ricotta, lemon, and thyme.

1 leek, trimmed and halved lengthwise
1 Tbsp butter
3 Tbsp olive oil
Sea salt and freshly ground black pepper
2 cups all-purpose flour, plus extra for dusting

TO SERVE
¾ cup ricotta cheese
1 thyme sprig, leaves only
Zest of ½ lemon

1. Thinly slice the leek into half-moons. Sauté in a medium-hot pan with the butter, a tablespoon of the oil, and some salt and pepper. Cook for 3–4 minutes until tender and wilted. Remove from the heat.

2. Meanwhile, mix together the flour, the remaining olive oil, and a couple of pinches of salt and pepper. Add the leeks and bring the mixture together with approximately ½ cup warm water, being careful to mix in any lumps of flour thoroughly. If the mixture is too sticky, add a little more flour.

3. Knead the dough for 2–3 minutes on a clean floured work surface until smooth and elastic. Cover and leave to rest for 20 minutes.

4. Divide the rested dough into 4 balls and roll these out on a floured work surface until ⅛ inch thick.

5. Heat a dry, nonstick frying pan and cook the flatbreads one at a time over medium heat for 1–2 minutes on each side until they begin to bubble slightly and turn golden brown. Keep warm and cook the remaining flatbreads in the same way.

6. Serve the flatbreads warm with spoonfuls of ricotta and sprinkled with thyme leaves and lemon zest along with a pinch of salt and pepper.

FRESH GINGER SPONGE CAKE

MAKES 8 SLICES

Every cook should master how to make a light, even sponge. Once you have, you can use it as a canvas for any flavors you like. Chocolate and ginger is a classic combination that works really well here.

¾ cup (1½ sticks) butter, at room temperature, plus extra for greasing
1½ cups all-purpose flour, plus extra for dusting
¾ cup sugar
3 eggs
1 tsp vanilla extract
1 tsp baking powder
About 2 Tbsp milk, to loosen, if needed

FOR THE ICING
7 ounces chocolate, finely chopped
2 Tbsp unsalted butter
¼ cup heavy cream
2 Tbsp dark corn syrup

FOR THE GINGER CREAM FILLING
1¼ cups heavy cream
2 Tbsp confectioners' sugar
1-inch piece of fresh ginger, peeled and finely grated

1. Preheat the oven to 350°F. Lightly butter and flour a deep 8-inch removable-bottomed cake pan.

2. Cream the butter and sugar until light and fluffy. Beat in the eggs one at a time, add the vanilla extract, and mix well.

3. Sift in the flour and baking powder and fold in gently using a spatula until completely combined. Add a little milk, if necessary, to create a batter of dropping consistency.

4. Pour the mixture into the cake pan, smoothing it down with the back of a spatula. Knock the pan on the work surface to get rid of any air pockets and to create a level batter. Bake in the preheated oven for 25 minutes until golden and just firm to the touch.

5. To test if the cake is cooked, insert a knife or metal skewer into the middle: it should come out clean. Remove from the oven and leave to cool in the pan for 10 minutes before turning out onto a wire rack to cool completely.

6. Make the icing while the cake is baking because it needs to thicken for 30 minutes before use. (If it is too runny, it will pour off the sides and look messy.) Put the chocolate and butter into a heatproof bowl. Place the cream and corn syrup in a saucepan and stir over medium heat until they come just to a boil. Pour immediately into the bowl, stirring until the chocolate and butter have completely melted, and the mixture is thick and glossy. Set aside.

7. To make the filling, whip the cream and confectioners' sugar to soft peaks, then mix in the ginger.

8. Once the sponge is cool, cut it in half horizontally. Spread the ginger cream over one half, then place the other half on top, pressing down lightly to push the cream to the edges.

9. Using a spatula, spread the icing over the cake and allow to set before serving.

HOMEMADE CRUMPET

SERVES 2–4

Dripping with butter and jam, crumpets were the sort of teatime treat we Brits all grew up with and loved. Making individual crumpets can be a hassle, so it's much more fun to make a giant one to share. Topped with a quick homemade strawberry jam and a dollop of crème fraîche, the crumpet truly is worth rediscovering.

1½ cups white bread flour
¼ tsp salt
Pinch of sugar
½ tsp baking soda
1 tsp active dry yeast
½ cup milk mixed with ⅔ cup water, warmed to 105–115°F
Neutral oil
Butter
Crème fraîche, to serve

FOR THE QUICK STRAWBERRY JAM
2 heaping Tbsp sugar
1½ cups strawberries, hulled and sliced in half
Zest of 1 lemon and juice of ¼
½–1 tsp balsamic vinegar

HOW TO MAKE INDIVIDUAL CRUMPETS
If you want to make several small crumpets, drop individual spoonfuls of the batter into the pan and reduce the cooking time to 7–10 minutes before flipping over. You might want to use a greased metal ring or cookie cutter to help hold the mixture and prevent the crumpets from coming out too thin.

1. Sift the flour, salt, sugar, and baking soda into a bowl. Make a well in the middle, add the yeast, and slowly pour in the warm milk and water mixture. Draw the flour into the center, mixing thoroughly, and beat to a thick batter. (You may need to add up to another ½ cup warm water if the mixture is very thick.) Whisk for a couple of minutes until smooth. Cover with a clean dish towel and leave to rise in a warm place for about 1 hour, until it has almost doubled in size and has a spongy consistency.

2. Meanwhile, make the jam. Heat the sugar in a frying pan over medium–high heat for 3–4 minutes until caramelized and golden. Turn the heat down and add the strawberries, coating them in the caramel. Cook for about 10 minutes until the strawberries are tender and collapsing slightly and the sauce is nice and syrupy. Add the lemon zest and juice followed by a drizzle of balsamic vinegar. Continue to heat for 5–7 minutes until the mixture has reduced to the consistency of jam. Leave to cool.

3. Heat a very large nonstick frying pan (or use 2 medium pans) over medium heat and add a little oil. Stir the batter and pour into the pan. Cook for 10–15 minutes on low heat to prevent burning until the batter is dry and the surface is set with little holes. Dot a few little pieces of butter around the outside edge of the crumpet, and when it has melted, flip the crumpet over and cook on the other side for 5 minutes, until lightly browned.

4. Serve the crumpet with the quick strawberry jam and crème fraîche.

LEMON POLENTA CAKE

SERVES 16

This is a classic cake that works well as an afternoon snack but even better as a dessert served with a spoonful of mascarpone or crème fraîche spiked with vanilla seeds. The almonds give the cake a moistness you just don't get with flour, and the polenta contributes a slight crunch as well as a rich yellow color.

2¼ sticks unsalted butter, softened, plus extra
   for greasing
½ cup fine polenta
1 tsp baking powder
Pinch of sea salt
2 cups almond flour
1½ cups sugar
3 large eggs
Zest of 3 lemons and juice of 2
1 vanilla pod, split

1. Preheat the oven to 350°F. Butter a 9-inch round cake pan and line with wax paper.

2. Mix the polenta, baking powder, salt, and almond flour in a bowl and set aside.

3. Using an electric mixer or wooden spoon, beat together the butter and 1 cup of the sugar for 5–10 minutes until light and fluffy. Lightly beat the eggs, then beat them into the butter mixture a spoonful at a time, making sure it is well incorporated before adding the next spoonful. (If the mixture looks like it's splitting, beat in a spoonful of the polenta mixture before continuing with the eggs.)

4. When the eggs have been combined, beat in the polenta mixture. Finally, add the lemon zest and the juice of 1 lemon.

5. Bake in the preheated oven for 40–60 minutes until golden brown and just firm to the touch. To test if the cake is cooked, insert a knife or metal skewer into the middle: it should come out clean and the edge of the cake should come away easily from the side of the pan. Remove from the oven and leave to cool in the pan.

6. Make a syrup by heating the remaining lemon juice and sugar with the vanilla pod in a saucepan until the sugar has dissolved. Remove the vanilla pod and save for another use. Prick the top of the cake with a fork and pour the syrup over it. Leave to cool completely before turning out of the pan.

LEMON THYME SHORTBREAD

MAKES ABOUT 24 FINGERS

You can add all sorts of flavorings to shortbread, from vanilla and cocoa powder to hazelnuts and almonds. Herbs are good too: rosemary and lavender both work well, as does lemon thyme, which gives the shortbread a lovely delicate perfume.

2½ cups all-purpose flour, plus extra for rolling
¼ tsp fine sea salt
1 cup (2 sticks) unsalted butter, softened, plus extra for greasing
⅔ cup superfine sugar, plus extra to sprinkle
2 Tbsp finely chopped lemon thyme

1. Sift the flour into a bowl with the salt and set aside. Put the butter and sugar in a mixing bowl and beat with an electric mixer until smooth and creamy.

2. Turn the mixer to its lowest setting and, with the motor running, add the lemon thyme, then the flour, a little at a time, until combined. Shape into a flattened ball with your hands, wrap in plastic wrap, and chill for at least 20 minutes.

3. Meanwhile, preheat the oven to 325°F.

4. For shortbread fingers, gently pack the dough into a lightly buttered Swiss roll pan (roughly 12 x 8 inches). Score the surface to mark out the fingers and prick all over with a fork. If you want to make circular cookies, roll out the dough on a lightly floured work surface to ¼ inch thick, then stamp out the rounds using a 2½-inch cutter. (You can gather together the scraps and reroll them once.) Transfer to 2 lightly buttered baking sheets, leaving a little space between the cookies, then prick them with a fork.

5. Bake for 15–20 minutes until pale golden, checking often as ovens vary and the shortbread can easily burn. Cool in the pan or on the sheet until firm, then transfer to a wire rack to cool completely.

6. Sprinkle with superfine sugar, if you like, and store in an airtight container.

INDULGENT MINI CHOCOLATE TARTS WITH PEANUT BRITTLE

MAKES 8

These small chocolate tarts are fantastic for a midafternoon break, the perfect combination of rich, crumbly pastry, smooth ganache, and crunchy peanut topping. It's so easy to make your own sweet pastry in a processor, but store-bought pastry made with all butter will work as well.

Oil, for greasing
14 ounces dark chocolate, broken up
½ cup heavy cream
4 Tbsp butter, cubed
2 Tbsp sugar (optional)

FOR THE SWEET PASTRY
½ cup (1 stick) butter, chilled and cut into pieces
½ cup sugar
1 egg
1¾ cups all-purpose flour, plus extra for dusting

FOR THE PEANUT BRITTLE
⅔ cup sugar
1½ cups salted peanuts, roughly chopped

1. First make the pastry. Combine the butter and sugar in a food processor and process until just combined. Add the egg and process for 30 seconds. Add the flour and process for a few seconds until the dough just comes together (add 1 tablespoon of cold water if it seems too dry). Knead lightly on a floured surface, then shape into a flat disc. Wrap in plastic wrap and chill for at least 30 minutes.

2. Preheat the oven to 375°F. Lightly grease ten 3-inch fluted removable-bottom mini tart pans. Roll out the pastry ⅛ inch thick on a floured work surface and cut out 8 small discs using a 5-inch fluted cutter. Line the pans with the pastry, allowing it to overhang the edges, then prick the base with a fork and let rest for at least 20 minutes in the fridge. (They should be really firm and cold so they don't burn when they are baked.)

3. Bake the rested tart cases on a baking sheet in the preheated oven for 12 minutes until golden. Use a sharp knife to trim off the excess pastry, then cool the cases in their pans on a wire rack.

4. While the tarts are cooking, make the peanut brittle. Line a baking sheet with wax paper or a lightly oiled sheet of foil. Put the sugar into a dry wide frying pan over medium-high heat for 3–4 minutes and allow it to caramelize without stirring. Once the caramel begins to form, swirl it around the pan to make sure it colors evenly. After 2–3 minutes, when it's beginning to turn light brown, add the peanuts and swirl to coat. Pour onto the prepared baking sheet, tilting it so that the peanut mixture spreads out thinly and evenly. It should harden almost immediately. Set aside for about 10 minutes to cool.

5. Meanwhile, make the chocolate ganache. Put the chocolate, cream, butter, and sugar if using, into a heatproof bowl and place over a pan of gently boiling water for 7–8 minutes, stirring to combine once melted. (Taste and add a little more sugar if you prefer a sweeter ganache.)

6. Spoon the ganache mixture into the cooled tart cases and top with broken shards of peanut brittle. (Save the remaining brittle for snacking.) Chill for 20 minutes, then serve.

MALT CHOCOLATE DOUGHNUTS

MAKES 12

I know deep-fried doughnuts don't strictly count as baking, but I've included them here because they start with a dough, and they taste too good to leave out, especially made with a chocolate ganache filling instead of the usual jam.

¼ cup sugar, plus 2–3 heaping Tbsp
   for dusting
⅔ cup whole milk
One ¼-ounce package active dry yeast
3½ Tbsp unsalted butter
2½ cups all-purpose flour, plus extra for dusting
Pinch of sea salt
2 egg yolks
2–3 heaping Tbsp malt powder, such as Ovaltine,
   for dusting
Vegetable oil, for deep-frying

FOR THE FILLING
1 cup heavy cream
2–4 Tbsp runny honey, to taste
9 ounces dark chocolate, chopped
4 Tbsp unsalted cold butter, cubed

1. Heat the sugar and milk in a pan for about 5 minutes until the milk is warm—105–115°F—and the sugar has dissolved. Place the yeast into a bowl, pour in half the warm milk, then mix and set aside. Place the remaining milk back on the heat and add the butter. Heat gently for about 3 minutes (be careful not to let the milk boil).

2. Sift the flour and salt into a large bowl and make a well in the center. Add the egg yolks, yeasted milk, and the hot milk. Mix together, drawing in the surrounding flour to make a dough.

3. Tip the dough onto a floured work surface and knead with floured hands for a few minutes until the dough is smooth and elastic. Dust with a little extra

flour if the mix is too sticky. Place in a clean bowl dusted with flour. Cover with plastic wrap to keep the dough from forming a skin on top and leave to rise in a warm place for 1–1½ hours until doubled in size.

4. When the dough has risen, knock it back by giving it a thump and knead lightly on a floured work surface. Roll out the dough with a floured rolling pin to a thickness of about ¾ inch and shape it into a 9 x 6-inch rectangle. Using a sharp knife, cut the dough into 12 rectangular pillows, then place on a baking sheet lined with parchment paper and leave to rise again for 30–40 minutes until doubled in size. (This will make the doughnuts light and fluffy once cooked.)

5. Meanwhile, make the filling. Put the cream in a pan and mix in the honey to taste. Put the chocolate and butter into a heatproof bowl. When the cream is almost boiling, pour it over the chocolate mixture and stir until well mixed, smooth, and glossy.

6. Combine the remaining sugar with the malt powder in a bowl and set aside. Put the oil in a deep-fat fryer and heat to 340°F, or fill a large saucepan one third full with vegetable oil and heat over medium-high heat until a cube of bread dropped in it sizzles and turns golden brown in 30 seconds. Fry the doughnuts, in batches, for 3–4 minutes until evenly golden brown and cooked through, turning them in the oil once or twice. (You will need to moderate the heat between batches according to whether the doughnuts brown too quickly or too slowly.) Using a slotted spoon, remove the doughnuts from the hot oil and roll in the malt sugar to coat.

7. To fill the doughnuts, spoon the warm chocolate filling into a piping bag fitted with a small plain nozzle. Make sure you pipe the chocolate filling while it's still warm. If it cools down too much, it will set and be difficult to work with. Insert the nozzle into the doughnut and gently squeeze in the filling. Serve right away.

BASIC
SKILLS

WHAT IT SOMETIMES TAKES EVEN PROFESSIONAL CHEFS AWHILE TO LEARN IS THAT COOKING IS A CRAFT RATHER THAN AN ART.

By that I mean it is about learning a set of rules, the right way to do things, rather than simply flying by the seat of your pants. The vast majority of what you do in a kitchen is based on a series of basic techniques that come up again and again, and it's not until you have understood and mastered these core skills that you can start to experiment a bit more and get creative.

During the filming of my TV series *Kitchen Nightmares* a few years back, when I'd travel the country putting failing restaurants back on their feet, the biggest problem I came across was chefs who were trying to run before they could walk. They'd come into the kitchen full of swagger and start trying to stamp their personality on the menu, yet they had no idea how to do the most basic things like cook an omelette or make a stock. There they were, trying to reinvent the Caesar salad with scallops or lobster, and yet they couldn't even dress the salad properly. They were putting out truffled wild mushroom lasagne but didn't know how to make a béchamel sauce.

They were on their way to nowhere, of course. All cooking has to be underpinned by an understanding of the basics. These are the building blocks you need to construct a dish. And, like any building, without them your cooking will always fall flat. In this chapter you'll find nine recipes that demonstrate different techniques or processes that come up again and again in cooking. Whether it's poaching an egg or making a beautiful glossy mayonnaise, these are skills needed in countless recipes. Get them right and you'll already be a better cook than an alarming number of so-called professionals.

POACHING EGGS

This seems to defeat so many people, but couldn't be simpler, provided you follow a couple of rules. First, use really fresh eggs. The fresher the egg, the more viscous the white will be, and the better it will cling to the yolk. Second, use a deep saucepan of very gently simmering water: deep because the egg will take longer to fall through the water, which will give more time for the white to set around the yolk, gently simmering because a rolling boil will disperse the white and make it rise to the surface in a horrible scum. You can, as an extra precaution, add a splash of white wine vinegar to the water, which helps the white to coagulate, but it shouldn't be necessary if you get the other elements right—and there's always the danger you'll taste it in the final dish.

Once your water is simmering, crack the egg into a cup and use a slotted spoon to swirl the water around, like a mini-whirlpool, creating a well in the center. Now, very gently, ease the egg into the water. It should be carried by the current and slowly spin to the bottom. Don't drop it from too high or the yolk will fall through the white: the idea is that it becomes enrobed as it falls. You can cook up to four eggs at a time, but make sure the water is spinning before you add each one. You can either cook these fully at this point, for 3–4 minutes, or do as we do in the restaurants and remove them after 1½–2 minutes and "shock" them in iced water to stop the cooking process. Then you can drain them on paper towels and trim the white to neaten them up. Cover them with plastic wrap and store in the fridge until needed. To reheat, either plunge them into boiling water for a minute; or baste them in hot butter, perhaps flavored with thyme or scallions, in a pan, for a richer, creamier result.

The recipe for Noodle Soup with Poached Egg (page 294) is an opportunity to practice your poaching technique.

SOUFFLÉS

Soufflés are one of those dishes that people can't help but be impressed by. They see that beautifully risen crust and assume they are in the presence of a master chef. It's true that soufflés take a certain amount of practice and confidence to pull off, but they are not actually that difficult.

The secret is to make sure that the egg whites are folded evenly through the mixture for an even rise, but to take care that you don't knock the air out of them while doing so. The other trick is to apply a double layer of softened butter to the ramekins in upward strokes. This will also encourage the soufflés to rise evenly. You can then dust the butter with flour, grated chocolate, blended dried blueberries— whatever suits the style of soufflé. If you get your soufflé mixture to the right consistency, it will hold in the fridge for up to 1½ hours, so you can make it before your guests arrive and cook it at the last minute. The final trick before cooking is to run your finger around the edge of the soufflé to make a slight indent just inside the rim. This also will help it to rise. Try the recipe on page 293.

ROUX

The Macaroni and Cauliflower Bake with Three Cheeses (page 297) incorporates one of the most important kitchen skills, namely, making a béchamel or white sauce. You'll come across this again and again in things such as moussaka, lasagne, or fish pies. You combine equal parts butter and flour in a pan and cook them together over medium heat until they turn golden, then you add your liquid—normally milk or stock. The secret for a smooth sauce is to add the liquid very gradually, especially at the beginning, and to whisk it in completely after each addition. If you add all the liquid at once, it is much harder to get rid of any lumps. Once all the liquid has been incorporated, the sauce needs to be gently simmered to cook out the flavor of raw flour.

OMELETTES

The secret to any good omelette is to use a lightly oiled heavy-bottomed pan. Add a bit of butter and only once it starts to foam do you add the eggs. Then you stir the eggs constantly to beat in some air, and tilt the pan from side to side to make any uncooked egg run to the sides. If you are adding lots of fillings to your omelette—ham, leeks, tomato, or bacon, for example—make sure these are all well caramelized *before* you add the lightly beaten eggs, which will cook in 2–3 minutes. I tend to use a fork to gently stir the mixture to make sure it is evenly distributed. Once the top is almost set but still moist and creamy (we call it *baveuse* in professional kitchens), lift the edges of the omelette to see if you have gotten a touch of color on the bottom and then take right off the heat.

The traditional way to serve an omelette is folded three ways. You tilt the pan away from you and flip the edge closest to the handle to the middle, and then roll the omelette so it folds over itself. But to be honest, I often don't bother. There's nothing wrong with an open omelette, especially if you've got a nice vibrant filling such as shrimp, feta, and tomato (see page 298).

MAYONNAISE

It's worth learning how to make a basic mayonnaise because it is such a versatile condiment that you can take in so many directions. I'll often flavor mine with basil or tarragon, garlic, lemon, lime, capers, watercress—even anchovies (see the lovely variation on page 305).

You start with your egg yolks, vinegar, mustard, and salt and then very gradually add your oil, whisking furiously all the time, to create a rich, thick sauce. The greatest danger is that your sauce will "split" (it will look curdled and the oil won't emulsify with the egg yolk). To prevent this from happening, make sure your ingredients are all at room temperature to begin with, and add the oil almost drop by drop at the beginning and never at more than a slow trickle. If the worst does happen, simply beat another egg yolk in a clean bowl and slowly add your split mixture, whisking all the time. It will soon come together and re-emulsify.

You can use any oil you like in mayonnaise. I find extra virgin olive too rich and overpowering so I like to use peanut, which has a very neutral flavor. An additional way to make it less cloying is to thin it out at the end with a couple of tablespoons of iced water. This will not only make it a nice white color, but means it will coat salad greens more easily.

CHICKEN STOCK

Classic French cooking used to rely on lots of heavily reduced veal and beef stocks, but the fashion now is to use more chicken stock, which gives a far lighter result. This is good news for the home cook because of all the stocks, chicken is the easiest to make, yet will absolutely transform your cooking. There are times when you can just about get away with a good stock cube—making gravy, for example, where the pan juices will already have plenty of meaty oomph—but nothing comes close to providing the same body and depth of flavor that you get from a proper homemade stock. If you eat a lot of chicken in your house, the biggest favor you can do yourself is always to buy whole birds, use the meat as you want—roasted whole or cut up as you need it (see page 85)—and then use the carcass to make the most fantastic versatile stock. This will be your secret weapon, your way of injecting so much more flavor into your cooking—and, as I've said elsewhere, that is half the battle. The Spiced Lentil Soup on page 301 is a good example of using stock to great effect, as the lentils readily take up the extra flavor it provides.

There are two styles of chicken stock: white and brown. White is made with uncooked carcasses and vegetables, and produces a much paler, more delicate stock, which is used for light broths, risottos, and the like, where you are looking for a lighter flavor. Brown stock is made with roasted carcasses and vegetables, sometimes with the addition of tomato purée. The result is much richer and more intense, and is great for sauces, stews, and hearty soups such as French onion. Both are made in roughly the same way. I reckon on making about a quart of stock from one carcass.

For a white stock, place your carcass bones plus any white vegetables in a large saucepan. Onions, leeks, celery, garlic, and turnips are all good additions, but not potatoes as they'll make the final stock cloudy. Add a bay leaf, a sprig of thyme, and a few peppercorns, then pour in just enough cold water to cover the carcass, and slowly bring it all to a simmer. The water must be cold to begin with so that any fat will solidify and rise to the surface, where you can skim it off. Bring the stock to the gentlest simmer, so you can see just the occasional bubble breaking the surface, and cook for up to 4 hours, skimming foam from the surface regularly. Pass the finished stock through a sieve, leave to cool, and keep in the fridge for up to a week or in the freezer for up to three months.

A brown stock is made in just the same way, but you need to roast the carcass and vegetables first. Place the carcass in a roasting pan and roast for 15 minutes at 400°F, then dust it with a couple of tablespoons of flour and cook for another 5 minutes. The flour will not only act as a thickening agent, but will also absorb the fat and keep your stock from being greasy. Meanwhile, chop your vegetables into rough chunks (this time including carrots if you like, as well), and sauté them in oil in your stockpot for a few minutes, stirring regularly, until golden. Add a tablespoon or two of puréed tomatoes or a small squeeze of concentrated tomato purée, and cook for 5 minutes. Then add the roasted bones and continue as for white chicken stock, but cook for about 1 hour instead of 4.

VINAIGRETTE

A vinaigrette is so much more than just a dressing for salad. We use it in my restaurants to finish anything from fish, and even meat, to spring vegetables (see the recipe on page 302). It's a lovely way of bringing freshness to a dish and is much healthier than covering everything in butter. You can also use it to mark the seasons, adding citrus flavors in the summer and robust herbs like rosemary and thyme in the winter. It helps to think of it more as a seasoning than just a dressing.

A classic vinaigrette is made with 3–4 parts olive oil to 1 part white wine vinegar, but that is only the starting point. You can change the oil—sesame, hazelnut, canola; change the vinegar—red wine, balsamic, sherry, lemon juice; change the flavorings— shallots, red pepper, mustard, honey, lemongrass, garlic. There really is no end. Sometimes I find using all olive oil too heavy. It becomes cloying and almost sticks to the roof of your mouth. When you have some beautiful young salad greens, the last thing you want to do is kill them with a heavy vinaigrette, so I usually substitute a third of the olive oil with some sunflower or peanut oil to thin it out a bit. I'll even sometimes add 2 or 3 tablespoons of iced water, which is a really nice way of lightening the vinaigrette even more and means a salad will stay fresh longer.

HOLLANDAISE SAUCE

Hollandaise is best known for that breakfast classic of eggs Benedict, but is also great with cold trout or salmon and steamed vegetables. Like vinaigrette, you can steer it in plenty of different directions by adding different citrus flavors—grapefruit or lemon, for example—or different herbs (see the recipe for Asparagus with Lemon and Tarragon Hollandaise, page 306). With mint it makes a particularly good accompaniment to barbecued lamb.

For a traditional hollandaise, you whisk egg yolks with a splash of water and white wine vinegar in a bowl set over a pan of boiling water. Once it is pale and creamy and forms ribbons, you remove it from the heat and whisk in large quantities of clarified butter (where the milk solids and fat have been separated by gentle heating). The key is to keep the sauce warm until you serve it as once it cools, it will solidify and will be very difficult to make creamy again.

In truth, very few chefs still make hollandaise in this way, but use olive oil instead of butter to make a kind of cooked mayonnaise. This results in a much more practical and stable sauce and it's also less cloying. I like to dilute it more with lemon juice or water at the end.

CUSTARD

Making a proper egg custard is one of the things that really mark out a competent home cook. It's worth perfecting as it is the base for so many things, from ice cream to crème patissière, and the difference between homemade and instant is like night and day. Making your own also allows you to flavor it as you like by infusing the milk with mint, lemongrass, basil, bay leaves, rosemary, thyme, cinnamon, star anise…you name it. (Also see the recipe for Lemongrass Custard Cups on page 309.)

There are three golden rules here. First, when you bring your milk and cream to a boil, make sure you take it off the heat the moment it starts to bubble. Even another 30 seconds will completely change the consistency and stop the custard from thickening. Second, don't add the sugar to the egg yolks until the last second before you are ready to whisk in the milk; otherwise, the sugar will dissolve into the egg and lose the strength that you need to make the custard thicken as you heat it.

The third, and most important, rule is not to allow the egg mixture to boil. If it does, you'll end up with a pan of sweet scrambled eggs. Most cookbooks will advise you to thicken your custard in a bain-marie, a bowl set over a pan of boiling water. The idea is that the indirect heat makes it less likely to boil. The trouble is, you'll be there for 20 minutes waiting for it to thicken, and can easily get distracted at the key moment. I think the quicker you cook it, the safer it is. That means in a saucepan over direct heat, stirring constantly and making sure you really get into the corners of the pan to keep all the custard moving and avoiding any hot spots. If you keep it moving, it will always thicken before it overheats, so provided you take it off the heat as soon as it starts to coat the back of your spoon and you immediately pour the custard through a sieve into another bowl standing by, you'll have a perfectly smooth, thickened custard.

ORANGE SOUFFLÉS

SERVES 4

Soufflés have a reputation for being difficult to pull off, but they really aren't so long as you fold the egg whites carefully into the base so they retain their air, and you have your oven at the right temperature. My other trick is to apply a double layer of softened butter to the ramekins in upward strokes to help them rise evenly. If you get the soufflé mixture to the right consistency, it will hold in the fridge for up to 1½ hours, so you can make it in advance and bake it just when you need to.

⅔ cup milk
½ cup heavy cream
½ cup sugar
3 large egg yolks
2 Tbsp all-purpose flour
4 tsp cornstarch

3 Tbsp unsalted softened butter, for brushing
1 ounce dark chocolate, finely grated
4 large egg whites
Zest and juice of 1 large lemon
Zest and juice of 1 orange
Confectioners' sugar, for dusting

1. Begin by making the soufflé base. Pour the milk and cream into a pan. Bring to the scalding point (just below boiling), then remove from the heat. Place half the sugar in a bowl, add the egg yolks, and whisk until pale and thick. Sift in the flour and cornstarch and whisk again. Gradually add the scalded milk, whisking as you go.

2. Pour the mixture back into the pan and place over low heat. Stir constantly with a wooden spoon for about 5 minutes until it thickens to a smooth, velvety consistency. Leave to cool to room temperature.

3. Brush four 8-ounce soufflé molds or ramekins with the softened butter, applied in upward vertical strokes. If your molds have a rim, make sure the butter covers this as well. Chill for a few minutes, then repeat with a second layer of butter. Sprinkle some of the grated chocolate into each mold, shaking it around to cover the inside completely. Tip out any excess and chill the molds until needed.

4. Preheat the oven to 400°F.

5. Put the egg whites in a bowl and whisk until they hold stiff peaks. Add a few drops of lemon juice to stabilize and whisk again. Gradually add the remaining sugar, a spoonful at a time, whisking constantly until you have a very thick and glossy mixture.

6. Whisk the lemon and orange zest into the soufflé base. Mix the lemon and orange juice together, measure out ½ cup, then whisk it in as well. Whisk a third of the egg white mixture into the soufflé base to loosen it. Carefully fold in the rest of the egg whites with a large metal spoon until evenly distributed. Fill each mold to the top and tap each one once on the work surface to get rid of any air bubbles.

7. Smooth the surface with a small palette knife. Run the tip of your finger around the inside edge of the molds to separate the mixture from the dish, then place on a baking sheet. Bake in the middle of the oven for 15–20 minutes or until risen with a slight wobble in the middle. Dust with confectioners' sugar and serve right away.

NOODLE SOUP WITH POACHED EGG

SERVES 2

In Asia they often finish off noodle or rice dishes with eggs, be they cooked in a wok or, as here, in a broth. This is a great dish for practicing your egg poaching skills (see page 288) as it doesn't matter if they break into strands.

2 Tbsp light/white miso paste, to taste
¾-inch piece of fresh ginger, peeled and grated
3 dried shiitake mushrooms, rehydrated then sliced
Soy sauce, to taste
4 ounces portobello mushrooms
8 ounces fresh noodles, such as udon
3 ounces baby spinach leaves
2 eggs
2 scallions, trimmed and finely chopped,
    to garnish

1. Pour 3 cups water into a saucepan and bring to a simmer over medium heat. Add the miso paste, ginger, sliced shiitake mushrooms, and a dash of soy sauce and simmer gently for 5 minutes to flavor.

2. Finely slice the portobello mushrooms. Divide them equally, along with the noodles and spinach, between 2 warm serving bowls. Pour over a ladleful of stock to wilt the spinach, and keep warm.

3. Break the eggs into individual ramekins or mugs and drop one at a time into the gently simmering stock. Poach for 2–3 minutes (it doesn't matter if they break up slightly).

4. Spoon the eggs into the serving bowls with a slotted spoon and pour the stock around them, dividing the shiitake mushrooms equally between the bowls.

5. Serve garnished with scallions and with extra soy sauce on the side to flavor as needed.

MACARONI AND CAULIFLOWER BAKE WITH THREE CHEESES

SERVES 4

This is my twist on the classic mac 'n' cheese, using a trio of cheeses. Sharp Cheddar adds a tangy depth of flavor to the base, while the Gruyère and Monterey Jack cheeses melt into a smooth and creamy sauce (a good opportunity to practice your roux technique, see page 289).

10 ounces cauliflower florets
10 ounces dried macaroni
4 Tbsp butter, plus a few extra chunks
¼ cup all-purpose flour
2 tsp English mustard powder
2½ cups whole milk
Pinch of cayenne pepper
Sea salt, to taste
4 ounces sharp Cheddar cheese, grated
3 ounces Gruyère cheese, grated
4 ounces Monterey Jack cheese, grated
3 Tbsp fresh white breadcrumbs
1 Tbsp thyme leaves

1. Bring a large pan of well-salted water to a boil. Add the cauliflower and cook for 4–5 minutes until tender. Remove with a slotted spoon and refresh in a bowl of ice-cold water to prevent it from cooking any further. Drain well.

2. Add the macaroni to the boiling salted water and cook until al dente, according to the package instructions. Drain, refresh under cold running water, and drain again. Mix the macaroni, cauliflower and a few chunks of butter together in a large bowl.

3. Preheat the oven to 400°F. Heat the 4 tablespoons butter in a pan, and stir in the flour and mustard powder to make a roux. Gradually add the milk, beating continuously with a balloon whisk until the mixture is smooth. Slowly bring to a boil over low heat, whisking frequently, until the mixture thickens. Season well with cayenne pepper and sea salt to taste.

4. Mix the three cheeses together and stir half into the white sauce. Mix well until the cheese has melted and the sauce is smooth again. Add the macaroni and cauliflower to the sauce and mix well to coat. Spread the mixture into a large, wide gratin dish.

5. Combine the remaining cheeses with the breadcrumbs and thyme leaves. Sprinkle over the top of the macaroni and cauliflower mixture. Bake for about 15–20 minutes until the topping is golden and crisp. Serve immediately.

SHRIMP AND FETA OMELETTE

SERVES 2

When you fill an omelette with so many good things, it makes no sense to fold it and hide them away. Just finish it off under the broiler and slip it from pan to plate.

Olive oil
1 ripe tomato, diced
1 scallion, trimmed and chopped
Sea salt and freshly ground black pepper
8 cooked large shrimp, peeled and deveined
    (see page 167)
Pinch of dried chile flakes, to taste
4 eggs, beaten
1 tsp chopped fresh oregano or pinch of
    dried oregano
2 ounces feta cheese, crumbled

1. Preheat the broiler to medium.

2. In a small frying pan, heat a dash of oil and add the tomato and scallion. Season with salt and pepper and cook over medium heat for 2–3 minutes or until the tomatoes are starting to break down. Add the shrimp and chile flakes, mix well to coat in the tomatoes, and cook for 1 minute to warm through.

3. Meanwhile, heat a broiler-safe frying pan over medium heat. Add a little oil and, when hot, pour in the beaten eggs, seasoning them well with salt and pepper first. Cook for 1–2 minutes until the underside of the egg is beginning to set but the top remains runny.

4. Sprinkle the oregano over the omelette, then pour the tomato and shrimp mixture over the top, making sure the shrimp are in an even layer. Crumble over the feta cheese, season with salt and pepper, and add a drizzle of oil.

5. Place the omelette under the hot broiler and broil for 2–3 minutes until the egg is just cooked through. Remove and serve.

SPICED LENTIL SOUP
SERVES 4

With a good chicken stock at its base, you don't need many ingredients to create a delicious soup. Red lentils, onion, garlic, tomato purée, and a few spices are all it takes to create this stunning winter warmer.

10 ounces split red lentils
2 Tbsp olive oil
1 large onion, peeled and finely chopped
2 large garlic cloves, peeled and finely chopped
1 tsp ground cumin
1 tsp ground coriander
2 tsp garam masala
1–2 tsp ground ginger
½ tsp ground turmeric
1 Tbsp tomato purée
3½ cups chicken stock
Sea salt and freshly ground black pepper

TO SERVE
3–4 Tbsp plain yogurt
Cilantro leaves

1. Rinse the lentils under cold running water in a colander, drain well, and set aside.

2. Heat the olive oil in a pan and add the onion and garlic. Sauté for 4–6 minutes until lightly golden. Stir in the ground spices and tomato purée and cook for another 2 minutes.

3. Add the lentils and pour in the stock to cover. Bring to a boil, then lower the heat and simmer, uncovered, for 25–30 minutes, stirring every now and then, until the lentils are very soft. (You may need to top up with a little more water toward the end of cooking if the soup seems too thick.) Taste and adjust the seasoning.

4. Ladle half of the soup into a blender and blend to a purée, then pour back into the pan. The soup should be somewhat chunky. Adjust the consistency again if necessary, adding a little boiling water to thin it down.

5. Ladle the soup into warm bowls and top with a spoonful of yogurt and a few cilantro leaves.

HOW TO MAKE THE MOST OF HERBS
Fresh herbs are a great way to add maximum flavor on a budget. Make them last longer by standing the stems in a glass of water. They'll keep this way for up to 2 weeks in the fridge.

ROASTED RED ONION VINAIGRETTE WITH GREEN BEAN SALAD

SERVES 4–6

A lovely salad that works any time of the year alongside grilled meat or fish. By roasting the onions first, you add another layer of flavor to the dressing, which would go equally well with potatoes or cauliflower. If you dress the vegetables while they are still warm, they'll take on more flavor still.

9 ounces green beans
4 ounces sugarsnap peas
Roughly chopped mint and parsley

FOR THE VINAIGRETTE
2 red onions, peeled
⅔ cup extra virgin olive oil, plus extra for roasting
2 thyme sprigs
1 garlic clove, peeled and crushed
Sea salt and freshly ground black pepper
¼ cup sherry vinegar

1. First make the vinaigrette. Preheat the oven to 425°F.

2. Place the onions in a roasting pan with a little olive oil, the thyme, garlic, and a little salt and roast for 25–30 minutes until the onions are completely cooked and have a nice roasted flavor.

3. Remove the onions from the pan and chop into rough dice (you want the dressing to have a rustic texture).

4. Mix the onions with the ⅔ cup extra virgin olive oil and the sherry vinegar and season with a little salt and pepper to taste.

5. To make the salad, blanch the beans and peas by plunging them in boiling salted water for 1½ minutes until their rawness has been removed but they are still crunchy. Refresh immediately in cold water, then remove and put onto paper towels to absorb the moisture. Cut each bean into bite-sized pieces.

6. Put the chopped beans into a large bowl, stir in the red onion dressing, and toss with the mint and parsley. Serve immediately in chilled salad bowls.

FRITTO MISTO WITH GARLIC AND SAFFRON MAYONNAISE

SERVES 4

Battered and fried seafood dipped into garlicky mayonnaise is one of my favorite summer holiday dishes. But if you find the idea of preparing all that seafood too intimidating, it's a recipe that works just as well with vegetables.

Bunch of asparagus, woody ends snapped off
1 fennel bulb, sliced
1 head of radicchio, cut into small wedges
2 zucchinis, cut into thin sticks
All-purpose flour, for dusting
Vegetable oil
12 sage leaves

FOR THE BATTER
1¼ cups all-purpose flour, plus extra for dusting
Sea salt and freshly ground black pepper
1 Tbsp olive oil
1 egg
⅔ cup milk

FOR THE MAYONNAISE
Pinch of saffron strands
3 free-range egg yolks
1 Tbsp Dijon mustard
4 garlic cloves, peeled and crushed
Juice of ½ lemon
¾ cup vegetable oil
¾ cup olive oil
Sea salt and freshly ground black pepper

HOW TO CHOP GARLIC
Garlic is brilliantly versatile and can be used in many different ways. The smaller you cut it, the more potent but shorter-lived its flavor, so leave it whole or thickly sliced if you want a mellow backnote, but crush it for more oomph. The best way to chop it finely, as instructed above, is to cut it as you would an onion (see page 15).

1. First make the mayonnaise. Soak the saffron in 1 tablespoon of boiling water for 30 seconds. Beat the egg yolks with the mustard, garlic, lemon juice, and saffron plus a little of its water in a bowl (or blend in a food processor). Add the oils gradually in a slow, steady stream. Season with salt and pepper, adding a little more lemon juice if you like a sharp flavor. Set aside.

2. Heat a deep-fat fryer to 340°F, or fill a large saucepan a third full of oil and heat until a cube of bread dropped in the hot oil sizzles and turns golden in 30 seconds. (Alternatively, pan-fry with less oil, turning frequently.)

3. Put the flour for the batter into a bowl and season with salt and pepper. Mix in the olive oil, then make a well in the middle and slowly whisk in the egg, milk, and ⅔ cup water. Whisk for 2–3 minutes until smooth.

4. Dust the prepared vegetables in seasoned flour, shaking off any excess before dipping them into the batter. Fry in batches in the hot oil for about 2–3 minutes each or until golden. Remove with a slotted spoon and drain on paper towels, and repeat with the remaining vegetables. Finally, dip the sage leaves in the batter, shake off any excess, and fry for 20–30 seconds until crisp.

5. Serve the battered vegetables and sage leaves hot with the mayonnaise on the side for dipping.

ASPARAGUS WITH LEMON AND TARRAGON HOLLANDAISE

SERVES 4

We're all becoming more health conscious, and making hollandaise with olive oil instead of butter results in an equally rich sauce. You can flavor the hollandaise with any citrus fruit—grapefruit or orange, for example—but with asparagus I always like to keep it simple, with lemon and a sprinkling of tarragon.

1 pound asparagus, woody ends snapped off

FOR THE HOLLANDAISE SAUCE
3 large egg yolks
Squeeze of lemon juice, plus extra to taste
Sea salt and freshly ground black pepper
¾ cup olive oil
2 Tbsp chopped tarragon

1. First make the hollandaise sauce. Using a large balloon whisk, beat the egg yolks with a squeeze of lemon juice and salt and pepper to taste in a bowl set over a pan of simmering water. Beat vigorously for about 10 minutes until the mixture thickens. (To make sure the sauce doesn't overheat, take it on and off the heat while you whisk, scraping around the sides of the bowl with a plastic spatula.) The aim is to achieve a golden, airy sauce that forms ribbons on the surface when the whisk is lifted.

2. Warm the olive oil in a small pan, then set aside. Off the heat, gradually add a little of the warmed olive oil at a time to the egg mixture, then return the pan over a gentle heat to cook a little more. Remove from the heat again and whisk in another dash of warm oil. Repeat until all the oil is incorporated and the sauce has a thick, mayonnaise-like consistency.

3. Whisk in lemon juice, salt and pepper to taste, plus 2–3 tablespoons of warm water to give the mixture a pouring consistency, then add the chopped tarragon.

4. Blanch the asparagus by plunging it into boiling salted water for 2–3 minutes until its rawness has been removed but it is still crunchy. Drain well and serve with the hollandaise.

HOW TO USE UP LEFTOVER CITRUS FRUIT
Cut the fruit into wedges and freeze until needed. They're ideal for cooling drinks without watering them down as ice does, and also add flavor.

LEMONGRASS CUSTARD CUPS

MAKES 4

Instant custard is all very well, but nothing beats a proper crème anglaise, especially when it's perfumed with lemongrass. These cups make a fantastically elegant dessert, which can be made well in advance and finished off with a dusting of sugar and blast of a chef's blowtorch.

1⅔ cups heavy cream
¾ cup milk
2 large lemongrass stalks, split, chopped, and
   slightly crushed with the back of a knife or with a
   mortar and pestle
6 free-range egg yolks
⅓ cup granulated sugar
Dark brown sugar, for the topping

1. Combine the cream and milk with the lemongrass in a large saucepan and scald the mixture, pressing down on the lemongrass in the liquid to extract as much flavor as possible. Allow to cool and infuse for at least 1 hour, or cover and refrigerate overnight. Strain to remove the stalks. Return the mixture to the pan.

2. Beat the egg yolks in a large heatproof bowl set on a damp cloth to hold it steady. Scald the creamy milk again and when it is at the point of boiling, whisk it into the yolks in "slurps," beating well.

3. Preheat the oven to 300°F.

4. Return the mixture to the pan again, pouring through a fine sieve. Beat in the sugar. On very low heat, stir the liquid with a wooden spoon until it starts to coat the back of the spoon, about 15 minutes. Remove from the heat, immediately strain again, and pour into four 4-ounce ramekins or heatproof cups.

5. Place the ramekins in a roasting pan or high-sided ovenproof dish, pour in enough hot water to reach halfway up the sides of the ramekins, and bake for about 45 minutes until the mixture becomes slightly set. Remove, cool, and chill until firm, at least 2 hours or overnight.

6. When you are ready to serve, sprinkle the ramekins evenly with brown sugar and caramelize it with a kitchen torch or under a hot broiler.

HOW TO PREVENT THE CUSTARD FROM SPLITTING
Beating in the sugar after the eggs helps to stabilize the mixture and means it will thicken more quickly.

INDEX

ACKNOWLEDGMENTS

First and foremost, I would like to thank the brilliant team at Hodder—Nicky Ross, Sarah Hammond, Eleni Lawrence, Alasdair Oliver, Kate Brunt, Susan Spratt, and Joanna Seaton—for their belief and passion. Without them this book would not have been possible. And we are very glad that the US edition is being wonderfully supported and promoted by the team at Grand Central Life & Style—Karen Murgolo, Matthew Ballast, Tareth Mitch, and Leda Scheintaub.

Tony Turnbull has my sincerest gratitude for his invaluable guidance and advice on producing and completing this book.

A big thank you to Sarah Durdin Robertson and Lisa Harrison, who have both worked on so many of my books and programs and who worked across this project with endless energy and enthusiasm. Also thank you to Anna Burges-Lumsden for her great work and to my Group Executive Chef, Simon Gregory (who has aided me for many years) for his input and dedication.

This book has the most breathtaking photography courtesy of the talented Anders Schønnemann, aided by stylist Cynthia Inions, whose creativity has made the book so stylish.

I'm indebted to James Edgar at Post98 Design for his design and art direction—his inspired vision has led to a book that is both enticing and beautiful—and to Miren Lopategui, who copyedited the recipes with an eagle eye.

A massive thank you to all at One Potato Two Potato for producing another fabulous series, especially Pat Llewellyn, Ben Adler, Sue Murphy, Paul Ratcliffe, Kimberley Sangster, Karen Kelly, Colin Steele, Tom Clarke, and Anna Horsburgh, a team whose expert craftsmanship guaranteed a successful and exciting production. Thanks also to Charles Walker at United Agents.

I would also like to thank Jennifer Aves-Elliott, my tireless PA, who makes things possible and has the daunting and unenviable task of managing my calendar.

Finally, a huge thank you to my beautiful wife, Tana, for her unwavering support and our four incredible children, Megan, Jack, Holly, and Tilly, for being the best team a father could hope for.

ONE POTATO TWO POTATO

MANAGING DIRECTOR Pat Llewellyn
SERIES PRODUCER & DIRECTOR Paul Ratcliffe
HEAD OF POTATOES Sarah Durdin Robertson
ASSISTANT FOOD PRODUCER Anna Horsburgh